McGraw-Hill Publications in Psychology

CLIFFORD T. MORGAN, *Consulting Editor*

PSYCHOANALYTIC THEORIES OF PERSONALITY

McGRAW-HILL PUBLICATIONS IN PSYCHOLOGY

Clifford T. Morgan, CONSULTING EDITOR

Barker, Kounin, and Wright CHILD BEHAVIOR AND DEVELOPMENT
Bartley BEGINNING EXPERIMENTAL PSYCHOLOGY
Blum PSYCHOANALYTIC THEORIES OF PERSONALITY
Brown PSYCHOLOGY AND THE SOCIAL ORDER
Brown THE PSYCHODYNAMICS OF ABNORMAL BEHAVIOR
Cattell PERSONALITY
Cole GENERAL PSYCHOLOGY
Crafts, Schneirla, Robinson, and Gilbert RECENT EXPERIMENTS IN
 PSYCHOLOGY
Deese THE PSYCHOLOGY OF LEARNING
Dollard and Miller PERSONALITY AND PSYCHOTHERAPY
Dorcus and Jones HANDBOOK OF EMPLOYEE SELECTION
Ferguson PERSONALITY MEASUREMENT
Ghiselli and Brown PERSONNEL AND INDUSTRIAL PSYCHOLOGY
Gray PSYCHOLOGY IN HUMAN AFFAIRS
Gray PSYCHOLOGY IN INDUSTRY
Guilford FUNDAMENTAL STATISTICS IN PSYCHOLOGY AND EDUCATION
Guilford PSYCHOMETRIC METHODS
Hirsh THE MEASUREMENT OF HEARING
Hurlock ADOLESCENT DEVELOPMENT
Hurlock CHILD DEVELOPMENT
Johnson ESSENTIALS OF PSYCHOLOGY
Karn and Gilmer READINGS IN INDUSTRIAL AND BUSINESS PSYCHOLOGY
Krech and Crutchfield THEORY AND PROBLEMS OF SOCIAL PSYCHOLOGY
Lewin A DYNAMIC THEORY OF PERSONALITY
Lewin PRINCIPLES OF TOPOLOGICAL PSYCHOLOGY
Maier FRUSTRATION
Maier and Schneirla PRINCIPLES OF ANIMAL PSYCHOLOGY
Miller EXPERIMENTS IN SOCIAL PROCESS
Miller LANGUAGE AND COMMUNICATION
Moore PSYCHOLOGY FOR BUSINESS AND INDUSTRY
Morgan and Stellar PHYSIOLOGICAL PSYCHOLOGY
Page ABNORMAL PSYCHOLOGY
Reymert FEELINGS AND EMOTIONS
Richards MODERN CLINICAL PSYCHOLOGY
Seashore PSYCHOLOGY OF MUSIC
Seward SEX AND THE SOCIAL ORDER
Shaffer and Lazarus FUNDAMENTAL CONCEPTS IN CLINICAL PSYCHOLOGY
Stagner PSYCHOLOGY OF PERSONALITY
Vinacke THE PSYCHOLOGY OF THINKING
Wallin PERSONALITY MALADJUSTMENTS AND MENTAL HYGIENE

> *John F. Dashiell was Consulting Editor of this series
> from its inception in 1931 until January 1, 1950*

Psychoanalytic Theories

of Personality

GERALD S. BLUM UNIVERSITY OF MICHIGAN

1953

McGRAW-HILL BOOK COMPANY, INC.

New York   *Toronto*   *London*

PSYCHOANALYTIC THEORIES OF PERSONALITY

Copyright, 1953, by the McGraw-Hill Book Company, Inc. Printed in the United States of America. All rights reserved. This book, or parts thereof, may not be reproduced in any form without permission of the publishers.

Library of Congress Catalog Card Number: 52-12350

TO MY WIFE

Preface

Theories of personality are multiplying like the plague. The disease can take the form of types or traits, factors or fields, canalizations or cathexes. Unlike most epidemics, however, this one is allowed to rage unchecked. It almost seems to be more fun for the doctor to get the bug himself than to try to discover what caused the last victim to die. The prognosis in such cases must be deemed, in the vernacular, guarded.

In short, we are confronted with a proliferation of would-be theories and a paucity of should-be evidence. Attempts to verify or deny existing concepts seem far less attractive than the lure of fabricating new ones. Still more censurable is the fact that those theories which seem potentially capable of maturity are not even presented in systematic form conducive to research. The present book is written with the aim of helping to bridge the latter gap.

To approach the goal of an ultimately sound theory of personality, it seems reasonable to begin by organizing into a common framework those theories which have gained some measure of credibility in their field of application. For the majority of professional people whose work relates closely to the area of personality, psychoanalytic theory, conceived in its broadest sense, probably has fared the best. Social workers, psychiatrists, and clinical psychologists, among others, by and large are guided by psychoanalytic principles in their everyday practices. If an author feels called upon to justify further such a narrowing of his scope (which this one obviously does), he can also cite the fact that psychoanalytic theory is currently the most comprehensive one of its species. But from another point of view there is really very little reason to feel defensive about restricting one's efforts *only* to this theory. The breed has many, many strains, as the forthcoming pages will attest.

In sheer volume, roughly two-thirds of this endeavor is devoted to an exposition of various psychoanalytic theories of personality. The content obviously cannot be new, nor can it approach the primary sources in completeness. The unique contribution of the expository sections is presumed to lie in the way the materials are sifted and organized to facilitate comparison of diverse theoretical positions on the same issues. The first task in preparing the manuscript was to decide upon a broad framework which would be relevant for all theories. For this purpose the presentation of views according to a chronological sequence of personality formation seemed most appropriate. Besides following naturally from the fact that psychoanalytic writers have traditionally dealt with the developmental process, such a framework offered the further justification that an adequate theory must in the long run aid in the understanding, prediction, and control of emerging behavior.

Tracing the growth of personality through the years entailed a division into age levels beginning way back with possible prenatal and birth influences and eventually reaching adult character structure. Continuity from one level to the next was sought by utilizing wherever possible a common outline for subdividing the content: Ego and Superego Formation; Psychosexual Development; Relationships with Others; and Mechanisms. By starting each section with the Freudian viewpoint and following with the positions of earlier and later deviants from the orthodox psychoanalytic fold, it was hoped that the organization would be further enhanced.

At this point we should probably pause to identify briefly the cast of characters who figure prominently in the text. To say that psychoanalytic theory sprang from the brow of Sigmund Freud (or more precisely from the lips of his patients) shortly before the turn of the century will come as no great

revelation to the reader. Almost equally familiar are the se-
cessions of the "early deviants"—Adler, Jung, and Rank—
during the second and third decades of the twentieth century.
More recently we have seen the rise of various "neo-Freudian"
movements. These and other historical features, while significant in the evolution of psychoanalysis, have been amply
documented elsewhere (232, 252, 282) and are not directly
pertinent to the job at hand.

It is important, however, to try to clarify the distinctions
between currently orthodox and neo-Freudian theorists.
There are those who say that nowadays everyone is a neo-
Freudian in the sense that many of Freud's original formulations are almost universally held to be outmoded. His treatment of cultural influences, for example, has been altered considerably by such a leading modern orthodox disciple as Otto
Fenichel. But the neo-Freudians go still further in raising
objections on issues like libido theory, Freud's metaphorical
concepts, and the orthodox emphasis upon early psychosexual
development. Apart from sharing these general attitudes, the
neo-Freudians themselves are a heterogeneous group. Perhaps the least confusing manner of introduction is simply to
name the individuals who are commonly designated as neo-
Freudians: Karen Horney, Erich Fromm, Harry Stack Sullivan, Abram Kardiner, and Clara Thompson. At the opposite
extreme is Melanie Klein, leader of a British school of psychoanalysis, who is said to "out-Freud Freud" in many of her
formulations. Along with Freud and Fenichel in the so-called
"orthodox" group should be mentioned such currently emi-
nent figures as Anna Freud, Richard Sterba, Phyllis Greenacre, and Heinz Hartmann. More difficult to place are Erik
Homburger Erikson and Franz Alexander, each of whose
theories is close to the orthodox position but also borders on
the neo-Freudian.

The attempt to boil down and synthesize such a variety of
points of view, which unfortunately were not offered originally
with this criterion in mind, necessarily involves sins of omis-
sion. Some readers may feel that the unequal apportionment

of space to different theorists smacks of discrimination. Orthodox psychoanalytic theory, since it is the most carefully
worked out, tends to receive the lion's share. To the discon-
solates who may feel their favorite lamb has been badly shorn,
I reply with sincere apologies. Such has not been the conscious intent. Any offense of this nature can, I hope, be attributed to a deep-dyed dislike for lengthy tomes.

In summary, the text proper seeks to present descriptive
yet concise accounts of expert psychoanalytic opinions on
personality development, organized according to age levels.
The exposition itself is intended to be factual and objective.
It should be pointed out that many psychoanalytic formulations, especially in the areas of psychotherapy and psychopathology, do not fall within the boundaries set for this book.

Now back to the plaintive tale with which we began.
Psychoanalytic views, judging by their popularity in the applied fields, appear promising for an ultimately sound theory
of personality. The first suggested step toward the long-range
goal is to provide a meaningful organization of the content.
But what next? In the writer's opinion, the second phase
should contain a thorough evaluation of existing concepts in
order to sort out those which seem worthy of future research
exploration. This is not a one-man job. It requires the combined efforts of the clinician, the researcher, the logician, and
the theory builder. But perhaps it is permissible for an author
to take the liberty of making occasional forays into that sunny
field, without any pretense of carrying back systematic en-
lightenment. Such self-indulgence is given expression in the
"Notes" sections at the end of each chapter.

These notes, which occupy a third of the volume, are intended to be critical. They are oriented primarily toward the
research possibilities inherent in the content. Brief résumés of
existing experimental data, suggestive evidence from related
fields like cultural anthropology and learning theory, consideration of logical inconsistencies and semantic confusions,
and comparisons of overlapping views are interspersed
throughout. To borrow a phrase from *The New Yorker*, these

sections therefore might appropriately be labeled "Research Notes from All Over." That they do not furnish complete, well-knit integrations of theory and evidence is lamentable. Perhaps, though, the time for integration is not yet here. Before the endless concepts in the jigsaw of personality theory can be put together, it will probably be necessary to find out which were carved with precision and which came into being when the craftsman's hand slipped.

The book is intended for the following groups of readers: advanced undergraduate and graduate students in psychology and related disciplines, students in psychiatry and social service, and professional workers in these same fields. The expository sections should be of interest to all, whereas the notes are aimed especially at those individuals who wish to pursue a research orientation toward psychoanalytic theory.

In general, I wish to express my indebtedness to the graduate students and staff members in the Department of Psychology at the University of Michigan. The former have provided a perennial source of stimulating comments and questions, and the latter have made possible an intellectual climate which imprints on everyone its inestimable mark. Grateful acknowledgment for their critical reading of all or parts of the manuscript is extended to my Michigan colleagues—E. Lowell Kelly, Donald G. Marquis, Theodore M. Newcomb, Harold L. Raush, and Edward L. Walker—and to Ernest R. Hilgard of Stanford University. For her many hours spent in typing and editing the manuscript I want to thank Marietta Case, who was ably assisted by Ruth Carter Sullivan.

Of the many source materials which contributed to the preparation of the book, several should be singled out for special mention. Otto Fenichel's *Psychoanalytic Theory of Neurosis* provided an outstanding portrayal of orthodox psychoanalytic theory, and Clara Thompson's *Psychoanalysis: Evolution and Development* and Patrick Mullahy's *Oedipus Myth and Complex* were both valuable secondary sources on Adler, Jung, Rank, and the neo-Freudians. Permission to quote passages from their publications was graciously extended by the following publishers: W. W. Norton & Co., Hogarth Press, Josiah Macy, Jr. Foundation, International Universities Press, William Alanson White Psychiatric Foundation, Hermitage House, Alfred A. Knopf, Inc., and the American Orthopsychiatric Association.

GERALD S. BLUM

Ann Arbor, Mich.
June, 1952

Contents

PREFACE   vii

1. PRENATAL AND BIRTH INFLUENCES   1
   Theories of Prenatal Effects   1
       Greenacre
       Fodor
   The Birth Trauma   3
       Freud
       Rank
       Freud's Reply to Rank
       Greenacre
       Fodor
   Summary   7
   Notes   8

2. THE NEONATE'S PERSONALITY POTENTIAL   14
   Instincts and the Concept of Libido   14
       The Orthodox Biological Orientation: Fenichel and
          Sterba
       The Neo-Freudian Cultural Orientation: Thompson
          and Sullivan
   Views on the Death Instinct   17
       Freud
       Fenichel
       Thompson
   The Unconscious and the Id   19
       The Orthodox Formulation
          Definition and importance
          Freud's reasons for believing in the unconscious
          Attributes

Origin of content
Nature of content
Relationship to the id
Jung: "The Collective Unconscious"
Neo-Freudian Viewpoints
Primary Narcissism   25
Freud: The Orthodox View
Greenacre: Relationship to Anxiety and Birth
Fromm: A Neo-Freudian View
Summary   28
Notes   30

3. THE FIRST YEAR OF LIFE   33
Ego and Superego Formation   33
Orthodox Formulation: The Archaic Ego
Infantile perceptions
Self-esteem
Development of the sense of reality
Melanie Klein's Theory
Sullivan: The Prototaxic Mode
Psychosexual Development   37
Orthodox Approach: The Oral Stage
Klein's Position
Jung's Position
Neo-Freudian Views
Erikson: The Oral Zone, Incorporative Mode
Relationships with Others   43
Orthodox View: Mother as First Object
Klein's Theory
Sullivan: Empathy and the Significant Other
Mechanisms   46
Introductory Comments
Introjection, Primary Identification, and Projection
Orthodox formulation
Klein's formulation
Denial
Fixation and Regression
Orthodox concepts
Kleinian concepts
Summary   50
Notes   53

4. AGES ONE TO THREE YEARS 62
   Ego and Superego Formation 62
      Orthodox Views: Fenichel
         Development of active mastery
         Anxiety
         Belated mastery and "functional pleasure"
         Development of speech and thinking
         Defenses against impulses
         Forerunners of superego
      Neo-Freudian Views: Sullivan
         The parataxic mode
         Autistic language
         Anxiety and the beginnings of the self-dynamism
   Psychosexual Development 69
      Orthodox View: The Anal-sadistic Stage
      Neo-Freudian Views: Thompson and Sullivan
      Erikson: The Anal-urethral Zone, Retentive and
         Eliminative Modes
   Relationships with Others 72
      Orthodox View
         Ambivalence and bisexuality
         Sadism and masochism
      Sullivan's Theory
         Reflected appraisals
         Multiple "me-you patterns"
   Mechanisms 75
      Denial in Word and Act: Anna Freud
      Consensual Validation: Sullivan
   Summary 78
   Notes 80

5. FROM THREE TO FIVE 85
   Psychosexual Development 85
      Orthodox View: The Phallic Stage
         Urethral eroticism
         Castration anxiety in boys
         Penis envy in girls
         Masturbation
      Neo-Freudian Views
         Thompson on the phallic phase

Horney on penis envy
Erikson: The Phallic Zone, Intrusive Mode
Relationships with Others   91
    Orthodox Position
        The Oedipus complex
        Change of object in girls
    Other Views on the Oedipus Complex
        Adler
        Jung
        Rank
        Horney
        Fromm
        Sullivan
        Thompson
Ego and Superego Formation   96
    Orthodox View
        Development of the superego
        Functions of ego and superego
        Relationships of superego to ego and id
    Rank's Conception of the Superego
    Fromm: Authoritarian versus Humanistic Conscience
Mechanisms   102
    Orthodox Mechanisms of Defense
        Introductory comments
        Successful vs. unsuccessful ego defenses
        Sublimation: Fenichel vs. Sterba
        Repression
        Reaction formation
        Undoing
        Isolation
        Displacement
    Sullivan: Selective Inattention and Disassociation
    Fromm: Mechanisms of Escape
Summary   111
Notes   113

6. THE LATENCY PERIOD (AGE FIVE TO PREPUBERTY) 127
Orthodox View   127
    Ego and Superego Formation
    Psychosexual Development

Relationships with Others
Mechanisms
Neo-Freudian Views 131
Thompson
Sullivan
Summary 132
Notes 133

7. PREPUBERTY AND ADOLESCENCE 136
Orthodox Views 136
Psychosexual Development
Ego and Superego Formation
Relationships with Others
Mechanisms
Prepubertal defenses
Asceticism
Intellectualization
Creativity as a defense
Rankian View: Hankins 146
Neo-Freudian Views: Sullivan 147
Summary 148
Notes 150

8. ADULT CHARACTER STRUCTURE 156
Orthodox Position 156
Definition and Classification of "Character"
Character Types
The oral character
The anal character
The urethral character
The phallic character
The genital character
The Early Deviants 164
Adler
Jung
The extravert
The introvert
Rank
The average man
The neurotic
The creative man

More Recent Views   171
    Horney
        The compliant type
        The aggressive type
        The detached type
    Fromm
        The receptive orientation
        The exploitative orientation
        The hoarding orientation
        The marketing orientation
        The productive orientation
    Kardiner
    Alexander
    Erikson
    Summary   180
    Notes   182

9. POST-MORTEM   190

   BIBLIOGRAPHY   193

   NAME INDEX   207

   SUBJECT INDEX   211

CHAPTER 1 *Prenatal and Birth Influences*

The problem of deciding at what age to start studying personality development of the human organism is becoming increasingly difficult. At one time it seemed outrageous to propose that experiences during infancy were crucial to personality formation. Next the onset was pushed back to the birth process itself; and now there is a growing area of interest in prenatal influences on personality. This text begins, therefore, with the exposition of several psychoanalytic theories pertaining to the nebulous realm of life's earliest events.

THEORIES OF PRENATAL EFFECTS

Greenacre

Probably the leading psychoanalytic exponent of prenatal effects is Greenacre (120),[1] who is quite modest in presenting her opinions as little more than speculations supported by some experimental and clinical findings. She concludes that constitution, prenatal experience, birth, and the situation immediately after birth all play a part in creating a predisposition to anxiety. This type of preanxiety, according to Greenacre, differs from later anxiety in that it lacks psychological content and operates at the reflex level. She points out that the fetus is capable of a wide variety of activities—moving, kicking, turning around, reacting to external stimuli by increased motion. She also cites the increases in fetal heart rate recorded after sharp loud noises have occurred near the

[1] Numbers in parentheses refer to the Bibliography at the end of the book.

1

mother. Sontag and Wallace found, for example, that there was marked increase in fetal movement in response to the noise of a doorbell buzzer (see Note 1).[2] Furthermore, the fetus may cry *in utero* if air has been accidentally admitted to the uterine cavity. All these reflex reactions to discomfort are interpreted by her as supportive evidence for the existence of an anxietylike pattern before birth (see Note 2). This pattern, which is further acted upon by birth and early postnatal experiences, is said to provide an organic potential which, when especially strong, may result in more severe reactions to psychological dangers later in life.

Fodor

Fodor's (80) approach to prenatal influences on personality is quite grandiose in comparison with Greenacre's, and in general is radically deviant from that of other analysts. He places exclusive emphasis on prenatal conditioning and the birth trauma, maintaining that there is a biological foundation behind many forms of neurotic behavior. He states that Otto Rank made the first attempt to "biologize" psychoanalysis but differentiates himself from Rank by saying that his own approach is clinical whereas Rank's was philosophical. Fodor's arguments are primarily reconstructions based upon fantasies and dreams obtained from patients in his own private practice—so-called "prenatal dreams."

According to Fodor, these prenatal dreams do not always reflect a state of rapture—the life of the unborn is not necessarily one of unbroken bliss, as traditional analytic theory has assumed. The unborn child is dependent on the mother's blood stream for oxygen, for food, and for the elimination of its waste products. There are many maternal afflictions that affect and perhaps weaken the child before birth, causing him to start postnatal life with a handicap. One significant type of external shock to the advanced fetus is the violence of parental intercourse, the traumatic effect of which is said to be clearly traceable in dreams throughout our life.

[2] Notes are given at the end of each chapter.

To account for these vestiges of prenatal existence, Fodor postulates an "organismic consciousness" which is the deepest level of mind—possibly, as he puts it, the very bedrock of the unconscious mind. He tries to dispense with the objection that, because of the lack of nerve connections between mother and child, the fetus cannot be affected by a shock which the mother suffers (see Note 3). The key to this dilemma, says Fodor, is the experimental work in telepathy at Duke University. Having granted the existence of telepathy, he goes on to state that it becomes easy to understand how the mother's fond expectations and wholesome feelings can have a healthful influence on the psyche of the unborn; and similarly, the unwanted child's loneliness can be traced back to its psychic isolation in the womb (see Note 4).

THE BIRTH TRAUMA

Freud

According to Freud (89), who first postulated the psychological significance of the birth process, the organism at birth emerges from a relatively calm and peaceful environment into an overwhelming situation. There is an intense exposure to outside stimulation which the newborn has no adequate way to handle. He cannot utilize any defense mechanisms to protect himself and consequently is flooded by excitation. This first danger situation becomes the prototype or model for all later anxiety. The common link in this sequence is separation from the mother, which at birth is purely biological and later is manifested in more psychological and symbolic ways.

Rank

Rank (234) differs from Freud in that he assigns a central role in personality development to the birth trauma. He sees birth as a profound shock on both the physiological and psychological levels. This shock creates a reservoir of anxiety, portions of which are released all through life. All neuroses stem from severe birth anxiety, and all later anxiety can be interpreted in terms of birth anxiety—not merely as a model but as the source itself. Separation from the mother is the original trauma, and later separations of any kind come to acquire a traumatic quality—for example, weaning involves separation from the breast, and castration fear means separation from the penis. The infant is actually aware of the separation at birth and forms visual impressions at the time. An illustration is the later horror of the female genitals which can be traced back to the visual impression received at birth.

According to Rank, every pleasure has as its final aim the reestablishment of intrauterine primal pleasure, the paradise lost by birth. The most satisfactory means of achieving the return is through the sex act, which represents a symbolic reunion with the mother. In sexual intercourse the male conceives of his penis as a child returning to the mother's womb, whereas the female achieves satisfaction by identifying with her own unborn child. Obstacles to this gratification are found in the original birth anxiety, which is a danger signal against returning to the mother's womb.

Freud's Reply to Rank

Freud objects to Rank's emphasis on the severity of the birth trauma as a main determinant. In his book, *The Problem of Anxiety*, he states (89, pp. 95–96):

The emphasis on the varying severity of the birth trauma leaves no room for the legitimate aetiological claim of constitutional factors. This severity is an organic factor, certainly, one which compared with constitution is a chance factor, and is itself dependent upon many influences which are to be termed accidental, such as for example timely obstetrical assistance. . . . If one were to allow for the importance of a constitutional factor, such as via the modification that it would depend much more upon how extensively the individual reacts to the variable severity of the birth trauma, one would deprive the theory of meaning and have reduced the new factor which Rank has introduced to a subordinate role. That which determines whether or not neurosis is the outcome lies, then, in some other area, and once again in an unknown one. . . . For no trustworthy investigation has ever been carried out to determine whether difficult and protracted birth is correlated in indisputable fashion with the development of neurosis—indeed, whether children whose birth has been of this character manifest even the nervousness of earliest infancy for a longer period or more intensely than others. If the assertion is made that precipitate births . . . may possibly have for the child the significance of a severe trauma, than *a fortiori* it would certainly be necessary that births resulting in asphyxia should produce beyond any doubt the consequences alleged. . . . I think it cannot yet be decided how large a contribution to the solution of the problem (of the fundamental basis of neurosis) it [*i.e.*, difficult birth] actually makes.

Freud also objects to the attribution of psychological meaning to the birth process in the following passage (89, p. 73):

But what is a "danger"? In the act of birth there is an objective danger to the preservation of life. . . . But psychologically it has no meaning at all. The danger attending birth has still no psychic content. . . . The foetus can be aware of nothing beyond a gross disturbance in the economy of its narcissistic libido. Large amounts of excitation press upon it, giving rise to novel sensations of unpleasure; numerous organs enforce increased cathexis soon to be initiated; what is there in all this that can be regarded as bearing the stamp of a "danger situation": . . . it is not credible that the child has preserved any other than tactile and general sensations from the act of birth (in contrast to Rank's assumption of visual impressions). . . . Intrauterine life and early infancy form a continuum to a far greater extent than the striking caesura of the act of birth would lead us to believe.

Greenacre

Greenacre (121) attempts to reconcile Freud and Rank by saying that there is no necessary opposition between them as far as the birth trauma is concerned. She disagrees with Freud's statement that Rank's position automatically excludes the possible effect of constitutional factors. She feels that there very likely is an interaction between the constitutional or inherited factors and the accidental factors which emerge during the birth process. Furthermore, if we are to assume, as Freud does, that the birth trauma is sufficiently significant to serve as the prototype of human anxiety, then it should follow that variations in the degree of trauma could affect later anxiety to a greater extent than he was willing to admit. As for Freud's criticism that there can be no content at birth, she offers her preanxiety response formulation, described earlier. In summary, Greenacre is of the opinion that the true influence of the birth trauma is probably somewhere between the positions of the two—not so exalted an effect as postulated by Rank and not so slight as believed by Freud and his current followers.

Fodor

Fodor (80), as we have seen, stresses prenatal experience and the trauma of birth as the primary forces affecting personality development. The change from prenatal to postnatal life is said to involve an ordeal as severe as dying. In fact, says Fodor, the fear of death begins at birth. The two are essentially similar—both are interchangeable symbols for the unconscious mind. Because of the terrific impact of birth, nature has provided an infantile amnesia by which the memory of the trauma is repressed. However, the imprint of the experience continues in the unconscious mind and exerts its devious influences all through life in the form of nightmares, phobias, symptoms, and the like. Many birth-fear symbols are so universal that they can be recognized immediately. The most general dream fantasies in which the trauma of birth may manifest itself, according to Fodor, are: creeping through narrow openings; being rooted to the ground or sinking into mud or sand; being crushed or compressed; drowning; being sucked down by whirlpools or dragged under by crabs, sharks, or alligators; fear of being devoured by wild animals or monsters; nightmares of suffocation or being buried alive; phobias of mutilation or of falling to one's death.

By way of summary, Fodor offers what he calls four principles of prenatal psychology:

1. In our present-day life, birth is traumatic in almost every instance.
2. The longer the labor, the more serious the physical complications, the greater the trauma of birth.
3. The intensity of the trauma of birth is proportionate to the shocks or injuries which the child suffers during labor or immediately following delivery.
4. The love and care which the child receives immediately after birth are decisive factors in the persistence and intensity of the traumatic pressure (see Note 5).

SUMMARY

Among the psychoanalysts, Greenacre and Fodor offer specific formulations relevant to the influence of prenatal environment upon subsequent personality development. While the two differ markedly in several respects, there are certain common threads running through their stated positions. Both stress the importance of prenatal effects on later personality; they agree that the prenatal environment can be traumatic at times; and both attribute the discomfort to external stimuli—for Greenacre such disturbances as loud noises, and for Fodor the violence of parental intercourse. Their major differences lie in the kinds of processes postulated and the types of evidence employed by each. Greenacre speaks of "preanxiety" operating at a simple reflex level, presumably through some process of conditioning, whereas Fodor resorts to a content-oriented "organismic consciousness," made possible by telepathic communications between mother and fetus. For evidence Greenacre calls upon a few clinical and experimental observations of fetal activity, while Fodor bases his views on interpretations of so-called "prenatal dreams" obtained from himself and his patients.

The significance of the birth experience itself is pointed out by Freud, Rank, and again Greenacre and Fodor. Freud's position is the most conservative. He mentions the danger involved in the initial flood of excitation from the outside world against which the newborn cannot defend himself adequately. The birth situation becomes the model for all later anxiety, originally in terms of biological separation from the mother but afterward manifested in more psychological ways. He tends to minimize the importance of accidents during the process of delivery and denies the possibility of awareness of actual content at that time.

Rank assigns a central role to the birth trauma, portrayed as a shock creating a reservoir of anxiety, portions of which are released all through life. The newborn child is said to form lasting visual impressions of this painful separation from the mother, so that future separations of any kind are seen as threatening. The goal of every pleasure later on is to regain the feeling of intrauterine contentment, an aim best achieved through the sex act, which symbolizes reunion with the mother.

Greenacre occupies an intermediate position between Freud and Rank on this issue. She concedes the operation of both constitutional and accidental factors emerging from the birth process but substitutes her preanxiety response formulation in place of Rank's notion of visual impressions. Fodor's view is the most extreme of all, for he considers the birth trauma, along with prenatal influences, as the primary, almost exclusive forces determining personality.

NOTES

1. *Susceptibility of the Fetus to External Stimulation.* Montagu's (211) summary of the experimental literature amply documents Greenacre's observation that the fetus reacts to external stimuli. The Fels Institute researchers have found that pregnant mothers undergoing periods of severe emotional distress have fetuses which show considerably increased activity. Likewise, mothers with the highest rates for functioning of parts of the autonomic nervous system have the most active fetuses. Kenworthy (167) suggests that fatigue in the mother produces hyperactivity, which is supported by the Harris and Harris (129) finding that fetal movement is greatest in the evening. The startle reflex to

which Greenacre refers has been elicited at 30 weeks in response to a doorbell buzzer. Montagu also lists these additional sources by which the maternal environment affects the fetus: nutritional states, drugs, infections, dysfunctions, sensitizations, age, and number of other children. On the basis of such findings, Sontag concludes that "the psychophysiological state of the mother exerts an influence upon the behavior pattern of the normal fetus."

2. *Conditioning the Fetus.* Spelt (266) has already demonstrated the possibility of fetal conditioning. Using 13 pregnant women and 3 nonpregnant controls, he was able to establish a conditioned response during the last two months of gestation. Paired stimulations from a loud noise and a vibrotactile device (doorbell with gong removed, applied to the mother's abdomen) eventually resulted in fetal movement from the vibrotactile stimulus alone. Experimental extinction, spontaneous recovery, and retention of the response over a three-week interval were shown, as well as a significant degree of agreement between direct records of fetal activity and maternal reports.

3. *Fetal Physiology.* Controversies concerning the physiological properties of the fetus are still numerous [see Carmichael (50)]. While it is true that there are no communicating fibers between the nervous systems of mother and fetus, Sontag (265) points out, however, that the fetus is an intimate part of a total psychosomatic organism. As such, it responds to the mother's somatized anxieties or fears, which modify the function of her endocrine organs, cell metabolism, and so forth. Through momentary or longer changes in the composition of the blood these gross chemical alterations can be transmitted to the fetus, since many maternal hormones are composed of molecules small enough to pass very readily through the placenta. Thus, "blood-borne" anxieties or stimulations can prove irritating to the fetus, as evidenced by an immediate increase in bodily activity. Repeated stimuli of this sort may maintain a state of irritability and hyperactivity during later intrauterine life.

4. *Research on the Consequences of Prenatal Influence for Personality Development.* It might be said that the evidence in this area is itself little more than embryonic. On the physical side there have been a few suggestive reports based mainly on observational material. Hall and Mohr (125), for example, note that emotional antagonism toward childbearing on the part of the

mother may result in premature birth. Richards and Newberry (244) found that those fetuses who were more active during the latter part of pregnancy tended to be more advanced in motor development during the first year of postnatal life. Sontag (263, 265) describes an association between prenatal disturbance and subsequent crying, irritability, and feeding difficulties.

With respect to personality development, crucial research would be very difficult to accomplish. We can readily dispense with Fodor's approach as unsuited to scientific investigation on a number of counts: the dubious validity of dream interpretations when used for this purpose; the highly questionable practice of reconstructing prenatal effects inferentially from the verbal reports of adults; and the unverified premise that telepathy can serve as a means of communication.

Presumably it might be possible to record fully the prenatal environment of an organism [see (171) for an example of an intensive study of expectant mothers] and then follow the growth of its postnatal personality. The apparent difficulties of thorough observation during the fetal period are more than matched by complications involved in later personality assessment. In addition to these measurement problems, there is the inescapable fact that mothers continue to affect the personalities of their children after birth. For example, how can we decide whether the anxieties of a four-year-old are due to the anxiety-ridden environment provided by an unhappy mother before birth or after?

One avenue might be adoption cases or any situation in which we could compare postnatal personality in two groups of children whose contact with the real mother ended at birth: one group having led what Greenacre might describe as a preanxiety type of fetal existence [see A. Freud and Burlingham (85) concerning wartime experiences of English children], and the other not. Since only the grossest kinds of control would be possible in such a study, it would have to be carried out on a large-scale basis. Assuming the two groups to be roughly equated for postnatal environment and differing only in prenatal experiences, we could attempt to compare them by a variety of techniques (play and other projective devices, observations, interviews, etc.) for relative anxiety levels in childhood.

An exploratory study of less ambitious scope has been reported by Wallin and Riley (284). Based on the assumption that many psychosomatic complaints by the mother during pregnancy reflect a more negative attitude toward the coming child, a series of questions about physical complaints during pregnancy was put to 100 recent mothers, 63 of whom had only the one child and 37 who had two children. This score on reactions to pregnancy was then compared with an infant adjustment score determined from questions on eating habits, bowel training, sleeping, crying, etc. A significant, positive relationship between the two sets of scores was found in the two-child group, *i.e.*, mothers with more psychosomatic complaints had more disturbed children, but not in the one-child group. The authors are duly cautious in their interpretation of the results, stressing the need for direct observation in order to validate the questionnaire approach, and the unknown reliabilities of the two scores. They offer three alternative possibilities to account for the inconsistent findings: mothers on the basis of their first childbearing experience may have become more negatively disposed to the second; the relative absence of compensating attention and indulgence on the part of the husband during the second pregnancy; and the economic pressures induced by having a second child.

Obviously we are not yet in a position to evaluate the consequences of the prenatal environment for later personality development. A fairly extreme summary statement is the following comment by Montagu (211, p. 169): ". . . the indications are that a child which as a fetus was traumatized by such factors as have already been discussed is likely to find the achievement of healthy personality development more difficult, other things being equal, than a child who as a fetus was not so traumatized. Some children, as Sontag has pointed out, are born 'neurotic' as a result of their intrauterine experiences."

Somewhat more conservative is this comparable quote by Windle (211, pp. 185–186): "There is no question that many varying factors in the mother's external environment, through her physiology, influence the physiology of her fetus. We must not assume that all of them are proved beyond doubt. True it is that external sounds appear to be perceived by the fetus; at least he responds by performing certain movements. But what real scientific proof have we that his postnatal existence is significantly altered by such perceptions and activities? We are guessing. Again, we may surmise that the mother's emotional state is capable of affecting her fetus, and I will grant that there is good reason to think that this may be true. However, I am sure that all investigators, and particularly Doctor Sontag, would like to have a much larger series of observations before drawing final conclusions in the matter."

5. *Evidence Relating Birth Experiences to Later Personality.* The evidence in this area is almost as inadequate as in the case of prenatal influence. The various approaches can be divided into several types.

CAESAREAN SECTION. Theoretically, the child delivered by Caesarean section might be expected to show fewer adverse effects from his birth experience. Kenworthy (167) reports that "the Caesarean sectioned child is prone to be less sensitized—he cries less, is markedly less irritated by the contacts of handling, etc.— than the first-born child delivered through the birth canal." She presents no data, nor do Mowrer and Kluckhohn (214), for their statement that "individuals who have been delivered by Caesarean section do not, as adults, differ temperamentally in any easily discernible way, from persons who have been normally born."

DURATION OF BIRTH. Pearson (226) compared the behavior of children whose birth time was brief (less than six hours) with those whose birth time was long (more than fourteen hours). Contrary to what might be anticipated according to theory, he found that the short-birth children were more "neurotic" than the others. Pearson himself notes as a limiting factor the uncontrolled variable of a greater number of youngest children in the short group.

PREMATURE BIRTHS. On the assumption that premature birth is more traumatic to the organism, we might expect more evidences of personality disturbance in such samples. Studies reported by Shirley (211) and Hirschl *et al.* (211) reveal that prematurely born children at nursery-school age are more highly emotional, shy, jumpy, and anxious than full-term children. Motor coordination tends to be poorer, and control of the sphincters is usually achieved later and with more difficulty. On the other hand, sensory acuity seems to be more highly developed in the premature group. Drillien (211) also found behavior disorders, especially with respect to feeding, to be more frequent in premature infants. Any causal connection between the birth situation per se and subsequent personality traits is again difficult to establish, since anxiety in the mother may contribute to the premature delivery as well as to postnatal personality.

DIFFICULT BIRTHS. Wile and Davis (286) compared 380 spontaneous births with 120 instrument deliveries. They found a greater incidence of aggressiveness, fears, and tics among the less difficult births, and more restlessness, irritability, and distractibility among the more difficult. As Cattell (51) points out, these results must be interpreted cautiously in view of the lack of experimental control, *e.g.*, family size, conditions of rating, statistical calculation of significance of differences.

From the brief survey presented above, it is apparent that we also do not yet have sufficient evidence on which to base any conclusions concerning the relationship of birth trauma to later personality. Many of the same difficulties face the investigator in this area as in prenatal research, particularly the problem of controlling the diversity of variables which affect personality once the child has been born. All the outlined approaches to studying birth trauma have some potential merit as methods. In the case of instrument deliveries it would be preferable to follow those children who turn out to be relatively free of injury, since we can assume that the presence of injury exerts a continuing influence on personality development. The chance of obtaining reliable measurements of the birth process offers a distinct advantage over fetal observations, but again large-scale sampling would be needed to offset the virtual impossibility of devising adequate controls for the criterion phase (personality assessment during childhood) of the design.

CHAPTER 2   *The Neonate's Personality Potential*

Orthodox psychoanalytic theory blesses the newborn child with instincts, libido, an emerging differentiation of levels of awareness, an intriguing reservoir called the id, and finally a condition described as primary narcissism. These formulations, along with the reactions of other psychoanalytically oriented theorists, will be the subject matter of this chapter.

INSTINCTS AND THE CONCEPT OF LIBIDO

The Orthodox Biological Orientation:
Fenichel and Sterba

Orthodox psychoanalytic theory explains mental phenomena as the result of a dynamic interaction of forces. Specifically, the interaction is between urging forces or instincts and the counterforces set up by the external environment. The distinction is made between stimuli coming from within the organism, such as hunger, thirst, and sex, and stimuli from the outside world (see Note 1).

Richard Sterba (271) defines instinct as the "psychic representative of a continuously active stimulus originating in the interior of the body and flowing into the psyche from the somatic field." It is a borderline term, between the psychic and somatic, since it deals with mental influences originating within the soma. An illustration is the nutritional instinct. Lack of food brings on certain chemicophysical changes or organic stimuli. These organic stimuli then have various mental manifestations, such as mood changes. The instinct is

14

described as the force acting upon the psyche to produce the mental changes. The phrase "continuously active" derives from the fact that somatic stimuli flow uninterruptedly into the brain and cannot be shut off internally. Stimuli from the outside, on the other hand, can be escaped through flight. In other words, if it starts to rain, you can avoid the problem of not having an umbrella by standing in a doorway; but if you are ravenously hungry, you have to deal with the problem more directly, by getting something to eat.

Fenichel (74) describes three characteristics of an instinct: (1) aim, (2) object, and (3) source. The aim of an instinct is its satisfaction, brought about by a discharge which dispels the physical condition of excitement. Therefore the aim is to reestablish a state in which there is no longer an instinctual need. The object of an instinct is something belonging to the outside world by which or through which the instinct reaches satisfaction—an instrument for attaining the aim. Food, for example, is an object for the nutritional instinct. The source of an instinct is said to be the chemicophysical status itself, about which we know relatively little. Sterba adds a fourth characteristic to these: "drive," which he defines as the quantity of energy which the instinct represents. This driving power of an instinct can be estimated from the degree and number of obstacles which it can overcome. In the case of starvation, the hunger drive becomes so powerful that normal inhibitions about eating practices are easily brushed aside.

Fenichel classifies instincts into two groups: (1) those dealing with simple physical needs; and (2) those dealing with sexual urges. Examples of the first category are breathing, hunger, thirst, defecation, and urination. The process by which such needs are satisfied is relatively uncomplicated. Somatic changes induce sensory experiences which lead to specific actions for eliminating the tension. The common feature in this group of instincts is their necessity for quick satisfaction which allows for very little variability among individuals. Therefore, says Fenichel, they are of minor importance for psychology.

The other group, the sexual instincts, operate in a broader and more complicated fashion. If not gratified in their original form, they have the capacity to change, to alter aims and objects, to disappear from consciousness, or to reappear in different disguises. Like the first group, they function from birth onward, and adult forms of sexuality are continuations of the infantile ones.

This leads us to the concept of libido, which is defined as the energy of sexual instincts. Everyone possesses a quantity of energy which serves as a reservoir for sexual expression in the broad sense. This quantity of libido is fixed in the case of each individual and presumably is present at birth. In the course of development, libido becomes attached to different body organs and undergoes a variety of transformations which Freud describes as the "vicissitudes of the libido" (directed outward or inward, fixation, regression, repression, sublimation).

The Neo-Freudian Cultural Orientation: Thompson and Sullivan

Notions concerning libido vary from Jung's at one extreme to the neo-Freudians' at the other. For Jung (157, 159) libido represents a primal energy underlying the dynamics of all mental life ("the foundation and regulator of all psychic existence"), not merely the sexual alone. This fundamental urge, or life-pushing force, covers nutrition, growth, sexuality, activities and interests, etc. The neo-Freudians, on the other hand, discard instincts and libido completely. They admit the significance of biological needs and their impact on the developmental process. However, they reject the idea of libido as a driving force leading to the primary pursuit of erotic bodily satisfaction. Instead they attempt to understand the biological development of the child in terms of growth and of interpersonal relations provided by the culture. According to Thompson (282), Freud's libido theory has proved unsatisfactory in attempting to explain aggression, perversions, and narcissism. These and other differences between the two schools will become clearer as we progress through the genetic sequence of personality formation.

However, the neo-Freudians do have some positive opinions about the personality potential of the neonate. For example, Harry Stack Sullivan (277), borrowing a term from Adler, postulates that everyone is born with "something of the power motive." The infant is not actually born with a fully developed power drive but has the capacity to be conditioned in this respect. Early frustrations of the biological strivings for power result in the formation of a drive aimed to overcome the inner sense of powerlessness. Sullivan's illustration is the infant who reaches for the moon the first time he sees it. His inability to succeed is a frustration of his feeling of power, which leads him to seek means of gaining further power as compensation. Power is said to be more important than the impulses resulting from feelings of hunger, thirst, or sexual lust because it underlies all of them. The power motive is so fundamental that the degree to which it is satisfied or frustrated determines the development of personality. In Sullivan's words (277, pp. 6–7):

The full development of personality along the lines of security is chiefly founded on the infant's discovery of his powerlessness to achieve certain desired end-states with the tools, the instrumentalities, which are at his disposal. From the disappointments in the very early stages of life outside the womb—in which all things are given—comes the beginning of this vast development of actions, thoughts, foresights, and so on, which are calculated to protect one from a feeling of insecurity and helplessness in the situation which confronts one. [See Note 2.]

VIEWS ON THE DEATH INSTINCT

Freud

Freud originally divided the instincts into two categories: (1) the self-preservation or ego instincts; and (2) the sexual instincts. The historical features in the development of his thinking are clearly outlined in Thompson (282) and need not concern us here. The end result was a division into the life instinct, Eros, and the death instinct, Thanatos. The life instinct included libido and part of the ego instincts; the death instinct was a new and separate concept, fully as important as Eros. The death instinct, active immediately upon birth, refers to the tendency of organic life to return to its prior inorganic state. The process of living involves tension and the drive toward death aims at release of this tension. By this concept Freud hoped to account for self-destructive urges (*e.g.*, suicide), aggression toward others (*e.g.*, war), and the compulsive tendency to repeat earlier painful experiences. All mental phenomena are thus explainable in terms of fusions or mixtures of the two basic instincts.

Fenichel

Fenichel accepts the existence of destructive urges and grants that they are the opposite of sexual desires for a love object. However, he deviates from Freud by maintaining that the two are merely differentiations of an originally common root. Both are expressions of what he calls the "constancy principle"—the need to strive for relaxation by getting rid of tensions. An illustration of how the constancy principle affects the erotic instincts is the hungry infant who awakens to satisfy his hunger and to fall asleep again. Aggressive drives, on the other hand, have no instinctual aims of their own but are rather a mode of responding to frustration. If tension is aroused by insufficient tolerance for a frustration, then aggression is simply a way of attempting to get rid of that tension. Fenichel concludes by iterating that there is no necessity to assume that instincts should be dichotomized. He suggests that an adequate, detailed classification of instincts will have to wait until physiology can provide better information concerning their sources.

Thompson

The neo-Freudians also reject the notion of an innate death instinct. Thompson (282) voices several objections to Freud's theory: (1) suicide and aggression toward others are more related to the frustrations of living and develop out of interpersonal difficulties; (2) the so-called destructiveness of the child may not really be intended as such but may result instead from curiosity, liking noise, or just plain ignorance; (3) the child born in a perfectly benign environment should, according to Freud's theory, still have a seriously destructive force within himself, which does not seem to be the case. According to Thompson, serious destructiveness seems to be developed by malevolent environments (see Note 3).

THE UNCONSCIOUS AND THE ID

The Orthodox Formulation

A second consideration involved in appraising the personality potential of the neonate is the concept of the unconscious. The split into levels of awareness—unconscious, preconscious, and conscious—is said to occur in the earliest part of childhood, probably in the first year according to Ernest Jones (155). So the neonate's mental life, therefore, may be characterized as an undifferentiated state, from which the levels of consciousness shortly begin to emerge.

Definition and Importance. The unconscious is defined as that vast quantity of mental life which either never was in consciousness or, if previously conscious, has been repressed. It is a dynamic concept in the sense that unconscious impulses are continually striving for conscious expression in a very active way. Its effects are far more powerful than those of the conscious mind, and it can profoundly alter ideas, emotions, and even somatic conditions without the individual's being aware of the influence. The importance of this concept for the theory is summed up by Fenichel as follows (74, p. 7):

The existence of the unconscious is an assumption that forced itself upon psychoanalytic research when it sought a scientific explanation and a comprehension of conscious phenomena. Without such an assumption the data of the conscious in their interrelationships remain incomprehensible; with such an assumption, that which characterizes the success of every science becomes possible: to predict the future and to exert systematic influence.

Freud's Reasons for Believing in the Unconscious

. . . (a) the post-hypnotic carrying out of suggestions held in the unconscious, (b) the evidences found through discovering the latent meaning of dreams, (c) the discoverable bases for common slips or errors of speech, memory, action, (d) the fact that ideas suddenly appear in the mind from somewhere outside consciousness or even that problems are solved without awareness, (e) the small amount in consciousness at any one time in comparison to the latent content of the mind, (f) the fact that through psychoanalytic technique various mental and physical symptoms are found to have their foundations in hidden mental life, and in general, the "analytic investigation reveals some of these latent processes as having characteristics and peculiarities that seem alien to us, or even incredible, and running directly counter to the well-known attributes of consciousness," (g) finally, "an incontrovertible proof" is found in that the assumption of the unconscious helps us to construct a highly successful practical method by which we are enabled to exert a useful influence upon the course of conscious processes [136, pp. 22, 24]. [See Note 4.]

Attributes. The unconscious has certain special characteristics which distinguish it from the preconscious (level close to consciousness, whose contents have a ready capacity for becoming conscious) and the conscious itself.

1. Wishes based on instinctual impulses reside in the unconscious and exist independently side by side with each other. In Freud's words, they are "exempt from mutual contradiction." When two wishes whose aims appear to be incompatible become active at the same time, they do not detract from or cancel one another. Instead they combine to form an intermediate compromise aim.
2. The processes of the unconscious are timeless—they are not altered by the passage of time and have no temporal sequence. Time relation is a function of the conscious (see Note 5).
3. Within the unconscious system there is no negation, no

doubt, and no varying degree of certainty. These rather are functions of the censorship which exists between the unconscious and the preconscious.

4. There is very little relation to external reality. Unconscious processes are regulated only by their own strength and by their conformity to the pleasure principle, that is, the seeking of pleasure and the avoidance of pain. In other words, the unconscious is amoral.

5. Energy belonging to unconscious ideas is far more mobile than in the preconscious or conscious. This free-floating energy is directed according to the "primary process," that is, unaffected by demands of reality, time, order, or logic. It can easily become condensed or displaced, following only the path of greater likelihood of discharge. This is in contrast to the more differentiated "secondary process" which is characteristic of the preconscious.

Origin of Content. The origin of the content of the unconscious remains a highly speculative issue. Freud speaks of "primal fantasies," which refer to fundamentally similar fantasies found so frequently that they assume a typical form. At first he felt that they could be traced to real experiences, but later he switched to a phylogenetic view, maintaining that the individual is capable through racial inheritance of reaching out "beyond his own life into the experiences of antiquity, where his own experience has become all too rudimentary." He adds that these unconscious fantasies "were once realities in the primeval existence of mankind and that the imaginative child is merely filling in the gaps of individual truth with prehistoric truth." (See Note 6.)

Nature of Content. According to Freud, the content of the unconscious consists only of ideas. It is incorrect to speak of unconscious instinctual impulses, emotions, and feelings. An instinct can never be an object of consciousness—only the idea that represents the instinct. Similarly, in the unconscious it can be represented only by the idea, for if the instinct did not attach itself to an idea, we could know nothing about it. He goes on to say that we do speak of an unconscious or a repressed instinctual impulse, but this is nothing more than a harmless looseness of phraseology.

Just as there can be no unconscious instinctual impulses, there also cannot be unconscious emotions. By definition, an emotion is something that has entered consciousness. The practice of referring to unconscious love, guilt, and anxiety is based upon a subtle type of process which is not in contradiction to the general principle. What happens is that a certain emotion is perceived but misconstrued. This distortion results in connecting the emotion with another idea, and the emotion is interpreted by the conscious mind as an expression of the second idea. In this sense the original emotion can be described as unconscious, though it was really its ideational representation which had been repressed.

Fenichel, on the other hand, feels that it is legitimate to speak of unconscious emotions. There are tensions in the organism which, if not blocked, would result in specific sensations. These can be viewed as unconscious predispositions, so that an individual unknowingly may have a readiness toward rage, sexual excitement, anxiety, or guilt.

Relationship to the Id. Freud later supplemented his notion of levels with a topographical division of personality structure into id, ego, and superego. At this point in our genetic sequence we need be concerned only with the id.

The exact relationship between the unconscious and the id has never been clearly formulated. Some writers use the two interchangeably, while others, including Freud, feel that the separation is a fruitful one. Perhaps the analysis can best be made by viewing the id as one segment of the unconscious. In other words, all of the id is unconscious, but not all of the unconscious is id.

The characteristics of the id may be described as follows:

1. It is the source of instinctual energy for the individual, forming his reservoir of libido (see Note 7).

2. It aims at gratification of libidinal urges, obeying the pleasure principle.
3. It is amoral and illogical, with no unity of purpose.
4. It contains all phylogenetic acquisitions.

Jung: "The Collective Unconscious"

Jung (158) offers his own version of the concept of the unconscious, which has some slight overlap with Freud's. First of all, Jung divides the unconscious into two parts: the personal unconscious and the collective unconscious. The personal unconscious is said to contain forgotten memories, suppressed painful ideas, apperceptions sometimes described as below threshold, and finally contents that are not yet ripe for consciousness. The main differences from Freud in this respect are: (1) Less emphasis upon repression. The personal unconscious for Jung is not so much the result of repression as it is a consequence of the tendency of every individual to develop one-sidedly. In adapting to life one part of his potentialities is neglected in favor of the other, and the neglected part tends to become unconscious. (2) Therefore unconscious aspects of a person are not necessarily undesirable traits, since positive features are easily relegated to the unconscious by this one-sided development.

The second part, the collective unconscious, refers to the racial inheritance of significant memories. It contains "irruptions from the deepest part of the unconscious," and that part of the unconscious that can never be made conscious. Jung writes (136, p. 27): "In every individual there are present (besides his personal memories) the great 'primordial images,' those potentialities of human representations of things as they have always been, inherited through the brain structure from one generation to the next." Concerning the inheritance of ideas, he says (136, p. 29): "I do not by any means assert the inheritance of ideas, but only of the possibilities or germs of ideas, something markedly different. I must own I have never yet found indisputable evidence of the inheritance of memory-images, but I do not regard it as positively excluded that besides these collective deposits, which contain nothing specifically individual, the psyche may also inherit memory acquisitions of a definite individual stamp." (See Note 8.)

These primordial images or archetypes become known through the symbolic interpretation of dreams. Beyond the personal level of association comes the collective unconscious meaning of the dream. The archetype is a universal category of intuition and apprehension, common to entire nations or even epochs. It is an inherited organization of psychic energy. Myths are favorite carriers of racial archetypes. Examples are the mother and father archetypes. The composite image of all preexisting mothers is a model or pattern of all the protecting, warming, nourishing influences which man has experienced or the child will experience. The protecting mother is also associated with the nourishing earth, the provident field, the warming hearth, the protecting cave, the surrounding vegetation, the milk-giving cow, and the herd. The symbol of the mother refers to a place of origin such as nature, to that which passively creates, to matter, to the unconscious, natural, and instinctive life. The archetype of the father, on the other hand, signifies such things as strength, power, authority, the creative breath, and all that is moving and dynamic in the world. The father image is associated with rivers, winds, storms, battles, raging animals like wild bulls, the violent and changing phenomena of the world, as well as the cause of all change.

This particular aspect of Jung's system, dealing with primordial images, has something in common with Freud's notions of phylogenetic inheritance, as in the example of the primal horde. However, Jung ascribes a very different role to the functioning of the unconscious. For him, the collective unconscious contains the wisdom of the ages lying dormant in the brain. Continually active, the unconscious creates combinations of its materials which serve to indicate the future path of the individual. These unconscious combinations are said to be superior both in refinement and extent to the conscious ones. Therefore he describes the collective unconscious as an "unparalleled guide" for human beings, ". . . the mighty spiritual inheritance of human development, reborn in every individual constitution."

Neo-Freudian Viewpoints

The neo-Freudians consider the concept of unconscious mental functioning to be one of Freud's greatest contributions. Thompson, for example, takes pains to point out that discarding libido and instincts in no way interferes with the acceptance of varying levels of awareness as a key theoretical construct. Their main criticism is that Freud's original treatment connotes the unconscious as a place, where instincts or their mental surrogates reside; and that his later conception of the id is even more guilty in this respect. Although Freud specifically states that the id is nothing more than a figure of speech and cannot be allocated to any area in the body, Thompson, reading between the lines, feels that the idea of finding a location held a strong appeal for him.

A more specific criticism is made of Freud's opinion that repressed experiences and id forces, by virtue of being together in the unconscious, somehow join forces in attempting to gain conscious expression. Repressed material, for example, may borrow some energy from the id to obtain an outlet, according to Freud. Thompson deems this area highly speculative and inherently incapable of being subjected to validation study.

PRIMARY NARCISSISM

Freud: The Orthodox View

Another condition which is part of the neonate's potential is the state of primary narcissism. Narcissism refers to the turning of libido upon the self rather than upon other persons or objects in the external world. Primary narcissism is the original state of the newborn, who is not capable of distinguishing between himself and external objects. Sexual aims in this period are entirely autoerotic, that is, concerned with self-love. The ego has not yet been differentiated, and the infant is omnipotent, since his needs are cared for as a matter of course. He is said to possess an "oceanic feeling." Later in life, individuals in the face of severe stress are tempted to regain the original idyllic feeling of security—an illustration being the catatonic schizophrenic. This return to self-love as a consequence of failure to make satisfactory attachments to others is termed "secondary narcissism."

Freud, in his paper entitled "On Narcissism" (1914), attempts to substantiate the concept of primary narcissism through deductions from the observation of parents. He writes (100, pp. 48–49):

If we look at the attitude of fond parents towards their childen, we cannot but perceive it as a revival and reproduction of their own, long since abandoned narcissism. Their feeling, as is well known, is characterized by over-estimation, that sure indication of a narcissistic feature in object-choice which we have already appreciated. Thus they are impelled to ascribe to the child all manner of perfections which sober observation would not confirm, to gloss over and forget all his shortcomings—a tendency with which, indeed, the denial of childish sexuality is connected. Moreover, they are inclined to suspend in the child's favor the operation of all those cultural acquirements which their own narcissism has been forced to respect, and to renew in his person the claims for privileges which were long ago given up by themselves. The child shall have things better than his parents; he shall not be subject to the necessities which they have recognized as dominating life. Illness, death, renunciation of enjoyment, restrictions on his own will, are not to touch him; the laws of nature, like those of society, are to be abrogated in his favor; he is really to be the center and heart of creation, "His Majesty the Baby," as once we fancied ourselves to be. He is to fulfill those dreams and wishes of his parents which they never carried out, to become a great man and a hero in his father's stead, or to marry a prince as a tardy compensation to the mother. At the weakest point of all in the narcissistic position, the immortality of the ego, which is so relentlessly assailed by reality, security is achieved by fleeing to the child. Parental love, which is so touching and at bottom so childish, is nothing but parental narcissism born again and, transformed though it be into object-love, it reveals its former character infallibly. [See Note 9.]

Greenacre: Relationship to Anxiety and Birth

Greenacre (121) links the concept of primary narcissism to her preanxiety response and also to the birth process itself. Figuratively speaking, she refers to primary narcissism in its relation to anxiety as surface tension which may be great or little according to the organism's needs. An increase in anxiety causes a corresponding increase in narcissism; and excess narcissism develops as part of the organism's attempt to overcome excess anxiety. One illustration of the link between the two is the cry of the newborn infant, which serves both as an expression of anxiety and soon afterward as a means of preserving omnipotence by summoning parents to the rescue.

The birth process serves as an organizer and catalyst in the transformation of the relaxed, relatively sleepy narcissistic state of the fetus into the primary narcissism of the neonate. For Greenacre, primary narcissism connotes more than the oceanic feeling of omnipotence. It also is characterized by the beginnings of a propulsive psychic drive based on the biological need for survival. In times of later biological stress, such as a trauma or deprivation, there is an increase in narcissism, which is described as the libidinal charge of the impulse to attack or to defend. She uses the analogy of an amoeba which, when hungry, sends out a pseudopod to engulf its food. The rudimentary form of this drive is present in the neonate as a result of the organizing action of birth.

Fromm: A Neo-Freudian View

The neo-Freudians' criticism of the concept of narcissism is directed against the notion of a fixed amount of libido. They say that, according to Freud, the more love an individual turns toward the outside world, the less love is left for himself, and vice versa. Fromm (107) objects to this formulation on the grounds that it leads to the untenable position of saying that the narcissist is a richer person than the individual capable of love. Instead of being exhausted by loving others, he actually becomes enriched. Also, in Fromm's opinion, a person capable of genuinely loving himself is therefore more capable of loving others. Similarly, the person incapable of love for others is also incapable of loving himself. Primary and secondary narcissism are totally different from each other, since primary refers to self-esteem and secondary to a defense against awareness of loss of self-esteem. Secondary narcissism, as manifested by conceit, attention to one's own body, and general self-centeredness, is not self-love, but rather self-hate, arising from the feeling of failure and not being loved (see Note 10).

SUMMARY

Orthodox psychoanalytic theory explains mental phenomena as the result of a dynamic interaction between urging forces or instincts within the organism and counterforces set up by the external environment. Instincts, described as psychic representatives of stimuli originating in the soma, already exist for the newborn child. Each instinct has its aim, object, and source. Fenichel classifies instincts generally into the simple physical needs and the sexual urges. The former, such as hunger, breathing, and thirst, are said to be less important for personality development since they require quick satisfaction and thus allow for very little variability among individuals. Sexual urges, conceived in the broadest sense, operate from birth onward so that adult forms of sexuality are continuations of the infantile ones. The energy of the sexual instincts is termed "libido," fixed quantities of which are presumed to be present in the neonate. Jung defines libido more broadly as a primal energy underlying all mental life, not merely the sexual. The neo-Freudians, on the other hand, reject the notions of instinct and libido, though Sullivan does speak of a "power motive."

Freud in his later writings also postulated an innate death instinct to account for aggression and self-destructive urges. However, Fenichel takes issue with this notion and prefers to explain aggression as a mode of response to frustration, growing like the sexual instincts out of a need for tension reduction. Similarly the neo-Freudians offer interpersonal difficulties as a better explanation than the death instinct for aggression and suicide.

Another major element in the personality potential of the neonate is the unconscious, a cornerstone of psychoanalytic theory. Its influence is purported to be far more powerful than that of the conscious mind, for unconscious impulses continually strive in a very active fashion for conscious expression. Processes in the unconscious are timeless and bear little relation to external reality. Incompatible wishes can exist side by side, and there are no considerations of doubt, negation, or uncertainty. The term "id" was added later to designate that portion of the unconscious which functions as a source of instinctual energy, forming a reservoir of libido. Freud's own view on the origin of content in the unconscious is phylogenetic, that is, through some form of racial inheritance. The latter resembles to some extent Jung's formulation of the collective unconscious, a product of the racial inheritance of significant memories or germs of ideas. Transmitted in the collective unconscious are primordial images or archetypes which, according to Jung, become known through the symbolic interpretation of dreams. Examples are the mother and father archetypes, dealing, respectively, with nourishment and strength. In addition to the collective unconscious each individual is said to possess a personal unconscious— forgotten memories which are a consequence, not so much of repression, but of one-sided development. Neo-Freudians accept the principle of unconscious function but criticize Freud's connotation of the unconscious as a place, where, for example, repressed experiences and id forces can combine with each other.

Finally orthodox theory ascribes to the neonate a condition known as "primary narcissism." The infant is unable to differentiate himself from external objects, so that sexual aims are autoerotic and libido is turned inward. Because of the magical gratification of his needs, the infant soon develops a feeling of omnipotence which later in life he may wishfully seek to regain. For Greenacre primary narcissism connotes more than this "oceanic feeling." She considers that narcissism, catalyzed by the birth processes, contains the beginnings of a propulsive drive based on the biological need for survival. An increase in anxiety is said to cause a corresponding defensive increase in narcissism. Fromm quarrels with the fixed-amount-of-libido notion and criticizes Freud's formulation of narcissism on the grounds that a person capable of genuinely loving himself is actually more capable of loving others.

NOTES

1. *The Term "Instinct."* It should be noted that "instinct" is considered a poor translation of Freud's *Trieb.* "Instinct" connotes something inherited, rigid, unchangeable, whereas *Trieb* actually refers to something which is changed and influenced by forces stemming from the environment (74). Perhaps the term "drive," or possibly "motive," as currently used in psychology would have been a happier choice.

2. *Sullivan's "Power Motive."* Although the neo-Freudians reject instinct and libido theory as a hindrance to scientific investigation, one wonders whether Sullivan's "power motive" is not open to the same criticism. A "biological striving for power" would be rather difficult to demonstrate. His attempt to cushion the concept by describing it as a capacity rather than a fully developed drive does not appear to make it any more productive.

3. *Thompson's Objections to the Death Instinct.* While we can agree wholeheartedly with Thompson's opposition to the notion of a death instinct, her three arguments seem to have a descending order of convincingness. The first—interpersonal difficulties as a

preferred explanation for aggression—makes good sense; the second—innocent destructiveness—is a bit dubious, purely on the basis of observation of children; and the third—children free of any destructive tendencies—is too hypothetical to imagine, since "perfectly benign environments" are probably scarce nowadays.

4. *Freud's Reasons for Believing in the Unconscious.* Acceptance of the existence of some sort of unconscious mental functioning is almost sufficiently widespread to obviate the necessity for further discussion. However, we might examine the relative merits of the seven points of evidence presented by Freud. The first three, dealing with posthypnotic suggestion, latent meaning of dreams, slips of the tongue, etc., have all received confirmation in clinical and experimental work. The next two—problem solving with awareness and the small amount in consciousness at any one time—are acceptable statements. However, they are not directly pertinent to the psychoanalytic contention that unconscious material is continually pushing to break through into consciousness; instead they simply support some notion of conscious and not conscious perception. Point six, the unconscious meaning of symptoms, is also an established clinical finding. The final bit of evidence, though, can and has been debated at length. Can successes in psychoanalytic therapy (assuming this is what Freud had in mind) be interpreted as a validation of psychoanalytic theory? This writer is willing to defend the negative for at least two reasons: first of all, we have no good evidence yet regarding a greater proportion of cures by psychoanalytic treatment than by other methods; and secondly, there is no way to determine, even in an eminently successful case, how much and in what ways the therapist's theoretical orientation contributed to the complex interpersonal relationship which resulted in the patient's improvement.

5. *Timelessness in the Unconscious.* This concept is difficult to comprehend, perhaps by virtue of our time-bound frame of reference. Any inference of timelessness must be based on derivatives observed in behavior, which is subject to time regulation. Also, it would be hard to establish that repressed ideas, as they prepare to emerge into consciousness, do not have some, however illogical, temporal relationship to one another.

6. *The Phylogenetic Origin of Content in the Unconscious.* The transmission of "primal fantasies" via racial inheritance can only be considered of historical interest, in terms of our present-day think-

ing. Explanations of this kind are sufficiently implausible and un-
testable to warrant their deletion. Note the similarity to Jung's
theories regarding the origin of the collective unconscious.

7. *The Id: Source, Reservoir, or What?* Earlier we were told
that the source of an instinct is the chemicophysical status itself
of the organism. Now the id is defined as the source of instinctual
energy, forming a reservoir of libido. Is the id, then, a chemicophysical status or a kind of receptacle for libido? This state of
metaphorical confusion makes one wonder about the ultimate
utility of concepts like id and libido. Their justification in the past
has been as handy labels whose nonreified meaning is clear to all
intimates of the theory. If even their clarity can be questioned,
perhaps we should dispense with the words themselves. [See Ellis
(66) for an extended discourse on the evils of Freud's topographical constructs.]

8. *Jung's Collective Unconscious.* The same comments apply
here as in Freud's phylogenetic explanations (see Note 6). The
main difference between the two is that Jung places major emphasis on the concept in both theory and practice, whereas Freud's
system does not suffer greatly by its elimination.

9. *Primary Narcissism.* While Freud's account of parental narcissism is keenly perceptive, its existence does not substantiate the
formulation of primary narcissism during infancy. The latter seems
destined to remain a postulate.

10. *Freud versus Fromm on Self-esteem.* One gets the feeling
that Freud and Fromm are using the same words with differing
connotations. Freud speaks of secondary narcissism as the withdrawal of cathexes from other individuals. The narcissistic person
no longer desires to gratify objects in his environment and, in a
constricting process, focuses on patching up his injured self-esteem.
Fromm views self-esteem more as a kind of positive fulfillment or
self-actualization, which enriches the individual and permits both
greater self-love and greater object love. This difference in approach to the concept of narcissism may account in part for the
conflicting statements.

CHAPTER 3 *The First Year of Life*

Once the human organism embarks on its postnatal career, things happen rapidly in a number of areas. This expansion and diversity of development in the first year is presumed to contribute mightily to personality organization. As a by-product, it also facilitates the organization of this book. We can now adopt a systematic outline which will encompass chronological events through the period of adolescence:

Ego and superego formation
Psychosexual development
Relationships with others
Mechanisms

EGO AND SUPEREGO FORMATION

Orthodox Formulation: The Archaic Ego

Infantile Perceptions. The newborn infant, as we have seen, does not have an ego. His ego becomes differentiated only under the influence of the external environment. He has no awareness of the outside world, and at best merely experiences sensations of pleasure and pain, or changes in tension. The first tendency is to get rid of the state of tension. Once this has been accomplished, by feeding him or making him warm and comfortable, he falls back asleep. At this time, relaxation goes together with loss of consciousness. The beginnings of ego functioning appear when the infant first realizes that something has to be done by the outside world in order to have his tensions reduced. He now longs for "objects" (persons or things)

33

to satisfy his wants—a condition described as "stimulus hunger." This introduces a basic contradiction between the longing for relaxation and the longing for objects, which is said to represent the undifferentiated forerunner of love and hate (see Note 1).

The distinction between self and environment centers about the indulgence and deprivation experienced at the hands of the mother. So long as all of the infant's needs are gratified, he continues to think only in terms of self. Some deprivation is essential before the distinction can be made. Theoretically, if every need could be immediately taken care of, a conception of reality would probably never develop. At the other extreme, intense deprivation also hinders ego development, for a certain amount of gratification is necessary (see Note 2). According to Hartmann, Kris, and Loewenstein (133), the optimal proportion for the maturation of the infant's perceptual equipment is a large amount of indulgence combined with a smaller amount of deprivation. These authors stress the fact that the distinction between self and object is also dependent upon the stage of development of the perceptual apparatus itself.

Fenichel (74) describes what the infantile perceptions are probably like, based on observations of regressed psychotics (see Note 3): objects are not sharply distinguished; images are large and inexact; perception and motility are inseparable; and the perceptions of many sense organs overlap. The more primitive sensations, such as the kinesthetic, are said to prevail. Infantile perceptions are also different in content as well as form. One source of content difference is due to the small size of the infant and to his spatial experiences. A second and more important source is the distortion resulting from the one-sided view of the world either as a possible provider of satisfaction or as a possible threat. Pleasure seeking is incompatible with correct judgment, which is based on consideration and postponement of reactions.

Self-esteem. The first regulator of self-esteem is the supply of nourishment (in a broad sense) from the external world.

This process operates as follows: the first longing for objects is in the nature of a longing for the removal of disturbing stimuli; satisfaction by the object does away with the longing and revives the feeling of primary narcissism or, in other words, restores self-esteem. This is possible because at the early period the longing for the return of omnipotence and the longing for the removal of instinctual tension are not yet differentiated from each other.

Later, when the child is forced to give up his feeling of omnipotence, he tends to share in the adult's omnipotence. At this stage, instinctual satisfactions do become differentiated from omnipotence, and each token of love from the more powerful adult has the same effect as the supply of milk formerly had. The small child loses self-esteem when he loses love and attains it when he regains love. This period, following the omnipotent stage of primary narcissism, is described as one of "passive-receptive mastery," since difficulties are overcome by inducing powerful external objects to deliver the desired supplies.

Development of the Sense of Reality. As the infant matures, his growing intellectual capacities lead him beyond mere concern with indulgence or deprivation. The pleasure principle gradually is replaced by the reality principle. This is a learning process in which he becomes aware of probable changes in his environment and can anticipate future considerations. He can now figure to himself: "When I behave in a certain way, my environment will react in a certain way"—and proceeds to regulate his behavior accordingly. The reality principle, therefore, refers to the ability to substitute future for immediate gratification. In terms of psychic energy, libidinal energy becomes transformed into aim-inhibited libidinal energy.

Ferenczi (75), in 1913, delineated four preliminary stages in the development of the sense of reality:

1. "Unconditional omnipotence"—the situation of the child before birth when all wishes are gratified.

2. "Magic hallucinatory omnipotence"—the period immediately after birth when the infant feels that all he has to do is wish for something and it will appear.
3. "Omnipotence by magic gestures"—later he learns that he can overcome disappointments by cries and gestures.
4. "Magic thoughts and words"—finally he attaches magical significance to thoughts and words (see Note 4).

Melanie Klein's Theory

Orthodox analytic theory characterizes the first year as witnessing the early tentative phases in the formation of ego structure. The superego is completely nonexistent at this time. Melanie Klein (172, 174, 177), the leader of a British school of psychoanalysis, postulates the active functioning of a well-developed ego and superego in the first year. Klein's system is predicated upon the assumption of unconscious fantasies, which she inferred from her work in analyzing neurotic children. These unconscious fantasies are said to be the primary content of all mental processes, underlying all unconscious and conscious thought. In the first few months of life Klein sees evidence for a wide range of highly differentiated object relations, some libidinal and some aggressive. The infant, at six months, already loves, hates, desires, attacks, and wishes to destroy and to dismember his mother. Being afraid of his destructive impulses, he attributes them to an external object and then fantasies swallowing the object in order to destroy it. This results in his carrying around with him a severe superego or conscience which offsets the destructive impulses. Numerous complications follow—such as the possibility of spitting out or ejecting the superego—but we need not concern ourselves with these now. Details of Klein's system will be added in subsequent discussions of psychosexual development, relationships, and mechanisms (see Note 5).

Sullivan: The Prototaxic Mode

Sullivan (277) describes three modes of experience which are involved in ego formation: prototaxic, parataxic, and syntaxic. In the first year of life the prototaxic mode is operating. At first the infant has no ego or sense of self-awareness. He vaguely feels or "prehends" earlier and later states without realizing any serial connection between them. There are no distinctions of time and place. All that he knows are momentary states, and his experiences are "cosmic" in the sense that they are undefined and unlimited. After a while he perceives or "prehends" the "mothering one." This is a very vague image which gradually gets distinguished as not being a part of himself. The mothering one who contributes to a feeling of wellbeing or euphoria is characterized as the "Good Mother." When she disturbs him in some way, another "complexus of impressions" becomes the "Bad Mother." The nipple of the breast becomes an attribute of the "Good Mother" and represents her in a hazy fashion. Such momentary experiences of the prototaxic mode form the basis of memory. In Sullivan's words (277, p. 52):

Memory is the relatively enduring record of all the momentary states of the organismic configuration. In less abstract language, living beings *fix*, somewhere and somehow, meaningful traces of everything they live through, not as "perceptions" or "states of excitation of the cortex" or the like, but rather as the pattern of how the organism-and-significant-environment existed at the moment. [See Note 6.]

PSYCHOSEXUAL DEVELOPMENT

Orthodox Approach: The Oral Stage

An integral part of orthodox psychoanalytic thinking is the theory of infantile sexuality (91). The small child is said to be "polymorphous perverse," which means that he is an instinctual creature dominated by undifferentiated, loosely organized sexuality. Infantile differs from adult sexuality in three ways: (1) the areas of greatest sensitivity need not be the genitals—other erogenous zones (areas which afford sexual pleasure) come to the fore, such as the mouth; (2) the aims differ in that infantile sexuality does not lead toward sexual intercourse, lingering instead at activities that later play a role in forepleasure; (3) infantile sexuality tends to be autoerotic rather than directed toward objects.

This pregenital period can be described in terms of several developmental stages. These phases are not clear-cut or separate from each other. Rather, all stages gradually pass into one another and overlap. Initially there is the oral stage, which extends all through and beyond the first year of life. The beginning expression of the sexual instinct is the act of sucking. The mother's breast is said to be the original object of the infant's sexual desire. In addition to satisfying hunger needs, the act of sucking itself gives pleasure. The infant learns this first while feeding but soon after discovers that excitation of the mouth and lips is gratifying even without food. An illustration is the thumbsucking of the infant. Thumbsucking presumably shows that the pleasure from breast or bottle is not based solely on the satisfaction of hunger but also on the stimulation of the mucous membranes of the mouth. Otherwise, the infant would remove his thumb, since it doesn't provide milk (see Note 7).

The first aim in this period of oral eroticism, therefore, is the pleasurable autoerotic stimulation of the erogenous zone. Later another aim is added—the desire to incorporate objects. Individuals are looked upon only as food or providers of food, and the infant fantasies being united with his source of supply by swallowing or incorporating it, thus making the object a part of himself. Fenichel (74) cites as evidence for this type of illogical association various religious rites in which by eating the same food a person magically "becomes the same substance," or the belief that he becomes similar to the object he has eaten. Corresponding to these incorporation aims are specific oral fears, such as the fear of being eaten. Common expressions like "You're so cute I could just eat you up!" are illustrations of the significance of incorporation.

The oral period is now thought of as being divided into two phases, following the lead of Abraham (1). The first phase is the one just described—pleasure sucking and oral incorporation. The second commences with the eruption of teeth. In response to frustrations at this time, usually in the area of feeding, the child attempts to retaliate by biting. This desire to injure or destroy the object is termed "oral sadism," in contrast to the earlier oral eroticism. The complications introduced by such impulses will be discussed when we come to the problem of relationships with others during the first year.

Klein's Position

For Melanie Klein (172, 177), most of the psychosexual developments which orthodox analysts ascribe to the whole period of early childhood are represented before age one. From the middle of the first year onward, the oral frustrations of the child, together with the increase in oral sadism, cause the release of oedipal impulses. The immediate consequence of oral frustration is the desire to incorporate the father's penis. But this is accompanied by the fantasy that the mother incorporates and retains possession of the father's penis. The impulse is then aroused to destroy in various primitive ways the mother's body and its contents. In the case of the girl, the impulse to destroy the mother's body gives rise to a danger situation equivalent to the castration anxiety of the boy, namely, fear of destruction of her own body. Oral frustration also arouses an unconscious knowledge that the parents enjoy mutual sexual pleasures (at first thought of in oral terms), and the oral envy aroused makes the child wish to push into the mother's body. These fantasied attacks are directed in particular at the orally incorporated penis of the father. The boy, for example, is afraid of the mother's body because it contains the father's penis.

Modification of these early anxieties is brought about through the libido and through relations to real objects. Even the earliest turning from the mother's breast to the father's penis is a libidinal step forward from an anxiety situation, although not a very successful step at first. The stages in the development of the libido really represent positions won by the libido in its struggle with destructive impulses (*e.g.*, the girl's attention to the father's penis is considered a precursor of the Oedipus complex).

Jung's Position

Jung (157) differs radically from the Freudian view of early psychosexual development. As we have already seen, he rejects the notion of libido as a sexual force. In addition, he defines infantile sexuality in a much narrower way. Jung divides the life of the individual into three developmental phases: (1) the presexual, comprising the first three to five years; (2) the prepubertal, from later childhood until puberty; and (3) the period of maturity, extending from puberty on. According to his view, the first signs of sexuality do not begin until the end of the presexual phase. The earliest phase is characterized almost exclusively by nutrition and growth. The libido passes over gradually and with great difficulty from the nutritive to the sexual function. The sequence is as follows: originally food is taken in the act of sucking, with certain rhythmic movements associated with it. Gradually the sucking passes beyond nutrition to gaining pleasure and satisfaction in rhythmic activity per se. Eventually the pleasure zones change and the rhythmic aspect becomes attached to the genital component. The progress of the libido from the function of nutrition to the sexual zone carries with it traits of the former, which accounts for the close association between nutritive and sexual functions (see Note 8).

Neo-Freudian Views

The neo-Freudians depart from orthodox analytic theory in minimizing the sexual or erotic aspect of early development. Instead they emphasize the cultural and developmental, with the sexual accorded an incidental or subsidiary role. They feel that Freud was correct in his observations of the general order of development but that his interpretation must be reevaluated. Concerning the oral stage, Thompson writes (282, pp. 35–36):

The oral stage seems to be chiefly determined by biological development. The newborn infant is chiefly a mouth. The most developed part of the cortex at birth is that which governs the oral zone. We are justified in assuming that the infant contacts the world and comprehends it in the beginning primarily in terms of mouth. We, however, question whether the erotic satisfaction obtained is the determining factor. It seems more likely that he contacts the world by mouth because it is his most adequate organ. Thus the oral stage is organically determined but not primarily because of its pleasure value.

Moreover, the kind of world contacted through the mouth is not universally the same, and the differences in experience make a more significant impression on personality development than does the organic fact of a period of oral primacy. There occur in different cultures variations as to the length of time a child is customarily breast fed and also variations in frequency of feeding. In some a child may nurse over a period of many years in contrast to our own system where the tendency has been to shorten the period of nursing as much as possible. Also among many peoples the child is fed whenever he cries, while with us until very recently a rigid schedule was not only enforced but considered good for the child. Moloney, in his study of the Okinawans, maintains that the free nursing habits of these people are the basis of their flexible, loving, anxiety-free personalities. Thus although there is an organic base for the oral stage, its effect on the personality of the child is undoubtedly greatly influenced by the cultural attitude towards it. [See Note 9.]

Erikson: The Oral Zone, Incorporative Mode

Erikson (70) elaborates the orthodox theory of psychosexual development by describing "zones" and "modes." He differentiates three zones: (1) "oral-sensory," which includes the facial apertures and the upper nutritional organs; (2) "anal," the excremental organs; and (3) the genitalia. The four modes of approach to these zones are the incorporative, retentive, eliminative, and intrusive.

During the first stage, the oral-sensory zone is dominated by the mode of incorporation. The infant not only sucks and swallows appropriate objects, but "takes in" with his eyes what enters his visual field, opens and closes his fist as if to hold onto things, and even seems to take in what feels good to his tactile senses. The other modes function in an auxiliary way at this time: clamping down with jaw and gums (later incorporative mode); spitting up and out (eliminative); closing up of the lips (retentive); and, in vigorous babies, a tendency to fasten upon the nipple (intrusive). These auxiliary modes "remain subordinate to the first incorporative mode unless the mutual regulation of the zone with the providing mother is disturbed either by a loss of inner control in the baby or by unfunctional behavior on the part of the mother." An example of the former is pyloric spasm, which thrusts food out again shortly after intake. Here the oral-eliminative mode assumes considerable importance and may result in an overly retentive approach to the world. Oral "closing up" becomes a generalized mistrust of whatever comes in because it is not apt to stay. An example of the second kind of loss of mutual regulation is a mother's habitual withdrawal of the nipple because she has been bitten or fears she will be. This may cause a premature biting reflex which, in later interpersonal relations, results in trying reflexively to hold on and to take from an unwilling source.

The second oral stage is characterized as the mode of incorporation by biting. The development of teeth is accompanied by pleasure in biting *on* hard things, in biting *through* things, and in biting pieces *off* things. Other activities are also subsumed: the eyes learn to focus and to "grasp" objects, the ears localize sounds and guide appropriate changes in position; and the arms and hands reach out to grasp more purposefully. Interpersonal relations center in the social modality of taking and holding onto things—things which are more or less freely offered and given, as well as things which have more or less of a tendency to slip away.

RELATIONSHIPS WITH OTHERS

Orthodox View: Mother as First Object

A third general category for describing personality development is "relationships with others" or, in technical terms, "object relations." According to orthodox theory, the first object of every individual is the mother. (The word "mother" is used in the broad sense to include that person who performs most of the care-taking functions as far as the infant is concerned.) As we have previously mentioned, the neonate cannot distinguish himself from others. He has no idea of mother as an individual. The process whereby this recognition comes about is a gradual one. It is assumed that the first ideas concern the things which bring satisfaction and are also momentarily absent. These may include the mother's breast or the bottle, the person of the mother, or parts of the child's own body. The actual perception of a "person" does not yet exist. Later the infant learns to differentiate impressions, with the first differentiation probably between "trusted" and "strange" impressions. "Strange" is felt as dangerous, whereas supplies are expected from "trusted" sources. The trusted parts of the mother are loved, and then gradually the mother is recognized as a whole, and oral union with the mother becomes the aim.

As the child learns to distinguish between himself and the mother, he develops understanding for her communications. Little is known about the detailed processes by which this understanding is established. Reactions to the actual handling of the child by the mother, to touch and bodily pressure, must play a part. Gradually, the understanding of the child for the mother's facial expression grows. All the cognitive features are said to be part of the libidinal tie between the two.

In the second part of the oral stage, when sadistic impulses occur, a new type of relationship is introduced. This is termed "ambivalence," which refers to the fact that two opposing attitudes—one friendly and one hostile—can exist concurrently toward a person. Thus the infant in the biting stage longs for pleasurable union with his mother and yet, in times of frustration, also wishes to destroy her. This oral-sadistic relationship is said to be the most extreme form of ambivalence. Love and hate are later derivatives of this process.

Freud felt that a possible explanation of the origin of ambivalence lay in its being a necessary protection of the infant against destructive impulses within himself. Externalizing these impulses, by attacking the object, is therefore a prerequisite for survival. Hartmann, Kris, and Loewenstein (133) advance another hypothesis to account for ambivalence. In the earliest phases of the infant's life, any transition from indulgence to deprivation tends to elicit aggressive responses. The child's ambivalence toward his first love objects corresponds to their position within the continuum leading from indulgence to deprivation. All human relations, according to this view, are permanently colored by the fact that the earliest love relations in the child's life were formed at a time when those whom the child loves are those to whom it owes both indulgence and deprivation.

Klein's Theory

Consistent with her radical departures concerning ego formation and psychosexual development, Klein also postulates the establishment of very early relationships. She states (177):

The hypothesis that the infant's first experiences of feeding and of his mother's presence initiate an object-relation to her is one of the basic concepts put forward in this book. This relation is at first a relation to a part-object, for both oral-libidinal and oral-destructive impulses from the beginning of life are directed toward the mother's breast in particular. . . . [177, p. 199.]

There are grounds to assume that as soon as the infant turns his interest towards objects other than the mother's breast—such as parts of her body, other objects around him, parts of his own body, etc.—a process starts which is fundamental for the growth of sublimations and object-relations. Love, desires (both aggressive and libidinal), and anxieties are transferred from the first and unique object, the mother, to other objects; and new interests develop which become substitutes for the relation to the primary object. This primary object is, however, not only the external but also the internalized good breast; and this deflection of the emotions and creative feelings, which become related to the external world, is bound up with projection. In all these processes, the function of symbol-formation and phantasy activity is of great significance. When depressive anxiety arises, and particularly with the onset of the depressive position, the ego feels driven to project, deflect and distribute desires and emotions, as well as guilt and the urge to make reparation, on to new objects and interests. These processes, in my view, are a mainspring for sublimations throughout life. It is, however, a precondition for a successful development of sublimations (as well as of object-relations and of the libidinal organization), that love for the first objects can be maintained while desires and anxieties are deflected and distributed. For, if grievance and hatred towards the first objects predominate, they tend to endanger sublimations and the relation to substitute objects. [177, pp. 224–225.]

Sullivan: Empathy and the Significant Other

The "significant other" is a term which Sullivan (277) uses to denote the most influential person in the child's world, usually the mother. We have already described in the section on ego formation how the infant first receives an impression of the "mothering one" which gradually differentiates into a "Good Mother" and a "Bad Mother." Sullivan treats another concept in the area of infantile relationships—the concept of empathy.

Empathy refers to a "peculiar emotional linkage" between the infant and significant other. Long before he can understand what is happening to him, this "emotional contagion or communion" exists. Its greatest importance is said to be from six months to twenty-seven months, but it endures through life in some people. An example of empathy is a feeding situation in which a fright experienced by the mother results in eating disturbances on the part of the child. A vicious circle is set up, since the mother's anxiety decreases the infant's feeling of euphoria, which consequently makes the mother more anxious.

The basis for this unclear mode of emotional communication is thought to be biological, since animals exhibit a similar phenomenon. However, the process is felt to be very important for understanding acculturation (see Note 10).

MECHANISMS

Introductory Comments

A fourth general category deals with mechanisms, which are the specific processes by which the individual operates. There has been a minor controversy over whether the term "dynamism" should be substituted for "mechanism." Healy, Bronner, and Bowers (136) urge the adoption of "dynamism" because they feel that mechanism merely connotes an arrangement of parts not necessarily doing anything, whereas dynamism refers to a specific force operating in a specific direction. However, "mechanism" is in more common usage, although Sullivan also prefers "dynamism."

The mechanisms functioning in the first year of life are considered forerunners of the later defense mechanisms. These early mechanisms include introjection, projection, denial, fixation, and regression. For most of these, there is only the orthodox formulation. Klein, as we have seen, offers her own viewpoint on several, but the neo-Freudians have no specific contributions. Sullivan does provide a definition of dynamism, which we might inject at this point—"a relatively enduring configuration of energy which manifests itself in characterizable processes in interpersonal relations." It refers to the way energy is organized and channeled in the human organism and implies only a relatively enduring capacity to bring about change.

Introjection, Primary Identification, and Projection

Orthodox Formulation. The first judgment of the ego is said to be the distinction between edible and nonedible objects: the first acceptance is swallowing; the first rejection is spitting out. Introjection is a derivative of the former, projection of the latter. In the early stage of development of the ego, everything pleasurable is experienced as belonging to the ego (something to be swallowed), while everything painful is experienced as being nonego (something to be spat out).

Originally, then, introjection or incorporation is an oral mechanism aimed at instinctual satisfaction. Later, when the infant no longer feels omnipotent, oral introjection of the powerful adult serves to regain the feeling. Still later, when incorporation is seen as destroying the independent existence of the outside person, the mechanism functions in a hostile manner as the executive of destructive impulses.

At this point it might be well to attempt to clarify the terms "introjection," "incorporation," and "identification." Introjection and incorporation are generally used synonymously; some also employ identification in the same way. However, identification usually connotes a type of relationship to objects, in other words, a state rather than a process. Thus, oral introjection is said to be the executive of the "primary identification." By introjecting or incorporating, one achieves a state of identification. Primary identification refers to the first relationship to objects, whereas secondary identification is a later repetition of the earlier one.

Projection starts as a primitive method of getting rid of pain, by attributing unpleasant stimuli to the outside world. It is a sort of reverse introjection—instead of the ego's being perceived as having the object's characteristics, the environment is perceived as having the ego's characteristics. In these early phases of development, the mechanism can function without difficulty. Later it requires a serious impairment of the sense of reality for it to play a major role. The essentially archaic nature of projection is illustrated by its prominence in animistic mythologies (see Note 11).

Klein's Formulation. Klein (177, p. 200) describes the operation of introjection and projection in the first year as follows:

In addition to the experiences of gratification and frustration derived from external factors, a variety of endopsychic processes—primarily introjection and projection—contribute to the twofold relation to the first object. The infant projects his love impulses and attributes them to the gratifying (good) breast, just as he projects his destructive impulses outwards and attributes them to the frustrating (bad) breast. Simultaneously, by introjection, a good breast and a bad breast are established inside.[1] Thus the picture of the object, external and internalized, is distorted in the infant's mind by his phantasies, which are bound up with the projection of his impulses on to the object. The good breast—external and internal—becomes the prototype of all helpful and gratifying objects, the bad breast the prototype of all external and internal persecutory objects. The various factors which enter into the infant's feeling of being gratified, such as the alleviation of hunger, the pleasure of sucking, the freedom from discomfort and tension, *i.e.*, from privations, and the experience of being loved —all these are attributed to the good breast. Conversely, every frustration and discomfort are attributed to the bad (persecuting) breast.

Denial

Another very primitive mechanism is denial, which is said to be as old as the feeling of pain itself. The ability to deny unpleasant parts of reality is the counterpart of the hallucinatory wish fulfillment. In a sense it amounts to closing one's eyes to the real state of affairs. Like projection, denial is a normal phase in the development of the infantile ego, but if it recurs extensively in later life it indicates an advanced stage of mental disease. Denial and reality are incompatible, so that, as perception and memory improve, denial becomes more difficult.

[1] Klein's footnote: "These first introjected objects form the core of the super-ego. In my view the super-ego starts with the earliest introjection processes and builds itself up from the good and bad figures which are internalized in love and hatred in various stages of development and are gradually assimilated and integrated by the ego."

Fixation and Regression

Orthodox Concepts. Two other mechanisms which operate in the first year are fixation and regression. In psychosexual development progress to a higher stage never takes place completely, for characteristics of the lower level persist to some extent. Disturbances may result in an arresting of development at any stage, which is termed "fixation," or they may cause the retention of an abnormal number of characteristics of an earlier stage, to which the individual will return if difficulties arise—the latter process being known as "regression." Thus fixation and regression are said to be complementary to each other. The stronger a fixation, the more easily will a regression take place if difficulties arise.

According to Fenichel (74), fixations are probably due both to constitutional factors, about which we know very little, and to any of a variety of experiential factors (see Note 12). The following are the kinds of experience which lead to fixation:

1. The most common cause is the simultaneous satisfaction of an instinctual drive and the need for security—in other words, a type of reassurance in the face of anxiety which also serves some instinctual gratification. An example predisposing to an oral fixation (characteristic of this early period) would be giving a bottle of milk to a child whenever he wakes up crying in the middle of the night.
2. Excessive gratification or overindulgence, so that the stage is given up with reluctance.
3. Excessive frustration or deprivation, leading to a continuing demand for gratification.
4. Alternating excessive gratification and excessive frustration.
5. Sudden changes from excessive gratification to excessive frustration.

The consequence of fixation is the hindering of future development. Oral fixations arising in the first year or so tie up a large amount of libido, so that an adequate supply of energy is not available to combat the difficulties of the next phase.

Regression in the first year is only a forerunner of the later concept of regression, which serves as a type of defense. In infancy it refers to the regular transformation of psychic functioning which accompanies the daily cycle from wakefulness to sleep (see Note 13).

Kleinian Concepts. Melanie Klein relates fixation and regression to infantile anxiety. The destructive impulses of the child in the oral and anal phases, accompanied by persecutory and depressive anxiety, are said to be the major cause of libido fixation. Thus fixation is to be understood partly as a defense against anxiety. Regression also takes place as the outcome of a failure of the libido to master the destructive impulses and anxiety aroused by frustration. Essential roles in the regressive process are played by introjected objects and the superego. The complicated function of anxiety is summarized by Klein (177, pp. 222–223) as follows:

The libidinal development is thus at every step influenced by anxiety. For anxiety leads to fixation to pre-genital stages and again and again to regression to them. On the other hand, anxiety and guilt and the ensuing reparative tendency add impetus to libidinal desires and stimulate the forward trend of the libido; for giving and experiencing libidinal gratification alleviate anxiety and also satisfy the urge to make reparation. Anxiety and guilt, therefore, at times check, and at other times enhance the libidinal development. This varies not only between one individual and another but may vary in one and the same individual, according to the intricate interaction between internal and external factors at any given time.

SUMMARY

According to orthodox psychoanalytic theory, the newborn child has no awareness of the outside world and can experience only changes in his own tension state. The beginnings of ego functioning appear when he longs for something to be done by the external world to satisfy his wants. This distinction between self and environment is said to occur in the context of indulgence and deprivation, with some amount of the latter essential for development. Self-esteem, one of the properties of the ego, is first regulated by the supply of nourishment from the outside, a magical source which leads the infant to feel omnipotent. Later there follows a period of passive-receptive mastery, in which he shares in the newly discovered omnipotence of adults and passively induces them to deliver the desired supplies. As the child grows, the earliest forms of pure pleasure seeking are gradually replaced by the reality principle—the ability to substitute future for immediate gratification.

Melanie Klein deviates from orthodox theory by postulating the active functioning of both ego and superego during the first year of life. Her theories are predicated upon the assumption of powerful unconscious fantasies at this time. Sullivan, in the neo-Freudian school, describes the first year as belonging to the prototaxic mode of experience. At first the infant knows only momentary states, with no distinctions of time and place. After a while he perceives or "prehends" the mother, mainly in terms of good and bad.

With respect to psychosexual development, the orthodox theory of infantile sexuality portrays the child as "polymorphous perverse." The beginning expression of the sexual instinct is said to be the act of sucking in the early oral-passive stage. Pleasure from this activity is soon discovered apart from the feeding situation, so that the first aim is autoerotic stimulation of the membranes of the mouth. Later the desire to incorporate persons and things is added. Individuals are looked upon primarily as food or providers of food in terms of these fantasies of incorporation, which are often accompanied by oral fears like the fear of being eaten. The second aspect of the oral stage, commencing with the eruption of teeth, is the sadistic, during which the child seeks to retaliate for frustration by biting.

Klein describes a wide array of sexual and aggressive fantasies in the first year, including oedipal impulses, the desire to incorporate the father's penis, the wish to destroy the mother's body, and so on. For Jung the earliest phase is characterized almost exclusively by nutrition and growth. The link between these nutritive functions and later sexuality is presumed to be rhythmic activity. The neo-Freudians also minimize the erotic element and stress instead cultural and developmental manifestations of orality. Erikson, closer to the orthodox position, adds the concepts of zones and modes, in this case the oral zone and incorporative mode.

In the area of relationships to people, orthodox theory traces a gradual transition from the infant's missing of things which bring satisfaction, to his differentiation of trusted and strange impressions, and finally to his recognition of the mother as a whole object. The notion of ambivalence is introduced in the oral-sadistic stage, at which period he longs for pleasurable union with the mother and yet in times of frustration wishes to attack her. Klein states that the mother probably exists as a whole object from the very beginning, but in vague outline. She tends to emphasize the child's fear of losing the love object. Sullivan concentrates his description of early relationships on the process of empathy—a peculiar nonverbal, emotional communication between parent and child, said to be strongest between the ages of six and twenty-seven months.

Mechanisms used in the first year include introjection, projection, denial, fixation, and regression. Introjection, based on swallowing or taking in food, is aimed first at instinctual satisfaction, later at regaining omnipotence, and still later at destroying the hated object by oral incorporation. Projection, stemming from spitting out the unpleasant, involves the attribution of painful stimuli to the outside world. Denial, also a very primitive mechanism, means the avoidance of unpleasant reality simply by closing one's eyes to it and pretending it does not exist. Fixation and regression refer to the retention of an abnormal number of characteristics of an earlier stage, to which the individual is predisposed to return if difficulties arise. All the preceding mechanisms, as they operate in the first year, are considered forerunners of the later defense mechanisms.

NOTES

1. *Love and Hate.* Freud's outmoded concern over polarities—love versus hate, life versus death, etc.—appears especially flimsy in this context. His need for developmental closure results here in the very strained interpretation of stimulus hunger as representing the "undifferentiated forerunner of love and hate."

2. *The Effects of Intense Deprivation.* Observational studies of infants by Spitz and Ribble have been widely cited for their demonstration of the harmful effects of insufficient "mothering." Spitz (268, 269) compared infants in a foundling home, where seven or more were in the charge of one adult, to those in the nursery of a penal institution, where each child was cared for by its own mother. The former showed a higher incidence of mortality, sickness, malnutrition, intellectual retardation, etc., despite excellent medical facilities. In addition, Spitz (270) has described a pattern of "anaclitic depression," occurring in children separated from their mothers in the latter half of the first year. Ribble (242, 243) concludes, on the basis of her observations of 600 infants, that a close, affectionate relationship between mother and child is essential for physical as well as mental health. She stresses the importance of such activities as cuddling, rocking, and singing softly to the infant in order to foster functional organization, relieve muscular tension, prime the breathing mechanisms, and, in general, promote a sense of security. Despite specific criticism of the quality of evidence in these observational studies [see Orlansky (224)], there seems to be general acceptance of the view that intense deprivation of love during the first year has deleterious effects. [For an extensive summary of research on maternal deprivation, see Bowlby (40).]

3. *Sources of Evidence.* Fenichel (74) comments that most of our knowledge about primitive ego development has been deduced from psychoanalyses of regressed, adult psychotics. Reconstructions from the treatment of adult neurotic patients are said to be very elusive, because of the undifferentiated nature of early mental reactions. Also, it is frequently not necessary to ex-

plore the earliest levels in order to cure the patient. Observations of infants have been of some help, he adds, but in most cases the studies have not been psychoanalytically oriented. With the latter statement we can agree heartily. Research psychologists in particular have, until recently, been much more fascinated with the acquisition of motor skill than the development of the ego. The growing emphasis on early interpersonal relationships, stimulated by such workers as Ribble and Spitz, would seem to offer considerably more promise in this area than necessarily tenuous inferences from the infantile behavior of adult psychotics. Anna Freud (84) also stresses the need for direct, continuing observations of children in the light of a variety of relationships with parents (*e.g.*, separation from parents at different ages).

4. *Ferenczi's Stages in the Development of the Sense of Reality.* The four stages are susceptible to varying degrees of credibility: "unconditional omnipotence" is challenged by the theories of prenatal influence discussed in the first chapter; "magic hallucinatory omnipotence" suffers from its implication of psychic content immediately after birth, as well as its basic unverifiability; whereas the last two—"omnipotence by magic gestures" and "magic thoughts and words"—can be affirmed by anyone who has ever watched children.

5. *Melanie Klein and Unconscious Fantasies.* While the clinical evidence for unconscious fantasies in children is well accepted, their extensive operation in the first few months of life taxes one's gullibility. Some harsh individuals may be willing to characterize the six-month-old as an ungrateful wretch who wishes to "dismember mama," but most of us will probably prefer to delay this appellation for a year or two, at which time we can watch him carefully aim a rock at her head.

6. *Sullivan's Prototaxic Mode.* Harry Stack Sullivan's descriptions of ego development, though viewed with some justification as old thoughts in new disguise, do seem to provide a more colorful and lucid account. Unfortunately the same cannot be said for his very confusing explanation of memory given in the text.

7. *The Act of Sucking.* The literature contains numerous references suggesting the existence of a sucking drive which operates independent of the nutritional process. Levy (187, 188) has reported two studies bearing on this point. In the first he found that the frequency of thumbsucking in infancy was higher among those

who had less sucking opportunity during the feeding process itself, as a result of overly quick withdrawal from the breast or bottle. In his classic experiment on sucking in puppies, those animals
which drank from bottles with large-holed nipples (short feeders)
did more body sucking and chewing between meals than did the
long feeders and breast feeders. Similarly, Roberts (245) observed that finger-sucking infants sucked fewer minutes per day
during their daily feeding than did nonsuckers. More recently
Ross (250) studied sucking behavior in newborn puppies, some
of whom had been separated at birth from the bitch and fed by
dropper and by bottle. Again the results indicated that more nonnutritional sucking took place in these animals than in the nursing ones.

The crucial theoretical question, however, concerns the genesis
of this so-called "oral drive." Orthodox psychoanalytic theory, as
we have seen, proposes an explanation in terms of physiological
pleasure deriving from stimulation of the mucous membranes of
the mouth. In support of this contention of a primary "instinctual"
response can be cited the very early evidences of nonnutritional
sucking. Pratt, Nelson, and Sun (231), Blanton (33), and Halverson (126) have all reported its occurrence shortly after birth. An
alternative explanation, based on learning theory, is offered by
Sears and Wise (259, pp. 123–124), who state: "In his discussion
of thumb-sucking, Freud [91] presented the hypothesis that the
lips and mouth become erotogenic, *i.e.*, capable of giving pleasurable sensations when stimulated, as a result of the association of
the act of sucking with the act of food taking. He recognized the
difficulty, from a systematic standpoint, of explaining how the
sensory apparatus of the lips and mucosa obtained their pleasure-
giving power from this association. This difficulty disappears if
the concept of erotogenesis is disregarded, and if the relationship
between sucking and nourishment is described in terms of instrumental acts and goal responses. Any instrumental act consistently
leading to a goal response (consummatory act, gratification, reward) develops the properties of a goal response in its own right;
i.e., it becomes a final act in a motivated behavior sequence. There
can then be said to be a *secondary*, or learned, drive to make that
response. Freud's hypothesis may be restated as follows: Sucking
is an almost universal instrumental act in infant feeding. It is
closely followed on nearly every occasion by the goal response of

eating. Sucking therefore becomes a secondary goal response, and children may be said to possess an oral drive that instigates sucking and other related oral manipulatory actions.

"A question may be raised as to whether there is not also an oral drive that is primary and unlearned. From a technical standpoint, this is difficult to answer. Nonnutritional sucking occurs soon after birth, but such behavior does not, by itself, guarantee the presence of an oral drive; it could result from an accidental juxtaposition of hand and mouth, and the sucking response could be reflexly instigated either by lip contact or by hunger stimulation. Kunst [182] has recently shown that even as late as the ninth to twelfth months thumb-sucking occurs more frequently when the child is hungry than when not." In their own research Sears and Wise (259) found that oral drive, as measured by amount of sucking, tends to be increased by longer practice at breast or bottle feeding. The question of genesis remains largely unanswered. If we can accept a seemingly more parsimonious explanation of nonnutritional sucking on the basis of a secondary, learned drive, then libido theory loses much of its attractiveness.

8. *Jung on Rhythm.* Jung here adds a third possible interpretation of sucking gratification—the associated rhythmic movement. Although many have been heard to voice the opinion that "all God's chillun" have rhythm, there is some difficulty in visualizing how rhythm-saturated libido carries nutritive traits to the sexual zone.

9. *Anthropological Evidence Relating to Feeding Practices.* The neo-Freudian emphasis on cultural variations in feeding practices is well taken. The Okinawans (210), Tchambuli (202), Comanches (164), and Arapesh (202), for example, are extremely indulgent in the nursing relationship, whereas the Mundugumor (202) child has to fight to obtain enough food and the Marquesan (163) is fed lying on his back on the cold ground. Weaning among the Alorese (62) is early and harsh, in direct contrast to the Motus (28). This impact of cultural experiences upon bodily functions would seem to be a vital consideration for personality theory. Implications of such child-rearing practices for adult personality characteristics will be reserved for discussion in Chapter 8.

10. *Research on Empathy.* Apart from a few limited observational studies and some anthropological descriptions, this in-

triguing area of nonverbal communication in young children remains to be explored. Fries (105) found many more startle
reactions among infants when weighed and bathed by active,
compulsive nurses than when handled by quiet ones. Similarly,
Escalona (72) noted that eight out of ten infants who refused the
breast at four weeks had high-strung and excitable mothers. The
most widely quoted evidence for empathy has been Escalona's
investigation of infant food preferences. Infants' likes and dislikes
for orange and tomato juice coincided in 15 cases with the preferences of their adult feeders in a penal institution. In three cases
where a baby was transferred to a feeder with the opposite dislike,
the infant switched his own choice. Also, emotional distress of
mothers who were not released on parole days seemed to be reflected in an increase of eating disturbances. From anthropological data (207) comes such suggestive evidence as the Arapesh
mother's violent reaction to being soiled by her child, which is
later associated with loss of sphincter control by the Arapesh adult
in emotionally charged situations.

More extensive experimentation along the lines of Escalona's
food-preference study would seem to be very worth while. Assuming that further research confirms the existence of empathy
in young children, we might then proceed to examine the various
conditions which are conducive to empathic response or not,
as well as to investigate the age levels (Sullivan says six to
twenty-seven months) at which the process operates. In any case,
explanation of empathy in terms of reaction to subliminal cues
appears more satisfactory than Sullivan's stress on a biological
basis.

11. *Studies of Projection.* The mechanism of projection is well
established clinically in the case of the paranoid individual, and
it also receives extensive illustration in animistic mythologies. The
experimental literature is again sparse. Sears (257) obtained ratings of self and others from nearly a hundred college fraternity
men on traits of stinginess, obstinacy, disorderliness, and bashful-
ness. Using a rough measure of insight (discrepancy between self
and other ratings), he found that those men who possessed more
than the average amount of a trait tended to attribute more than
average amount to others, provided insight was lacking. The projection occurred, however, at the positive as well as the negative
ends of the rated dimensions, *e.g.*, with generosity as well as stingi-

ness. This latter result is in contradiction to the theoretical statement that *unacceptable* impulses are the ones projected on to others. In an experiment utilizing the Thematic Apperception Test, Bellak (20) found that subjects whose stories were criticized tended to introduce more aggression in subsequent stories, thereby projecting their hostility to the examiner. Wright (290) asked eight-year-old children to give up either one of a pair of toys (one a preferred toy, the other not) to a friend. Immediately afterward they were asked which toy the friend would have given away. The proportion of times that the friend was considered generous was much less than in a control situation where the child did not have to give away a toy. The inference drawn from this finding is that guilt can initiate projection.

Another experimental approach has been to study the relationship between paranoia and homosexuality which, according to psychoanalytic theory, contains the mechanism of projection as a mediating variable. Gardner (109) noted that 47 per cent of a group of hospitalized paranoid patients showed clear-cut evidence of homosexuality. However, Miller (206) and Klein and Horwitz (170) report very minor concern with homosexuality in their paranoid samples. Page and Warkentin (225) administered the Terman-Miles Masculinity-Femininity Test to 50 paranoids, whose scores were said to resemble those of passive homosexuals more than those of either the normal male population or active homosexuals. Recently, in a more systematic study, Aronson (15) has given a battery of psychological tests to a group of paranoid schizophrenics and control groups of normals and nonparanoid schizophrenics. Many of the findings, particularly from the Blacky Pictures (35) technique and the Wheeler signs of homosexuality on the Rorschach Test, substantiated the commonly held association between paranoia and homosexuality.

The latter group of studies, of course, is open to the criticism that no direct evidence is provided for the operation of projection. Furthermore, Anna Freud (84) has attacked the Sears type of research on the grounds that projection, in its original meaning, does not normally occur in adults. Being a primitive mechanism, it can be found only in young children or psychotics; therefore, such experiments are necessarily irrelevant to the concept. However, all need not be black research-wise in the writer's opinion, for the area of projective testing may offer a way out of the dilemma. For the description of a projective approach to the mechanisms of defense (including projection), see Note 13 in Chapter 5.

12. *The Constitutional "Fudge" Factor.* Psychoanalytic literature is replete with references to the importance of "constitutional factors about which we know very little." One cannot escape the feeling that repeated lip service to constitution, which may at some future date be demonstrated to have specific relevance for psychoanalytic concepts, does not further the cause much at this time.

13. *Experiments on Regression.* Most of the experimental work on regression has been done with animals. Sears (258) has reviewed a number of such studies under the heading of "instrumental act regression." Probably the best known animal regression experiment is the one performed by Wolf (289). He taped the ears of one group of rats during infancy, and the eyes of another. Later the restraints were removed and the animals grew up normally. As adults, when placed in competition with control animals for food in response to a light stimulus, the previously blinded group had trouble seeing; when a sound stimulus was used, the previously deaf animals failed. Other animals whose senses had been impaired later than infancy did not fail in the adult situation.

Before proceeding to the work done with human subjects, the writer feels a need to inject his bias concerning the value of animal research generally for personality theory. All such studies are patently liable to the dangers of artificiality and oversimplification, since it is impossible to duplicate the complexity of interpersonal relations in the animal laboratory. The typical argument in defense is that animal research is an excellent source of hypotheses, hunches, etc., which can then be applied to humans. A counterproposal might be that an equivalent amount of time and energy, devoted to explorations with human subjects, might easily yield a more profitable harvest. Without much question experiments on animals *have* proved to be indispensable for the advancement of learning theory and, since learning theory and personality theory must ultimately be integrated, anyone who wants to badly enough can make a very indirect case on this basis.

The Barker, Dembo, and Lewin (17) experiment on regression in children has also received wide attention. These authors observed that the constructiveness of play decreased during a frustrating experience in which more attractive toys were made inaccessible by a wire-net barrier. Anna Freud (84) makes the same criticism here as in the projection experiments, namely, irrelevance of the operational definition of the psychoanalytic concept. She states that the vast differences between disturbance in play and disturbance occasioned by an intense emotional event, such as the loss of the mother, cannot be viewed merely as quantitative differences. Kris (181) objects to the experiment on the basis that it does not answer under what conditions an individual will react to frustration with regression. He goes on to say that a child's reaction to his mother's saying, "No, no, you can't have that!" in a toy department will depend on a complex interaction of the child's relationship to the mother, his tolerance of deprivation, and the mother's own feelings in the situation. In any case, the Barker, Dembo, and Lewin concept of "primitivation" seems to correspond closely to the Freudian notion of "ego regression" and does not pertain to psychosexual or "libido regression," in which later difficulties cause a return to behavior characteristic of an earlier developmental stage.

A very different approach is the attempt to produce regression experimentally through the use of hypnosis. Investigations in this area have typically employed intelligence tests to measure the accuracy of hypnotic age regression. Platonow (230) hypnotized three adults, told them they were three years old, and then found that their test performance approximated the three-year level. Later Young (291) questioned these findings on the basis of his own experiments, in which the same instructions yielded mental ages close to six years rather than three. In addition, a control group, asked to simulate consciously the behavior of three-year-olds, showed mental ages around five and a half. Recently Sarbin (253) has criticized Young's design on the grounds that no objective data were available to check the validity of the Stanford-Binet responses and that no systematic effort was made to consider the effect of variations in the depth of hypnosis. In his own research Sarbin also found no authentic regression to earlier age roles, but the hypnotized group performed more accurately than the controls. Depth of hypnosis showed a high degree of relationship to regression.

A more promising area for research on regression lies in the study of psychotic children and adults. At least two peripheral attempts have been reported in the literature: a study by Cameron

(47) showing that schizophrenic thought processes are not analogous to thinking in children; and one by Du Bois and Forbes (63) revealing the infrequent use of fetal postures by catatonics during sleep. However, it should be possible to design research dealing more directly with the highly charged affective elements which the theory ascribes to regression.

Between one and three the child discards his infantile ways and actively proceeds to carve his distinctive niche in the world. This is the period when his capacities for walking, talking, thinking, controlling his sphincters, and the like, develop rapidly. Along with these increased motor and perceptual abilities come a host of associated interpersonal skills and, of course, complications.

EGO AND SUPEREGO FORMATION

Orthodox Views: Fenichel

Development of Active Mastery. The child gradually progresses from the period of passive-receptive mastery, in which difficulties were overcome by inducing powerful adults to deliver supplies, to one of active mastery. In this later phase actions are substituted for simple discharge reactions, and there is an ability to postpone gratifications and to tolerate tensions. Two prerequisites are involved in the development of active mastery: (1) mastery of the motor apparatus of the body; and (2) growth of the function of judgment. The main features in motor development are learning to walk, to talk, and to keep clean. Walking and sphincter control are said to form the foundation of the child's independence. Speech introduces the function of anticipation, since events can be planned in the world of words. This advance leads to the second prerequisite for active mastery—judgment, which refers

to a general function of the ego known as "reality-testing."
The latter is the ability to anticipate the future in the imagination by trying actively in small doses what might happen
passively and in unknown doses in the real world. Reality
testing and tolerance for tensions go hand in hand as functions
of the ego.

Anxiety. Another problem which the ego faces is anxiety.
We have seen that anxiety may exist before the differentiation
of the ego—possibly in prenatal life, next as a result of the
birth trauma, and also shortly after birth. This early or primary anxiety, involving a flooding with excitation, becomes
modified as the reality-testing ego grows. Along with anticipatory imagination and action planning comes the idea of
danger. The judging ego now has the capacity to view a situation as potentially traumatic or threatening. Such a judgment
sets up only a moderate, controllable state of anxiety, which
is significantly less than would actually be experienced in the
situation. This anticipatory anxiety serves as a protective signal to the child, advising him that here is something with
which he must cope.

The content of childhood anxiety also undergoes changes.
The most fundamental anxiety is supposed to be connected to
the infant's physiological inability to satisfy his drives himself.
The first fear is the fear of experiencing further traumatic
states, which is the basis for the idea that one's own instinctual
demands might be dangerous. Complicating this early picture
of anxiety is the primitive talion principle. In his animistic
thinking the young child believes that others want to do to
him what he wishes to do to them. If a child fantasies devour-
ing his environment, he subsequently may fear being eaten by
his parents. The fantastic anxieties of physical destruction are
presumed to originate with the talion principle.

Another source of anxiety is the fear that the gratifications
which the child requires from others may not be forthcoming.
This is called "fear over loss of love"—love in this case meaning help and protection. Since self-esteem is regulated by
external supplies, anxieties in this area are especially intense.

A strong ego is said to be one that is loved, whereas a weak ego is deserted and exposed to danger.

Belated Mastery and "Functional Pleasure." Young children cope with anxiety in a very characteristic manner. They attempt to overcome tensions by active repetitions of the original anxiety-producing situation, both in games and in dreams. This "belated mastery" differs from the earlier anxiety experience in that the child behaves actively rather than passively and determines himself when and how strong the repetition should be. Later, he not only dramatizes the past in his play but also anticipates what he expects to happen in the future (see Note 1).

The pleasure obtained from overcoming anxiety is called "functional pleasure," since gratification is based on the exercise of a function rather than on satisfaction of an instinct. A familiar illustration is the phenomenon in which children enjoy endless repetitions of the same game or the same story, which has to be told in exactly the same words.

According to Fenichel, functional pleasure usually occurs in combination with an erogenous pleasure. He cites the example of a child being tossed in the air by an adult and caught. On the one hand, the child feels erogenous pleasure in his equilibrium sensations, and on the other, functional pleasure due to overcoming the fear of falling. Courage is built up gradually, starting with an adult in whom the child has confidence and at a height which is not too great.

Development of Speech and Thinking. The acquisition of speech represents a decisive advance in the formation of the ego. In being able to tie together words and ideas, the ego is better equipped to handle the external world as well as impulses from within. There arises a magical belief that one can master what one can name. Again it is a common observation that children at this age level incessantly demand objects to be named for them. Thus, a striving for mastery of instinctual drives contributes in this way to intellectual development (see Note 2). The achievement of speech is said to be experienced as a great new power which turns the earlier "omnipotence of thought" into an "omnipotence of words." The child's earliest speech is a charm directed toward forcing the external world to do those things which have been conjured up in words. The magical power of words, according to the theory, is retained in oaths, obscenities, and poetry.

Thinking is described as a further elaboration of judgments, first between edible and nonedible, and later between harmless and dangerous. It involves postponing actions, which is done on a small-scale mental-trial basis. Thinking serves to tame two earlier automatic reactions: (1) the drive to discharge tensions, which is slowed down; and (2) the tendency to hallucinatory wish fulfillment, which is reduced to the imagination of prospective events and subsequently to abstract symbols of the events. At this stage of development, thinking processes are not free of these two tendencies, however. There are prelogical emotional elements which encourage disorganization, contradictions, and misconceptions. In this primitive phase, imagination consists more of concrete, pictorial representations, whereas more advanced thinking is based more on words. Later in life, prelogical thinking occurs in persons who are tired, dreaming, intoxicated, or psychotic. Even in normal, wide-awake thinkers, every thought is presumed to run through such a phase (see Note 3).

A second characteristic of earliest thinking is symbolism. Comprehension of the world originally comes from viewing objects as sources either of gratification or of threat, so that stimuli which provoke the same reactions are looked upon as identical. One illustration is the common symbolic equation of "departure" with "death." A less obvious tie is between "money" and "feces." Both represent possessions which are alike for everyone (not individualized) and thus are in danger of being lost as one's own. In other words, both are deindividualized possessions which are in constant danger of losing their ego quality. Symbolism in young children is said to differ from adult symbolism in that penis and snake, for example, are perceived as one and the same. In adults, on the other hand, the process is one of distortion in which an objectionable idea (penis) is repressed and represented through a conscious symbol (snake). (See Note 4.)

To summarize: The growth of speech gradually transforms prelogical thinking into logical, organized, and adjusted thinking, which is a decisive step toward the reality principle.

Defenses against Impulses. With the development of the ego, the reality principle assumes a second function in addition to the ability to postpone reactions. Certain impulses not only have to be postponed but must actually be curtailed more or less permanently. The ego learns to ward off or defend against impulses that are either dangerous or inappropriate. The learning takes place as a result of such things as early traumatic situations in which instinctual emergencies were not taken care of by the mother, and threats and prohibitions from the external world which create fear of instinctual acts and their consequences. These defensive functions of the ego will be explored more fully as we proceed through the mechanisms.

Forerunners of Superego. In this period of personality development the early stages of superego formation take place through the internalization of parental prohibitions. The introjection of prohibitions arises from the fear of punishment and the fear of losing parental affection. A portion of the ego becomes an "inner mother," signaling the approach of situations which threaten loss of love. A common sight is the child who, on the verge of performing a forbidden act, looks to his mother, shakes a finger, and cries, "No, no!" Since toilet training is a frequent arena for such battles, Ferenczi designated superego forerunners as "sphincter morals" (synonyms are "toilet-training superego," "visceral ethics," etc.).

These internalized prohibitions, while strong in their threat of punishment, are weak in that they may be easily disobeyed when no one is looking. Also, they can readily be projected onto other individuals like policemen and bogeymen, who are said to stand for "externalized presuperegos." In general, there is no unified, organized character to the prohibitions.

Neo-Freudian Views: Sullivan

The Parataxic Mode. In the first year of life we saw the operation of the prototaxic mode of experience, in which the infant prehends the mothering one and then gradually distinguishes between good and bad mother. There is no conception of time and place, only the perception of undefined momentary states. As the infant matures, this undifferentiated wholeness of experience is broken down into parts, which are still not connected in any logical way. They "just happen" together or not, depending on circumstances. The process is analogous to the grammatical term "parataxic," which refers to the placing of clauses one after another without any connectives ("and," "or," "since," etc.) to show logical relations between them. What the child experiences he implicitly, without reflection, accepts as the natural way. There is no step-by-step process of symbolic activity, and inferences cannot be made. Experience is undergone as momentary, unconnected organismic states. Dreams are an illustration of parataxic thinking, which occurs mainly through visual and auditory channels.

Parataxic distortion in the interpersonal situation happens when the child reacts to others on an unrealistic basis. It is described as any attitude toward another person based on fantasy or identification of him with other figures. The transference reaction of patient to therapist, in which the patient behaves toward the therapist as he originally did toward his parents, is an example of parataxic distortion.

Autistic Language. According to Sullivan (277) the learning of language plays a vital part in the development of the self and the acculturation process. Language gradually takes over where empathy leaves off, as far as communication is concerned. This early use of words is highly autistic, that is, words have a very personal, private meaning for the child. The autistic is said to be a verbal manifestation of the parataxic. Communication at this level is naturally difficult, since his symbol activity goes unchecked and untested. Imagination is not curbed to conform to reality. Mullahy (216) says, however, that autistic symbols are of some use in recall and foresight.

The difficulties which children face in the acquisition of language are illustrated by a confusion of objects, pictures, and words. Cat, for example, refers to an animal running around the house, a picture in a book, and the letters c-a-t under the picture. Sullivan comments as follows (277, p. 16):

> I am sure no child who can learn has not noticed an enormous discrepancy between this immobile representation in the book which, perhaps, resembles one of the momentary states that kitty has been in on some occasion. I am certain that every child knows that there is something very strange in this printed representation being so closely connected with the same word that seems to cover adequately the troublesome, amusing, and very active pet. Yet, because of unnumbered, sometimes subtle, sometimes crude experiences with the carrier of culture, the parent, the child finally comes to accept as valid and useful a reference to the picture as "kitty" and to the creature as "kitty."

The child thus learns some of the more complicated implications of a symbol in contradistinction to the actuality to which the symbol refers, which is its referent; in other words, the distinction between the symbol and that which is symbolized. This occurs, however, before verbal formulation is possible.

Anxiety and the Beginnings of the Self-dynamism. Anxiety is a further development of the loss of euphoria experienced by the infant via the process of empathy. Euphoria and anxiety are inversely related. Anxiety arises from the rewards and punishments involved in the socialization of the child. When parents approve of his behavior in the toilet-training situation, for example, he feels secure and satisfied with their expressions of tenderness; euphoria is increased. When they disapprove of nonconformity, he feels insecure and anxious; euphoria is decreased.

Even devices which earlier served to obtain satisfaction, such as crying for food, can now produce parental disapproval. Thus patterns of established behavior must be inhibited, with resulting heightened tension of the muscles formerly concerned in the activity. For example, inhibition of crying produces tension of the throat muscles. Muscle tensions of this sort are an essential condition of the experience of anxiety (see Note 5).

The introduction of disapproval, with its concomitant anxiety, leads the child to modify his behavior. He learns to recall incidents which preceded the experience of anxiety. As his observation improves, his grasp on the patterns of approval and disapproval becomes more refined. He learns that, when anxiety is present and something is done which brings tenderness, the painful discomfort vanishes.

Anxiety is a negative, restrictive force in the sense that it interferes with observation, diminishes the ability to discriminate, and works against effective recall and foresight. However, it does induce the child to emphasize those aspects of himself which are pleasing to significant adults. He tends to focus his alertness or awareness on those performances which bring approval or disapproval. Out of this focusing of alertness the self is evolved (see Note 6).

Three personifications of "me" gradually emerge—"good me," "bad me," and "not me." The "good me" is an organization of experiences of approval; the "bad me" relates to anxiety states; and the "not me" refers to parataxic experiences like horror, dread, loathing, and awe. The "I," or self, is composed of the "good me" and "bad me"—at times stressing one or the other, depending upon early life circumstances.

PSYCHOSEXUAL DEVELOPMENT

Orthodox View: The Anal-sadistic Stage

Beginning sometime in the second year and extending until the fourth, the anal zone comes to be of major significance for personality formation. Anal pleasure is present from the very beginning of life but does not occupy a prime position until this time. As in the case of the oral period, there are two anal phases—the earlier "expulsive" and the later "retentive."

The aim of the expulsive phase is the enjoyment of pleasurable sensations in excretion. Besides discharging tension, elimination stimulates the mucous membrane of the lower intestine, yielding sensual pleasure comparable with that provided by sucking in the oral stage (see Note 7). In addition to the natural pleasure involved, further stimulation is often obtained as a consequence of parental emphasis on anal functions. Excessive attention by adults leads the child to increase his active interest. He learns to retain his feces in order to experience a more pleasurable expulsion later on. Frequent enemas given by anxious mothers are another source of intense stimulation. The sadistic aspect of the first anal phase derives originally from the act of expulsion itself. Feces are regarded as objects which are destroyed by elimination. Later, social factors play a part, since the child can make use of expulsiveness to defy parents who are intent upon training him to be clean.

In the second phase, the retentive, the chief pleasure changes from expelling to retaining feces. One reason is the discovery that retention can also provide intense stimulation of the mucous membrane. Another is the high value placed on bowel movements by adults. If these products are considered so precious by others, then the child wishes to keep rather than to give them. Here is where the sadistic element again enters the picture. The child can utilize his feces as a gift to demonstrate love, or he can retain them as a hostile gesture toward parents who are concerned over his producing (see Note 8).

Neo-Freudian Views: Thompson and Sullivan

The neo-Freudian interpretation of the anal-sadistic stage is again in terms of cultural and interpersonal forces. Thompson (282) grants the organic influence which determines the age at which the child can easily master his anal sphincter, but apart from this general consideration, the exact time of appearance is primarily a cultural phenomenon. Freud's description applies only to our own culture. The methods of toilet training differ in various cultures, so that time of occurrence and degree of importance are not at all constant. She feels that the emphasis should be placed, not on the pleasure obtained from expelling and retaining feces, but on the struggle with parents. There is a sharp conflict for the first time between the child's wishes and the plans of his parents. The pleasure which a child eventually discovers in controlling his feces is considered a kind of consolation for his compromise with the parents, instead of a cause of the biological stage of development. Another point which Thompson questions is the sequence of oral-anal-phallic. She agrees that there is an organic basis for anal following oral, but argues that the order of anal-phallic might be reversed in another culture, since nerve pathways in anus and penis mature at about the same time (see Note 9).

Sullivan (277) links anal functions to the power motive and quest for security. Just as the cry was originally the powerful tool of the infant, constipation becomes the powerful tool of the young child. Whereas talk does not get the child very far, refusing to defecate can usually be counted on to provide plenty of action and attention.

Erikson: The Anal-urethral Zone, Retentive and Eliminative Modes

Erikson's (70) treatment of the anal stage contains elements resembling both the orthodox and neo-Freudian positions. In common with the latter he stresses the importance of the cultural environment by citing the wide variations among societies with respect to toilet training. Like Fenichel he emphasizes the two conflicting modes of approach, retention and elimination. The development of the muscle system, of which the sphincters are a part, is said to give the child a much greater power over the environment in the ability to reach out and hold on, to throw and to push away, to appropriate things and to keep them at a distance. All these seemingly contradictory tendencies can be traced to the formula of the retentive-eliminative modes.

The new social modalities acquired at this time emphasize "letting go" and "holding on." Disturbances in the anal-urethral sphere may lead to a variety of disorders in the zone itself (spastic rectum or colon), in the muscle system (general flabbiness or rigidity), in obsessional fantasy (paranoid fear of inimical substances within one's body), and in the social spheres (attempts at controlling the environment by compulsive systematization). Just as "basic sense of trust" versus "basic sense of evil" was the nuclear conflict of the oral phase, the conflict in this anal period becomes "autonomy" versus "shame" and "doubt."

RELATIONSHIPS WITH OTHERS

Orthodox View

Ambivalence and Bisexuality. Object relations in the anal period continue to be ambivalent, as in the oral-sadistic stage. Anal ambivalence has its physiological basis in the contradictory attitude toward feces: on the one hand, the child expels the object from his body, and on the other, he retains it as a precious possession. A second anal type of relationship is bisexuality, which is also said to have a physiological root. The rectum is an excretory hollow organ. As an excretory organ it can actively expel something; as a hollow organ it can be stimulated by an entering foreign body. Masculine tendencies are derived from the former, and feminine tendencies from the latter.

The physiological basis becomes generalized to people through the relationships involved in toilet training, since there are ample opportunities for both sensual and hostile gratifications. Objects may be retained or introjected, as well as eliminated and pinched off, just as in the case of feces. Other anal relationships are said to be impulses to share anal activities with somebody else, such as defecating together, etc. All these are ambivalently oriented. They may express tenderness in an archaic way, or, after they have been condemned as dirty, they may represent hostility and contempt.

The anal phase is also presumed to witness the true beginning of love for another person. Love implies consideration for the happiness of another person, which in this period manifests itself in the willingness of the child to surrender his valued possession, feces, in order to please his parents (see Note 10).

At the opposite extreme, frustrations, due to such things as premature attempts at training, extremely rigid enforcement, inconsistent treatment, and the like, promote aggressive impulses toward others, as well as fixations. These anal-sadistic tendencies, through the operation of the primitive talion principle, lead to specific anal anxieties. Fears of physical injury of an anal nature develop, such as the fear of some violent ripping out of feces or of body contents.

Sadism and Masochism. We have seen that sadism, defined as pleasurable aggression against an object, is characteristic of this period. In addition, there is the introduction of masochism, at least in a rudimentary form. Masochism refers to the passive aim of achieving pleasure from painful experience. Both sadism and masochism are linked to physical beating, in which the buttocks is the preferred target at this time. Beating or spanking someone else is easily understood as an outlet for sadistic tendencies. The masochistic function is somewhat more complex. It can operate only under certain conditions—the pain must not be too strong or too serious. What happens is that being beaten excites children sexually because it is an intense excitation of the erogenous zones of the skin of the buttocks and of the muscles below the skin. Libido is said to be shifted from the anus to the skin. The relation between sadism and masochism can also become quite complicated. For example, a child may behave in a very active, aggressive manner in order to provoke others to beat him (see Note 11).

Sullivan's Theory

Reflected Appraisals. For Sullivan (277), the self is evolved from relationships with others. The child appraises himself as he is appraised by the significant adults. He lacks the equipment and experience necessary to form an accurate picture of himself, so his only guide is the reactions of others to him—so-called "reflected appraisals." There is very little cause for him to question these appraisals, and in any case he is far too helpless to challenge them or to rebel against them. He passively accepts the judgments, which are communicated empathically at first and by words, gestures, and deeds in this period. If a child is unwanted and is treated in a hostile and derogatory fashion by his parents, he acquires a hostile and derogatory self. From then on he reacts to others in the same hostile way. Similarly, if he is loved and respected by significant adults, he acquires a loving, respecting attitude toward himself. Thus, the self-attitudes learned early in life are carried forever by the individual, with some allowance for the influence of extraordinary environmental circumstances and modification through later experience.

Multiple "Me-you Patterns." Interpersonal relationships in the parataxic mode are characterized as multiple "me-you patterns." The self-system generates a matrix of me-you patterns. Limits to the number and kind of me-you patterns are set by the self-system, just as the personality sets the limits of the self. Multiple me-you patterns refer to attitudes toward others which are not congruent or objectively based. One example would be the individual who manifests different attitudes, such as hostility, affection, and fear in the same interpersonal situation. Another illustration is the incongruent reaction of hostility toward an affectionate person. In psychotherapy the patient reacts to the therapist in terms of his earlier me-you patterns, which are relived or integrated into the present in a parataxic way. A hostile patient behaves as he does because the significant adults in his early life convinced him that he was a person to be ridiculed and abused. Since he dislikes or even hates himself, he must dislike or hate others, despite partial attempts at disguise.

Actually, most children are not exposed to pure hostility. Typically, they experience a mixture of attitudes—affection and indifference, as well as hostility. One of these usually predominates, but nevertheless, children are raised with contradictory, inconsistent attitudes about themselves, and therefore about others. It is not surprising, then, that their interpersonal behavior is erratic and inconsistent.

MECHANISMS

The chronological sequence of the mechanisms of defense has been the subject of very little theorizing, to say nothing of attempted verification. Anna Freud, in her book, *The Ego and the Mechanisms of Defence* (83), analyzes various possible bases for a classification and finally concludes that we know hardly anything about the area. The period from age one to three is especially difficult to place along a genetic sequence of mechanisms. Although several mechanisms, such as reaction formation, isolation, and undoing, are said to be related to anal conflicts, all are intimately connected with repression, which fits more logically into the next developmental stage from three to five. Therefore, it seems to make better sense to reserve our extended treatment of defense mechanisms for the next section (see Note 12).

However, a couple of new contributions do seem to belong in this age level:

Denial in Word and Act: Anna Freud

The mechanism of denial in the first year was seen as a fantasy process, a sort of counterpart of hallucinatory wish fulfillment. As the child matures, this denial in fantasy, according to Anna Freud, changes into denial in word and act. The infantile ego, in order to get rid of unwelcome facts, utilizes all kinds of external objects in dramatizing the reversal of real situations. The denial of reality is one of the motives underlying children's play in general, and games of impersonation in particular. She writes (83, pp. 89–91):

I am reminded here of a little book of verses by an English writer, in which the juxtaposition of phantasy and fact in the life of its child-hero is described in a particularly delightful way. I refer to *When We Were Very Young* by A. A. Milne. In the nursery of this three-year-old there are four chairs. When he sits on the first, he *is* an explorer, sailing up the Amazon by night. On the second he is a lion, frightening his nurse with a roar; on the third he is a captain, steering his ship over the sea. But on the fourth, a child's high chair, he *tries to pretend* that he is simply himself, just a little boy. It is not difficult to see the author's meaning: the elements for the construction of a pleasurable world of phantasy lie ready to the child's hand, but his task and his achievement are to recognize and assimilate the facts of reality.

It is a curious thing that adults are so ready to make use of this very mechanism in their intercourse with children. Much of the pleasure which they give to children is derived from this kind of denial of reality. It is quite a common thing to tell even a small child "what a big boy" he is and to declare, contrary to the obvious facts, that he is as strong "as Father," as clever "as Mother," as brave "as a soldier" or as "tough" as his "big brother." It is more natural that, when people want to comfort a child, they resort to these reversals of the real facts. The grown-ups assure him, when he has hurt himself, that he is "better now" or that some food which he loathes "isn't a bit nasty" or, when he is distressed because somebody has gone away, we tell him that he or she will be "back soon." Some children actually pick up these consolatory formulae and employ a stereotyped phrase to describe what is painful. For instance, one little girl of two years used, whenever her mother left the room, to announce the fact by a mechanical murmur of "Mummy coming soon." Another (English) child used to call out in a lamentable voice whenever he had to take nasty medicine, "like it, like it"—a fragment of a sentence used by his nurse to encourage him to think that the drops tasted good.

Many of the presents brought to children by grown-up visitors minister to the same illusion. A small handbag or a tiny sunshade or umbrella is intended to help a little girl to pretend to be a "grown-up lady"; a walking-stick, a uniform and toy weapons of different sorts enable a little boy to ape manhood. Indeed, even dolls, besides being useful for all sorts of other games, create the fiction of motherhood, while railways, motors, and bricks not only serve to fulfil various wishes and provide opportunities for sublimation but produce in children's minds the agreeable phantasy that they can control the world.

The transition from fantasy to reality is difficult for the child, since parents expect an immediate switch corresponding to their own capacity. Anna Freud says (83, pp. 91–92):

Children are expected to keep the enacting of their phantasies within well-defined limits. A child who has just been a horse or an elephant, going about on all fours, neighing or trumpeting, must be prepared at a moment's notice to take his place at table and be quiet and well-behaved. The lion-tamer must himself be ready to obey his nursemaid, and the explorer or pirate must submit to be sent to bed just when the most interesting things are beginning to happen in the world of grown-ups. The indulgent attitude of the latter towards the child's mechanism of denial vanishes the moment that he ceases to make the transition from phantasy to reality readily, without any delay or hitch, or tries to shape his actual behavior according to his phantasies—to put it more exactly, the moment his phantasy-activity ceases to be a game and becomes an automatism or an obsession.

The mechanism of denial in word and act is subject to two restrictions. The first applies also to the earlier denial in fantasy: (1) It can be employed only so long as it can exist side by side with the capacity for reality testing without disturbing it. As the ego matures, denial and reality become incompatible, as we have mentioned previously. The second restriction applies only to this later form of denial: (2) In fantasies a child is supreme. Inasmuch as he does not tell them to anybody, no one has any reason to interfere. On the other hand, dramatization in word and act requires a stage in the outside world. So the child's use of this mechanism is conditioned by the extent to which those around him will fall in with his dramatization, just as it is conditioned internally by the degree of compatibility with the function of reality testing.

Consensual Validation: Sullivan

A process which begins to operate in association with Sullivan's parataxic stage is consensual validation (see Note 13).

This involves an attempt to correct parataxic distortion by evaluating one's own thoughts and feelings against those of others. With increasing use of the mechanism, the child comes closer to an approximation of the truth. He gradually catches on to patterns of relationships in his society, and in his language he becomes aware of grammatical structure. He discriminates more clearly that someone will respond to his verbalizations and soon learns to anticipate the responses of others. Responses thus become associated with the use of certain words and gestures, which are implicitly agreed upon by all. In this way his communications change from the autistic to the consensually validated. Through this process he ultimately learns the syntaxic mode of experience.

SUMMARY

In his discussion of ego formation at this age level Fenichel traces the development of active mastery and the handling of anxiety. As a result of both newly acquired control over his motor apparatus and the growth of the function of judgment (reality testing), the young child learns to cope actively with the environment. His ego becomes capable of judging potentially traumatic situations, so that anxiety serves as a protective warning signal. Common sources of anxiety at this time derive from the talion principle—the fear that others may do to him what he fantasies doing to them—and fear over the loss of love and protection. When anxiety-provoking situations have been experienced, the child through a process of belated mastery attempts to reduce tension by reliving the trauma over and over in games and dreams. The acquisition of speech and the advances in thinking contribute heavily to a new feeling of power. Thinking in this period is said to contain many prelogical and symbolic elements. Superego forerunners are also prominent in the form of internalized parental prohibitions.

Sullivan speaks of the parataxic mode, in which experience

is undergone as momentary, unconnected organismic states. The earlier prototaxic undifferentiated wholeness is now broken down into parts, but these have no logical relation to one another. Dreams and the transference reaction in psychotherapy are given as illustrations of parataxic distortion. Communication in ages one to three involves the use of autistic language, words having a personal, private meaning. Anxiety is described as a further development of the loss of euphoria and arises from rewards and punishments in the socialization of the child. It serves to make him focus his alertness on performances which bring approval or disapproval, and out of this focusing the self-dynamism is evolved. Three personifications of self gradually emerge: the "good me," "bad me," and "not me."

Psychosexual development in the orthodox system witnesses the anal-sadistic stage. Two trends are distinguished—the earlier expulsive and the later retentive. Expulsiveness is expressed in the physiological pleasure of excretion but can also serve aggressive purposes by defying the parents in their insistence on toilet training. The retentive phase derives from both stimulation of the mucous membrane and the social values placed upon conformity. The neo-Freudians maintain that the emphasis should be placed, not on the pleasure obtained from expelling and retaining feces, but rather on the struggle with parents. Erikson occupies an intermediate position with his stress upon the social modalities of "letting go" and "holding on."

Concomitant relationships, according to orthodox sources, entail ambivalence, bisexuality, sadism, and masochism. Anal ambivalence is said to arise from the contradictory attitude toward feces; bisexuality from the fact that the rectum is an excretory hollow organ; sadism from frustration in the toilet-training situation; and masochism from the erotic stimulation of the buttocks in spankings. Sullivan approaches interpersonal relationships from another angle. He describes the operation of "reflected appraisals," in which the child forms an opinion of himself mainly from the reactions of significant adults to him; and also multiple "me-you patterns," which refer to incongruent attitudes toward others.

Two new mechanisms at these ages include Anna Freud's "denial in word and act," a later counterpart of denial in fantasy, and Sullivan's "consensual validation," a process in which the individual tries to correct his parataxic distortions by evaluating his own thoughts and feelings against those of others.

NOTES

1. *The Process of Belated Mastery.* In belated mastery, anxiety produced by a traumatic event is handled afterward by active repetition of the original situation. The child who witnesses a frightening accident and later insists almost frantically that his father describe the details of the scene over and over again seems to be engaged in a process of deconditioning. The repeated narrations enable the child to "work through" his anxiety in the presence of a reassuring adult. Each repetition serves to decrease the amount of associated anxiety, until the need for mastery is itself finally extinguished.

2. *Contributions to Intellectual Growth.* Obviously the striving for control over instinctual drives cannot be viewed as the exclusive or even major contributor to intellectual development. Maturation of the intellectual apparatus, along with everyday experiences not charged with emotion, must be considered fundamental to the fulfillment of intellectual capacity. [See Piaget (229) for a discussion of factors determining the evolution of intellect.]

3. *A Prelogical Phase in Normal Thinking.* The existence of prelogical thinking under abnormal conditions is readily observed and accepted. However, its postulation as a part of every normal thought sequence requires some evidence. How to approach this problem is a knotty question, since we cannot easily gain access to the instantaneous, unconscious antecedents of a thought. The psychoanalytic technique of free association does not offer a solution because it too must be classed as a special condition. Perhaps we can dream about advances in the field of electroencephalography which might permit accurate recording of brain waves ac-

companying a thought sequence. If characteristic patterns were found to be reliably associated with prelogical as opposed to logical thinking, we could then test the proposition. From the developmental side, Piaget (228) distinguishes three stages in logical thinking: the autistic, egocentric, and communicable. Autistic thought occurs earliest and is least adapted to reality; egocentric typifies the age period from three to seven and operates more at an intuitive level; and communicable thought, which develops last, contains explicit logical relationships.

4. *Symbolism.* The fact that young children continually make use of symbolic equations can be confirmed directly from their verbal behavior. One striking demonstration, such as the two and a half-year-old who exclaimed devilishly upon being presented a frankfurter, "That's no hot dog sandwich—that's a penis sandwich!" is usually enough to convert the skeptic. In adults ample evidence can be secured from dreams and responses to projective tests like the Rorschach. The origins of symbolic ties, however, are not so obvious. Fenichel's explanation of "money = feces" in terms of deindividualized possessions in danger of being lost does not sound very convincing. Direct observations of the language and play activities of young children would probably yield worth-while clues in this connection. Anecdotal evidence (271) for the money = feces tie is found in the old practice of putting debtors in the pillory and giving them drastic purges in order to "make payment," and the one-time Christmas-tree decoration consisting of a chocolate man expelling gold pieces anally. Expressions like "cleaned out" and a colorful Army phrase concerning what the eagle does on pay-day are also prime examples.

5. *Muscle Tension and Anxiety.* It is not clear from Sullivan's writings what role muscle tension is presumed to play in relation to anxiety. If the link is merely one of physiological concomitance, then a host of other factors, such as rapid heartbeat, sweating, and quicker breathing, deserve equal mention. If, on the other hand, muscle tension is intended as a causal explanation, the currently unpopular James-Lange theory is being invoked—the feeling of anxiety would be in reality a reaction to an underlying physiological disturbance, in this case muscular.

6. *The Positive Function of Anxiety.* Sullivan's discussion of anxiety as a force inducing the child to focus his alertness is akin to the notion of "adaptive anxiety" proposed by Allison Davis (56)

and others. The experience of a tolerable amount of anxiety can, according to this view, have the advantage of stimulating the organism to constructive activity in order to avert more serious recurrences of anxiety. Note the similarity to the position that some deprivation in infancy is necessary for ego development (see Chapter 3).

7. *Physiological Pleasure and Anality.* A controversy parallel to that in the oral stage (see Chapter 3, Note 7) exists here: is anal pleasure primarily physiological or can it be explained better as a secondary learned drive? The absence of experimental evidence, in contrast to the more socially acceptable studies on sucking, is, of course, understandable. Perhaps a guess can be ventured that physiological pleasure per se probably does exist, but its significance for personality remains enigmatic.

8. *Toilet-training Practices.* Anthropological sources supply numerous examples of variation in toilet-training practices. In Plainville (164) the child is taught sphincter control after he has learned to speak, while the Tanalan (163) mother starts to train her child when he is two or three months old. Rigid bowel training in Japan (118) is reinforced by physical punishment and mockery, whereas the non-punitive Comanche (164) parent utilizes a combination of ineffectual threats, encouragement, and elaborate praise. Hartmann, Kris, and Loewenstein (133) suggest that the ease with which control is learned depends upon four factors: (1) the stage of maturation of the physical apparatus—the ability to sit up comfortably, to understand the reasons for regulation, and to communicate signals [Orlansky (224) raises some question about neurological evidence concerning the necessity for completed myelinization of the pyramidal tract in order to permit satisfactory bowel training, but generally these physical prerequisites are accepted]; (2) sympathetic parental attitudes and expectations; (3) the child's tolerance for deprivation; and (4) gratifications afforded by the processes of learning.

Research on the effects of toilet-training practices for childhood development (see Chapter 8, Note 4 for studies relating early anal habits to adult personality) is very limited. Huschka (147) investigated the influence of bowel training on 213 problem children at a New York hospital. Separating the group into two categories of "coercive" (training begun before eight months or completed before eighteen months) versus "adequate" (begun after eight months and completed after eighteen months), she found a greater incidence of constipation, anxiety, rage, etc., in the former. No normal children were studied, nor were there any attempts to match the environments of the two clinical samples. The reliability of the bowel-training data is also open to question, since the mothers' reports were obtained at a time when two-thirds of the children were already between six and thirteen years of age. Huschka recognizes the limitations of her study and merely points to its being provocative for further, more definitive research. Koch (179) observed 46 nursery-school children for frequency of nervous gestures and discovered positive correlations with parental ratings of constipation in boys, but not in girls. No causal inferences can be drawn from these findings, as Koch mentions, since fear and anger can reduce gastrointestinal motility and also result in nervous mannerisms.

The possibility of conducting systematic research in this area certainly exists. Observations of time and method of toilet training could be used to differentiate groups of children trained under various conditions but otherwise equated for home background, etc. The personality development of children in these groups could then be compared through the years. One detail worth checking would be the separation of cases where the parents reward the act of defecation from those where particular attention is paid to the product itself, the feces. Perhaps the theoretical statement of high value ascribed to feces by children would apply primarily to the latter group.

9. *The Anal-phallic Sequence.* Thompson's point concerning the possible influence of cultural practices upon chronological sequence of psychosexual stages is well taken. However, we would be more content with some evidence which is other than hypothetical.

10. *The True Beginning of Love.* If love is to be defined as consideration for the happiness of another person, then any attempt to establish its "true" onset seems arbitrary. Certainly there must be instances prior to sphincter training in which the child gives up valued possessions, *e.g.*, a bottle, in order to please his parents.

11. *Physical Beating and Masochism.* The role in masochism played by sexual excitation of the skin of the buttocks is very dubious. Simpler explanations in terms of the psychic gratification of punishment are more plausible. In any case, the physiological

hypothesis would be difficult to isolate and test, since spankings occur in an interpersonal context. Even a far-fetched condition of mechanical spanking, in the absence of other persons, would not be crucial in view of the already established symbolic meaning of punishment for the child.

12. *The Chronology of Repression.* In her recent address at Clark University, Anna Freud (84) does place the original use of repression in the anal period. There seems to be no consensus on this point.

13. *Consensual Validation as a Mechanism.* The reader should keep in mind that the sections in the text headed "Mechanisms" include more than the mechanisms concerned solely with ego defense. Sullivan's consensual validation concept, for example, belongs outside the latter category.

CHAPTER 5

From Three to Five

By this time the early physical processes of maturation are under control. The focus of our attention now shifts, especially in the orthodox framework, to newly accelerated sexual interests and their influence upon relationships within the family as well as upon the inner life of the child. Here we have the ramifications of the Oedipus, the major evolution of superego functioning, and the expanded use of ego defense mechanisms. The usual outline division is altered in this chapter to permit the more meaningful sequence of psychosexual development followed first by relationships with others, then ego and superego formation, and finally mechanisms.

PSYCHOSEXUAL DEVELOPMENT

Orthodox View: The Phallic Stage

Urethral Eroticism. Some orthodox analysts posit an intermediate stage between anal and phallic—the urethral. Fenichel (74) recognizes the significance of urethral eroticism but feels that it is interwoven with the phallic stage. The primary aim of urethral eroticism is said to be pleasure in urination. There is also a secondary pleasure, that of retention, analogous to anal retention. At first the pleasure is autoerotic; later it is turned toward objects in fantasies about urinating on others, and so on. In general, the pleasure may have a double meaning: (1) a sadistic connotation due to the active penetration, along with fantasies of damaging or destroying; or (2) a passive giving up and "letting flow." In boys the active part is soon replaced by normal genitality. In girls it later serves to express conflicts centered around penis envy. The passive meaning of "letting flow" often is displaced from urine to tears.

An important feature in urethral eroticism is the narcissistic pride in learning to control the sphincter of the bladder. This pride is said to be due to the fact that failures in urethral cleanliness are usually punished by putting the child to shame—much more so than failures in rectal cleanliness (see Note 1). Therefore, just as the idea of being eaten is the specific oral fear, and the idea of being robbed of the contents of the body is the specific anal fear, shame is the specific force directed against urethral temptations. Ambition is presumed to represent the fight against this shame (see Note 2).

Castration Anxiety in Boys. The child reaches the phallic phase usually in the third or fourth year. Interest in the genitals becomes magnified and manifests itself behaviorally in the higher frequency of masturbation; greater desire for physical contact with others, particularly with members of the opposite sex; and the predominance of exhibitionistic tendencies. Apart from these behavioral manifestations, there are all sorts of sexual fantasies, usually associated with masturbation (see Note 3).

It is said that the boy at the phallic phase has identified himself with his penis. This high narcissistic evaluation of the organ is explained by the fact that it becomes very rich in sensations, so that active pleasure-seeking impulses come to the fore. Genital impulses were present from birth, but at this age they become primary. As a product of this extreme narcissism, boys are afraid of some harm or damage being done to the penis. This specific fear in the phallic period is called "castration anxiety."

Freud originally stressed the idea of phylogenetic factors predisposing the individual to castration fear. Fenichel prefers to think of the basis in the talion principle: the organ that has sinned has to be punished. Hartmann and Kris (132, pp.

21–22) summarize their views on the origin of castration anxiety as follows:

Freud argues that the intensity of the fear of castration experienced by the male child in our civilization is unaccountable if we consider it as a reaction to the actual threats to which the boy is being exposed in the phallic phase; only the memory of the race will explain it. To this, we are inclined to reply with Freud's own arguments. While in many cases the child in our civilization is no longer being threatened with castration, the intensity of the veiled aggression of the adult against the child may still produce the same effect. One might say that there always is "castration" in the air. Adults who restrict the little boy act according to patterns rooted in their own upbringing. However symbolic or distant from actual castration their threats might be, they are likely to be interpreted by the little boy in terms of his own experiences. The tumescent penis with which he responds in erotic excitement, that strange phenomenon of a change in a part of his body that proves to be largely independent of his control, leads him to react not to the manifest content but rather to the latent meaning of the restriction with which his strivings for mother, sister, or girl-playmate meet. And then, what he may have seen frequently before, the genitals of the little girl, acquire a new meaning as evidence and corroboration of that fear. However, the intensity of fear is linked not only to his present experience, but also to similar experiences in his past. The dreaded retaliation of the environment revives memories of similar anxieties when desires for other gratifications were predominant and when the supreme fear was not that of being castrated but that of not being loved. [See Note 4.]

The castration anxiety of the little boy may generalize to a variety of things, such as a tonsillectomy, cutting off a chicken's head, or injury to the eye. Another class of fears concerns the notion that some harm may have been done to the penis as a consequence of masturbation, circumcision, or simply the sight of an adult's larger penis. Fenichel cites as supportive evidence the fact that adults joke about castration so readily. The interpretation is that frightening others is a way of calming one's own fears. In other words, "If I am powerful enough to frighten others, then I need not be afraid myself." (See Note 5.)

Penis Envy in Girls. The phallic phase in females is characterized by a physiological dominance of clitoris rather than vaginal sexuality, and a psychological conflict around penis envy. At this period of life the clitoris is the part of the genital apparatus that is richest in sensations and that attracts and discharges most sexual excitation. It is also the central focus of masturbatory practices. The shift from clitoris to vagina as the leading erogenous zone occurs later in life, usually around puberty.

Penis envy results when the little girl notes the anatomical differences in genitalia. She not only feels that she would like to have a penis, but that she probably once did have one and lost it. In her eyes, possession of a penis is thought to be superior to the clitoris for both masturbatory and urinary functions. Along with this idea is the feeling that the lack of a penis is a kind of punishment, whether deserved or not.

Fenichel acknowledges that this primary penis envy of the little girl is capable of undergoing major modification as a result of later experiences in the culture. He says (74, pp. 81–82):

In our culture, there are many reasons why women may envy men. Masculine strivings of any kind may be added to the primary penis envy, especially after unfortunate experiences, frustrations, and repressions in the feminine field. What is regarded as masculine and as feminine varies enormously in different cultures, and these cultural patterns and the conflicts around them complicate the "psychological consequences of the anatomical distinction." In this respect Fromm's summary seems wholly accurate: "Certain biological differences result in characterological differences; such differences are blended with those which are directly produced by social factors; the latter are much stronger in their effect and can either increase, eliminate, or reverse biologically rooted differences."

Masturbation. Masturbation is a normal accompaniment of early childhood. In the phallic period its frequency is increased, and fantasies concerning objects are introduced for the first time. In addition to the pleasurable aspects, it serves the function of gradually learning the active mastery of the experience of sexual excitation, just as play helps first to achieve belated mastery of intense impressions and later to anticipate future events. The fears and guilt feelings associated with masturbation are said to arise, not primarily from the activity itself, but rather from the nature of the accompanying fantasies, which are usually of an oedipal variety (see Note 6).

Neo-Freudian Views

Thompson on the Phallic Phase. Thompson feels that the phallic phase, like the oral and anal, has some organic basis. The boy does not concern himself with his penis until he is physically capable of having some control over it. At this time, children are absorbed in trying to find out what the penis can do and why boys are different from girls. They discover the pleasurable sensations which can be obtained from manipulating the genitals. Penis envy arises from the girl's jealousy of what the boy can do with his penis; for example, the fact that he can direct his urinary stream and shoot it farther than she can.

Parental attitudes also play an important part. Even today it is still common to encounter strong disapproval of genital play. When such is the case, it is easy to see how castration fears would arise. However, Thompson feels that it is by no means certain that children who have not been threatened would still feel anxiety merely from noticing the differences between the sexes.

Horney on Penis Envy. Horney, one of the foremost neo-Freudians, has not entered the text prior to this point, since she attaches relatively less importance to developments in early childhood. However, she does offer an opinion on the topic of penis envy. According to Horney (142), specific cultural conditions engender specific qualities in both men and women. The wish to have a penis or to be a man may express a desire to have those qualities which we in our culture regard as masculine: strength, courage, independence, success, sexual freedom, the right to choose a partner. It may be a disguise for repressed ambition. But it is not the result of sexual experiences in early childhood. Fear of their own femininity causes what Horney describes as a "flight from womanhood." This notion is similar to Adler's (5) "masculine protest," in which women react against their feelings of inferiority to men by trying to assume masculine roles.

Fenichel's reply to this view of a reactive rather than a primary penis envy is in terms of regression. He maintains that in women with strong penis envy there was originally a childhood conflict, which has been reactivated by later cultural experiences (see Note 7).

Erikson: The Phallic Zone, Intrusive Mode

Erikson (70) characterizes the "phallic-locomotor" stage in terms of a variety of similar activities and fantasies: intrusion into other bodies by physical attack; intrusion into other people's ears and minds by aggressive talking; intrusion into space by vigorous locomotion; and intrusion into the unknown by consuming curiosity. Adult sex acts are said to be viewed by children as dangerous indicators of mutual aggression, in which the male plays an intrusive role and the female a "spidery" incorporative one. Although children of both sexes partake of the general pattern of these ambulatory and intrusive patterns, girls tend to acquire patterns of "demanding inception" in a ratio determined by previous experience, temperament, and cultural emphasis. The girl who cannot accept and integrate the feminine modes of "inception" and "inclusion" tends to develop this teasing, grasping attitude.

The basic social modalities in both sexes during the phallic period are described as "being on the make": head-on attack, enjoyment of competition, insistence on goal, pleasure of conquest. The child thus learns the prerequisites for initiative, *i.e.*, for the selection of goals and perseverance in approaching them.

RELATIONSHIPS WITH OTHERS

Orthodox Position

The Oedipus Complex. The development of object relationships in the boy is relatively simple, since in the phallic stage he remains bound to his first object, the mother. The Oedipus complex, which implies sexual love for the parent of the opposite sex and hatred or even death wishes for the parent of the same sex, is called the climax of infantile sexuality. Overcoming oedipal strivings is a prerequisite for normal adult sexuality, whereas unconscious clinging to them lays the cornerstone of neurosis.

In its simplest form, the boy's already formed attachment to the mother unconsciously becomes tinged with the strongly emerging sexual impulses. To permit the gratification of these impulses, the father as an obstacle must be removed. This is accomplished by fantasying himself in the place of the rival father—the so-called "positive Oedipus complex." The negative complex occurs when love for the father prevails and the mother is hated as a disturbing element.

The special form which the Oedipus complex takes in each individual depends upon his experiences. Some of these influences are the following (74):

1. Traumatic events, such as premature seductions, actual or fantasied; observation of sexual scenes between parents or other adults ("primal scenes"); birth of a sibling who now demands more of mother's attention.
2. Unconscious sexual love by parents for their children, which arouses all sorts of temptation and guilt.
3. Only children suffer more intensely, since other siblings are not around to relieve the pressure.
4. Absence of one parent causes complications, in attitudes toward the remaining parent as well as the missing one.
5. Conflicts and arguments between the parents, especially concerning the child, intensify oedipal problems.

6. Family morals, such as attitudes toward masturbation, affect oedipal conflicts.
7. Social status of the parents alters the particular form of the Oedipus. Lower class children, for example, are exposed more to sexual and aggressive experiences.

According to Fenichel, the Oedipus complex is undoubtedly a product of family influence. If the institution of the family were to change, the pattern of the Oedipus complex would necessarily change also. Societies with family configurations different from our own actually have different Oedipus complexes. Fenichel quotes Freud's phylogenetic theory of the origin of the Oedipus complex—the "primal horde" in which a prehistoric chieftain was killed and eaten by his sons, following which came remorse and inhibition—but refrains from commenting on its usefulness.

Change of Object in Girls. In the girl the development of object relationships is more complicated, since a further step, the transfer from mother to father, is necessary. The most important experiences are disappointments which cause a turning away from the mother. Among these are weaning, toilet training, and the birth of siblings. In addition, there is a specific feminine disappointment which is still more significant —the impression that she once possessed a penis which the mother took away from her. The aim now is to get from the father the supplies that the mother had denied her. In fantasy the idea "penis" is replaced by the idea "child" and receptive longings replace the active ones. The Oedipus complex (sometimes called the Electra complex) of the girl, therefore, is analogous to that of the boy. She loves the father and wishes to have a child by him, and combined with this is a guilt-laden, jealous hatred of the mother. Some remnants of the earlier pre-oedipal mother attachment still persist, however, so that females are more ambivalent toward their mothers than males are toward their fathers (see Note 8).

Other Views on the Oedipus Complex

Adler. According to Adler (6), the Oedipus complex is to be understood in terms of the pampering of the child. The normal attitude of the child is an almost equal interest in father and mother, following the period of early infancy. External circumstances, however, may direct his interest to either one of the parents. For example, prolonged illness requiring constant care by the mother may create distance between child and father. If pampering on the part of the father predominates, the child turns away from the mother to him. For Adler, the Oedipus complex "is nothing else than one of the many forms that appear in the life of the pampered child."

The sexual element enters the picture in the following way: the spoiled child is sexually precocious, since his desires are never denied. He indulges in erotic fantasy and in masturbation beyond the normal degree, thus overstimulating his developing sexuality. Another factor increasing sexual excitation is the excessive kissing and caressing of the pampering mother. Inasmuch as the mother is his primary source of relationships, these sexual fantasies are directed toward her. The sexual pleasure, though, is incidental to the lust for power over the mother, whom he has discovered he can dominate. Thus, the Oedipus complex "is not a fundamental fact, but is simply a vicious unnatural result of maternal overindulgence."

Jung. To Jung (160) the Oedipus is really a possession complex. He explains that, in the early stage of undifferentiated sex, both the boy and the girl want the mother, who is felt as a source of delight, protection, and food, and desire to be rid of the father. The element of eroticism gradually increases, however, and the girl begins to develop a typical affection for the father with a corresponding jealous attitude toward the mother—the so-called "Electra complex." Eroticism reaches a new stage after puberty, when the emancipation from the parents is more or less attained. Jung sees in Freud's incest desire only a symbolic expression of the desire to return to the original source of life, to the arms of the mother for rest, or to the maternal womb for rebirth.

Rank. Rank (235) agrees with Jung's concept of the Oedipus complex as a rebirth fantasy, but he bases the unconscious sexual wish upon his theory of the birth trauma. The mother's body, as we have discussed previously (Chapter 1), is according to Rank a source of fear at birth. The young child now unconsciously senses an opportunity to transform the original source of pain, the mother's genitals, into a source of pleasure. Such attempts, however, are doomed to failure because of the severe anxieties attached to the birth trauma.

In addition to this interpretation, Rank places considerable emphasis on the given family situation. He feels that the term "Oedipus" should refer to the entire relation of the child to the parents—to desires to bring the parents together, as well as wanting to separate them. Any given family situation involves all sorts of needs, on the part of both the parents and the children. Parents may try to work out their marital problems by dragging the child into the conflict, and the child may exploit their guilt feelings for his own ends. Various complications arise as a result of the roles played by members of the family. Biological urges produce attractions on the part of parents to the child of the opposite sex, whereas psychological needs are directed toward the child of the same sex. The father, for example, loves the son more because he sees in him his direct successor and heir. The child's individuality becomes threatened, since he wishes to be more than just a continuation of the father's ego, so he turns to the mother for refuge and develops a mother fixation. For similar reasons, the daughter often leans toward the father. Rank states that "the parents fight openly or tacitly for the child's soul, whether in the biological (opposite sex) or in the egoistic sense (the same sex), and the child uses the parents correspondingly, and plays them one against the other, in order to save his individuality."

Horney. According to Horney (142), oedipal attachments arise from family relationships, not from biological reasons.

There are two main series of conditions: (1) sexual stimulation by the parents; and (2) anxiety aroused by a conflict between dependency needs and hostile impulses toward parents. The sexual stimulation may consist of a "gross sexual approach," sexually tinged caresses, or "an emotional hothouse atmosphere." The goal of the child is love, and his attachment goes to the parent who elicits love or sexual desires. In the second condition, anxiety causes the child to cling to one of the parents in order to get reassurance. His goal is security rather than love, and his attachment goes to the more powerful or more awesome parent. There may be a sexual coloring to the second condition, but it is not essential. Most neurotic attachments are of this type, says Horney.

Both cases represent "a response to provocations from the outside." Early relationships are the important factors. She doubts if sexual leanings toward parents reach an intensity sufficient to meet Freud's description of the classical Oedipus complex. Certainly the phenomena are not biologically based.

Fromm. Fromm (108) believes that Freud observed the facts of the Oedipus complex correctly but erred in his interpretation of them. He agrees that there are sexual strivings in children, that lasting dependency ties are formed, and that conflict between father and son is characteristic of patriarchal societies. However, the interpretation that father-son conflict is a result of sexual rivalry is incorrect, since recent data show: (1) that the Oedipus complex is not universal; (2) that the rivalry does not occur in societies where strong patriarchal authority does not exist; and (3) that the tie to the mother is not essentially sexual. Infantile sexuality need not be directed toward the mother, since it is normally satisfied autoerotically and by contact with other children. Furthermore, fixation on the mother is caused by a dominating attitude of the mother, which renders the child helpless and in greater need of her protection and love (see Note 9).

The conflict between father and son is a product of authoritarian patriarchal society, where the son is regarded as his father's property, whose interest he should serve "like a thing," like a chattel or a beast of burden. The conflict has little to do with sexual rivalry. Such an attitude, and the treatment by the father of the son which springs from it, are opposed to man's wish to be free and independent. The greater the pressure by the father to make his son a means to his own ends, the greater will be the conflict.

Sullivan. Sullivan explains the Oedipus complex in terms of familiarity and strangeness between parents and child. The feeling of familiarity which a parent has toward his or her child of the same sex is said to lead to an authoritarian attitude, which produces hostility and resentment in the child. On the other hand, because of the difference in sex, leading to a sense of strangeness, the parent treats his or her child of the opposite sex with "kid gloves," with more consideration. Freedom from pressure by the opposite-sex parent often results in a feeling of greater affection and attraction by the child for him.

Thompson. Thompson also accounts for the Oedipus complex through interpersonal relationships within the family. It includes much more than erotic reactions. The child plays the parents off against each other as a method of dividing and ruling, as well as feeling hostile to them whenever they obstruct the development of his interests. When sexual elements do enter the picture, they are a result of the expression of the parent's sexual needs, which are worked out on the child. This is made easy by the fact that the child's discovery of genital pleasures usually takes place in connection with physical contact with his parents.

EGO AND SUPEREGO FORMATION

Orthodox View

Development of the Superego. The superego, according to Freud (96), is the heir of the Oedipus complex. The boy gives up his sensual desires for the mother and hostile wishes toward the father because of castration fear. In Freud's words, the complex "is smashed to pieces by the shock of threatened castration." The girl renounces her Oedipus complex more gradually and less completely, as a result of fear over loss of the mother's love, which is not so dynamic or powerful a force as fear of castration. With the resolution of the Oedipus, object choices are regressively replaced by identifications. "Object choice" refers to a desire to possess the individual sexually (*e.g.*, the boy's attraction to the mother), whereas "identification" implies wanting to be like someone (*e.g.*, the boy's taking over of his father's characteristics). (See Note 10.)

The frustrations of the Oedipus complex are said to cause a regression from more differentiated types of object relationships to introjection and orality, and the sexual longing for an object is replaced by an asexual alteration within the ego. The introjected parents do not fuse with the rest of the ego because of the feeling of distance between parents and child. Instead they combine with the previously existing parental introjects or superego forerunners to form a precipitate within the ego. These later identifications differ from the forerunners in the following way: the child, in order to escape conflicts revolving about love, hate, guilt, and anxiety, does not identify with the parents as they are, but with the idealized parents. He purifies their conduct in his mind, and the identification proceeds as if they were consistently true to the principles they explicitly profess or aspire to observe. According to Freud, the child identifies with the superego of the parents. Idealization was present earlier in terms of attributing magical powers to parents, but now for the first time the idealization concerns moral behavior.

Fenichel admits that there are many unsolved problems relating to the formation of the superego. If the superego were simply an identification with the frustrating object of the Oedipus complex, then one would expect that the boy would develop a "motherly" superego and the girl a "fatherly" one. Although everyone does bear features of both parents in his superego, this is not the outcome. Under our cultural conditions, says Fenichel, the fatherly superego is generally decisive for both sexes (see Note 11). The outstanding identification takes place with that parent who was regarded as the source of decisive frustrations, usually the father in the case of boys and girls alike.

Functions of Ego and Superego. Functions of the ego, as we have seen, center around the relation to reality. It holds an executive position—the aim being to effect some sort of compromise between pressures from the id, the superego, and the outside world. The ego controls the apparatus of motility and perception, tests the properties of the present situation at hand, and anticipates properties of future situations. It mediates between these properties and requirements and the demands of the other psychic organizations.

Functions of the superego center around moral demands. Self-criticism and the formation of ideals are said to be the essential manifestations of the superego. It represents the incorporated standards of society, including parental attitudes as interpreted by the child and the person's own ideals for himself. To a great extent the superego is unconscious, since it was incorporated by the child very early and without awareness. The fact that it is largely unconscious and inaccessible for reality testing accounts partially for the irrational harshness of conscience. In a sense the superego is the agent through which Freud treats the influence of culture on behavior.

With the establishment of the superego, various mental functions are altered. Anxiety changes in part into guilt feelings. It is no longer an external danger—loss of love or castration—which is feared, but an inner representative of this danger. The "loss of the superego's protection" is felt as an extremely painful decrease in self-esteem. The privilege of granting or refusing the narcissistic supplies needed by the child to maintain his equilibrium is now taken over by the superego.

The superego is the heir of the parents, not only as a source of threats and punishments, but also as a source of protection and as a provider of reassuring love. Being on good or bad terms with one's superego becomes as important as being on good or bad terms with parents previously was. The change from parents to superego is a prerequisite for the establishment of independence. Self-esteem is no longer regulated by approval or rejection by external objects, but rather by the feeling of having done or not having done the right thing. Complying with the superego's demands brings feelings of pleasure and security of the same type that children experience from external supplies of love. Refusing this compliance brings feelings of guilt and remorse which are similar to the child's feelings of not being loved any more.

Relationships of Superego to Ego and Id. The superego and ego are related to each other in that both are based on the external world. The superego is sort of a second ego, with a more limited sphere of functioning. Since the incorporation of the external world in the superego occurs relatively late, the superego remains closest to the outside world. To support this statement, Fenichel says that many persons remain influenced in their behavior and self-esteem, not only by what they consider correct themselves, but also by the consideration of what others may think. Superego and objects that make demands are not always clearly distinguished. Superego functions may also be easily reprojected, *i.e.*, displaced onto newly appearing authority figures. Another fact to support the belief that the construction of the superego takes place on a higher level than the construction of the ego is the role played by auditory stimuli in each. For the ego, auditory stimuli or words become important after the kinesthetic and visual experiences of the archaic ego. For the superego, on the other hand, words are important at the very beginning of its formation, since parental attitudes are mainly incorporated by way of the ear.

The superego is related to the id through its genesis. The most essential objects of the id, the objects of the Oedipus complex, live on in the superego. This genesis is said to explain the urgent, instinctlike irrational character of many superego strivings, which in normal development must be overcome by reasonable judgments of the ego. In Freud's words, "the superego dips deeply into the id."

Rank's Conception of the Superego

Rank (136) considers the basis of the superego to be the mother-child relationship, and its function is built up genetically from inhibited sadism. There are three different superegos or three different stages in superego development: (1) the biological superego—very early in life there is a missing of the breast which arouses oral-sadistic libido; this libido is partially drained in the form of rage reactions against the mother, but the rest is dammed up in the ego and leads to the formation of inner privations or inhibitions; (2) the moral superego—this arises in the anal stage as a result of toilet training, which provides content for the sado-masochistic mechanism; and (3) the social superego—this comes into being in the oedipal period, with identification and the introjection of parental prohibitions.

For Rank, the real nucleus of the superego is the "strict mother"—not the actual mother, but the mother as sadistically conceived by the child. He distinguishes between a "primitive" superego and a "correctly functioning" one. The primitive superego shows up in a need for punishment, in a constant attempt to unload itself or to reestablish punishment from the outside.

He also differentiates the female and male superegos. The girl at the Oedipus retains the primary biological superego, whereas the boy builds up over the primary maternal superego the paternal social superego. Thus the female superego consists much more of inhibitions than guilt feeling, whereas in the male anxiety dominates (see Note 12).

Fromm: Authoritarian versus Humanistic Conscience

According to Fromm (107), the authoritarian conscience corresponds to Freud's superego. It is the voice of an internalized external authority, such as the parents, and differs from fear of punishment or hope for reward only in the sense that it has been internalized. Whether the child behaves in a good or bad direction depends solely upon the goodness or badness of his authority figures, nothing more. The force of the authoritarian conscience hinges on a continuing relationship with the external authority. If the external figures leave the scene, the conscience weakens and loses power. At the same time, the conscience influences the image which a person has of the external authorities, since there is a need to set up an ideal and to project perfection upon the authorities. Very often this interaction of internalization and projection results in an unshakable conviction in the ideal character of the authority, a conviction which is immune to all contradictory empirical evidence.

The contents of the authoritarian conscience are derived from the commands and taboos of the authority; its strength is rooted in the emotions of fear of and admiration for the authority. "Good conscience is consciousness of pleasing the authority; guilty conscience is the consciousness of displeasing it." The good authoritarian conscience produces a feeling of well-being and security, for it implies approval by the authority; the guilty conscience produces fear and insecurity, because acting against the will of the authority implies the danger of being punished and deserted.

Humanistic conscience, on the other hand, is not the internalized voice of an authority, but rather the voice of the individual himself. It is a reaction of the total personality to its proper functioning or dysfunctioning—a knowledge within oneself of success or failure in the art of living. Humanistic conscience is the expression of man's self-interest and integrity. Its goal is productiveness and happiness. Guilt feelings arise when the self goes unfulfilled, and they express themselves typically in fears of disapproval, or of death and old age. For example, if a person cannot approve of himself because he fails in the task of living productively, he has to substitute approval by others for approval by himself. Thus, unconscious guilt feeling leads to fear of disapproval.

Everyone, according to Fromm, has both an authoritarian and a humanistic conscience. The relative strength of each, as well as the relations between the two, depend upon the individual's experiences. One form of relationship is that in which guilt feelings are consciously felt in terms of the authoritarian conscience, while dynamically they are rooted in the humanistic conscience. A person may feel consciously guilty for not pleasing authorities, while unconsciously he feels guilty for not living up to his own expectations of himself. If the conscience is based upon rigid and unassailable irrational authority, the development of humanistic conscience can be almost entirely suppressed. Usually the authoritarian conscience exists as a precondition for the formation of humanistic conscience, but Fromm feels that this is not necessary in a nonauthoritarian society.

MECHANISMS

Orthodox Mechanisms of Defense

Introductory Comments. Before considering the defense mechanisms themselves, it is necessary to examine in more detail such notions as psychic energy, closed system, cathexis, and countercathexis. We recall that everyone presumably possesses a fixed quantity of psychic energy or libido, which becomes attached to different body organs and undergoes a variety of transformations. The source of the energy is the id, which is likened to a reservoir. Energy from this reservoir can be invested in objects ("object cathexis") or in the self ("ego cathexis"). Examples of the former would be a crush on a movie actress or intense pleasure from owning a new car. In other words, the external object, whether a person or a thing, is valued highly. An illustration of ego cathexis is narcissism or self-love, in which the libidinal energy is turned inward. So far the theory is relatively easy to follow. It begins to get fairly obscure when we come to the problem of energy distribution and interactions among id, ego, and superego. Granted that the original source of energy is the id—what about the energy available to the ego? Does it come to possess its own supply which can be handled relatively autonomously, or does it have to borrow continually from the id?

Likewise, does the superego possess its own share of energy?

As nearly as it is possible to figure out, the following seems to be the prevailing orthodox opinion: both the ego and super-ego in the course of their formation acquire amounts of energy which are specifically at their disposal. These energy systems are a sort of reserve which can be called into action when needed. Normally, the ego serves as a watchman or mediator between the id and the outer world, with the function of chan-nelizing or directing the energy of the id according to the de-mands of reality. Presumably, where this can be accomplished without difficulty, the ego's own forces are not called upon, or at most become passively allied with those of the id. In cases of conflict, however, the ego calls its reserves to active combat duty and attempts to fight off the invading id impulses. This is the notion of countercathexis—where the energy of the ego blocks the energy of the id from consciousness.

The superego can enter the fight on the side of either the ego or the id. After the superego has been established, it is responsible to a great extent for the decision as to which dis-charges are permitted and which are negated. When guilt feelings concerning instincts enter the field, the superego allies itself with the ego against the id. On the other hand, in severe cases, the ego has to defend itself against guilt feelings, thus allying the superego with the id.

Successful vs. Unsuccessful Ego Defenses. Fenichel makes a distinction between: (1) successful defenses which bring a cessation of the blocked or warded-off impulses; and (2) unsuccessful defenses which necessitate a continuing repeti-tion of the warding-off process to prevent eruption of the im-pulses. The border lines between the two categories are not sharply defined, and sometimes it is not possible to distin-guish between them. The successful defenses include the various types of sublimation; the unsuccessful or pathogenic include denial, projection, introjection, repression, reaction formation, undoing, isolation, regression, and displacement. Some of these have already been discussed. The remaining ones will be taken up in this section (see Note 13).

Sublimation: Fenichel vs. Sterba. Through sublimation the ego changes the aim or object (or both) of the id impulse without blocking its discharge. In contrast to the unsuccessful defenses, which make use of countercathexes, sublimated impulses find their outlet, though drained via an artificial route. The original impulse vanishes because its energy is withdrawn in favor of the cathexis of its substitute. The defensive forces of the ego do not meet the instinctual forces head on, as in the case of a countercathexis, but impinge at an angle, thus unifying instinctual and defensive energy. Along with the inhibition of instinctual aim goes a process of desexualization. However, Fenichel shies away from the view that this desexualization necessarily results in the choice of a higher, more socially acceptable channel of expression. He prefers to omit the valuative aspect from his definition, though most other writers, like Sterba, do include it.

The conditions under which sublimation can take place are also treated more rigorously by Fenichel. Sublimation deals only with pregenital strivings. He says that it is highly improbable that a sublimation of adult genital sexuality exists, since genitality provides for the achievement of complete discharge in the orgasm. Those pregenital strivings which do not reach sexual expression in the various forepleasures are eligible for sublimation, but only if the individual has attained the normal adult phase of "genital primacy." If, on the contrary, the pregenital strivings have been repressed and remain in the unconscious competing with genital primacy, they cannot be sublimated successfully.

Other orthodox analysts do not take the position that genitality is prerequisite to sublimation. Sterba (271), for example, cites as a simple illustration of sublimation the child who gives up playing with feces and instead plays creatively with a lump of clay (see Note 14). He adds that in sublimation the aim can be displaced at varying distances from the original instinctual aim. The substitute may still show some of the qualities of the original pleasure object, as in the clay modeling, or there can be more subtle and indirect ways of attaining satisfaction. An illustration of the latter is the interpretation of the scientist's activity as a sublimation of the child's desire for sexual knowledge. The greater the deviation from the original instinctual aim, the less intense the pleasure from the satisfaction. And, says Sterba, the pregenital tendencies of childhood and the genital forces of puberty and adolescence are the most easily sublimated, whereas the genital tendencies of the adult are more rigid in their instinctual aim and can therefore be sublimated only in small quantities (see Note 15).

Both Freud and Fenichel believe that sublimation may be intimately related to identification. The same characteristics, such as inhibition of aim, desexualization, and an alteration within the ego, apply to both sublimation and identification, as in the case of the formation of the superego. Another link is the fact that sublimations depend upon the presence of models supplied by the environment. Also, the cases of disturbances in the capacity to sublimate show that such an incapacity corresponds to difficulties in making identifications. As with certain identifications, sublimations too may more or less successfully combat and undo infantile destructive impulses.

Repression. The term "repression" was originally used by Freud (95) in 1894 as a synonym for the general concept of defense—the ego's struggle against painful ideas or emotions. In 1926 (89), he switched to a more specific view, classing repression along with the other mechanisms of defense. It refers to the exclusion of painful material from consciousness, including both material that never was conscious (primal repression) and material that was once conscious but has been pushed back into the unconscious (afterexpulsion). The latter process is known as "repression proper."

After repression proper, impulses continually strive to break through into consciousness, which necessitates a steady enervating countercathexis. The pattern is best illustrated in the case of forgetting, where a name or a fact is associated with an objectionable instinctual demand. That the repressed still persists is manifested by the feeling that one ought to know what has been forgotten, that it is on the tip of the tongue, and so on. Sometimes the facts themselves are remembered and their emotional significance is repressed.

Conflicts arise when new experiences occur that are connected with what had previously been repressed. There is then a tendency on the part of the repressed impulses to use the new event as an outlet or "derivative," whereupon secondary repression can set in. At times, derivatives of repressed material are alternately discharged and repressed. An example is daydreaming, which can be enjoyed in a highly emotional way up to a point, beyond which it must be entirely forgotten.

Repression is said to operate fairly late in childhood, since it depends upon a clear differentiation of the functions of the ego from the id. The most extensive evidences, such as outbursts of anxiety, occur after the formation of the superego. Fenichel (74) describes repression as an outgrowth of the more primitive denial. Actually, it is commonly used in conjunction with one or more of the other defense mechanisms. Anna Freud (83) states that, theoretically, repression may be subsumed under the general concept of defense and placed side by side with the other specific methods, but from the point of view of efficacy it occupies a unique position in comparison with the rest. In terms of quantity it accomplishes more than the others, by virtue of being able to master more powerful instinctual impulses. It has to act only once, though the countercathexis continues, whereas the other defenses have to be repeated whenever the id impulses threaten to break through.

But in addition to being the most effective mechanism, repression is also the most dangerous. According to Anna Freud (83, p. 54):

The dissociation from the ego entailed by the withdrawal of consciousness from whole tracts of instinctual and affective life may destroy the integrity of the personality for good and all. Thus repression becomes the basis of compromise-formation and neurosis. The consequences of the other defensive methods are not less serious but, even when they assume an acute form, they remain more within the limits of the normal [see Note 16].

Reaction Formation. Reaction formation occurs in conjunction with repression. It refers to the development in the ego of conscious socialized attitudes which are the direct opposite of repressed wishes in the unconscious. Although classed as a special case of repression, reaction formation differs from repression in that it involves a change in the total personality which happens "once and for all." An illustration is the excessive cleanliness of the compulsive, who is struggling against his instinctual demands for dirt and disorder. The person who has built up reaction formations does not develop certain defense mechanisms for use when an instinctual danger threatens; he has changed his personality structure as if the danger were continually present so that he can be ready should it occur.

Fenichel (74) distinguishes reaction formation from sublimation on the grounds that the original impulse is suppressed in the former rather than discharged. Also, reaction formation decreases the effectiveness of ego functioning, whereas sublimation increases it. He cites the illustration of two children who try to work out in their manner of writing their anal impulses to smear (see Note 17). The one who sublimates learns to write well and enjoys it very much; the one who uses reaction formation learns to write in a very constrained and meticulous fashion. Similarly, children's pleasure in playing with dirt may be sublimated into painting, sculpture, or cooking, or it may lead to the reaction of extreme cleanliness and tidiness (see Note 18).

Undoing. The mechanism of undoing is said to go one step beyond reaction formation. Something positive is done which is the opposite of something done before. This may occur on either the real or magical level. The notion of expiation is an example of belief in the possibility of a magical undoing. Another example is the compulsive who has to turn on the gas jet so that he can then turn it off again. Sometimes the undoing does not consist of a compulsion to do the opposite of what has been done previously, but rather a compulsion to repeat the very same act (repetition compulsion)—the aim being to shake free the painful unconscious meaning somehow.

The link between undoing and anal eroticism is said to be the possibility for simultaneous reassurance and pleasure. When a person with castration anxiety regresses to the anal level and substitutes the idea of losing feces for the idea of losing the penis, the frequent repetition of defecation gives reassurance that the loss is not permanent; while the ego is concerned in undoing the castration, the id by the same process is indulging in anal impulses.

Isolation. Isolation is a process by which the memories of unpleasant impressions or experiences are deprived of their emotional connections. Countercathexis operates to keep apart what actually belongs together. Isolation is an exaggeration of the process of logical thinking, which consists of the continued elimination of emotional associations in the interest of objectivity. The ideas themselves remain conscious; only their emotional significance disappears.

In addition to this characteristic emotional alteration, there are several other types of isolation. Fenichel (74) says that many children try to solve conflicts by isolating certain spheres of their lives from one another, such as school from home, or social life from the secrets of their loneliness. One of the two isolated spheres usually represents instinctual freedom and the other good behavior. They even split their personality and state that they are two children with different names, a good one and a bad one, and deny the good one's responsibility for the bad one's deeds.

Another type of isolation occurs in attempts to solve conflicts around ambivalence. By splitting the contradictory feelings so that one person is only loved and another one only hated, countercathexis prevents the two feelings from having contact with each other. Fenichel cites the illustration of the good mother and the wicked stepmother in fairy tales.

Still another type is the isolation of sensual and tender components of sexuality. As a consequence of the repression of the Oedipus complex, some individuals cannot attain sexual satisfaction in relationships with people toward whom they have tender feelings. Prostitutes furnish these individuals with an opportunity to isolate their objectionable sensuality from the rest of their life, thus relieving the necessity to repress it.

Displacement. The term "displacement" is used with two meanings. The first is in the general sense of a shifting of instinctual energy from one pathway of discharge to another, without any obstacle being in the way. The second is specifically as a mechanism of defense, in which emotions associated with one object are transferred to another object. In dreams, for example, displacement from one object to another is very common. The two definitions can be applied to the erogenous zones. The normal phase of development entails the general concept of displacement from one zone to the next; whereas barriers to discharge set up by the ego cause a specific displacement from one zone to another, as anal to oral.

Sullivan: Selective Inattention and Disassociation

Sullivan (277), in order to avoid what he considers to be distasteful topographical connotations of the preconscious and the unconscious, develops his own concepts of "selective inattention" and "disassociation." The child, as we discussed previously, learns to focus his awareness on situations involving approval and disapproval. Since he has to pay close attention to these, he necessarily must ignore or be inattentive to other situations which are not directly concerned with approval or disapproval from significant adults. He uses the analogy of someone deeply engrossed in a concert, not noticing what goes on around him. For the child, security is the vital issue in which he is engrossed, and all other issues exist outside awareness. However, under appropriate circumstances, the selectively inattended can become accessible to the self and enter awareness. A friend, for example, may point them out and they are subsequently accepted.

Disassociation represents an extreme form of selective in-attention. Here the self rejects and refuses awareness and recognition. Disassociated material remains inaccessible and, if pointed out by a friend, is likely to arouse anxiety, followed by anger and heated denial. Recall of experiences connected with it is usually not possible. Recognition of disassociated dynamisms involves a profound change in the basic direction and characteristics of the self. Ordinarily, disassociated tendencies are expressed in dreams, fantasies, and in unnoticed everyday behavior (see Note 19).

Fromm: Mechanisms of Escape

Fromm (106) feels that man's growth in freedom is accompanied by growth of a sense of isolation. Despite the material advantages of our free society, there is a longing to return to an earlier state of group solidarity. Consequently, the individual uses several irrational mechanisms to relate back to the group: sado-masochism, destructiveness, and automaton conformity (see Note 20).

1. In the sado-masochistic mechanism he forms a dependent relationship to a powerful authority who can be looked upon as a "magic helper" and whose resources can be exploited. In its extreme form the orientation involves the inflicting or receiving of physical or mental suffering at the hands of the partner, which is still said to provide protection from the feeling of loneliness.
2. When using the destructive mechanism, a person tries to cope with his feeling of powerlessness by removing all sources of comparison or competition. He seeks to eliminate or destroy the other person or object. This type of irrational destructiveness is to be distinguished from rational destructiveness, which occurs when a specific attack is made upon one's own life and integrity.
3. In automaton conformity the feeling of isolation is overcome by adopting blindly the pattern of the culture. Here

the person aims to think, feel, imagine, and act exactly like all others of his culture or class, in an attempt to wipe out the differences between himself and others.

SUMMARY

At ages three to five the orthodox scene shifts to the phallic stage of psychosexual development. Early in this period urethral preoccupations appear, first in the form of pleasurable autoeroticism and later in association with sadistic fantasies of urinating on others. Interest in the genitals increases, along with masturbation and exhibitionism. The extreme narcissistic value placed upon the penis by boys leads them to fear damage to that organ—castration anxiety—in retaliation for guilt-laden oedipal fantasies. In girls penis envy, arising from observation of differences in male and female genitals, is said to predominate. The lack of a penis is presumably felt as a punishment for some wrongdoing.

Among the neo-Freudians, Thompson questions whether observation of the genitals is sufficient to elicit castration anxiety unless reinforced by parental threats. Horney objects to the notion of primary penis envy in girls. She attributes envy in women to the desire for masculine qualities prized by the culture rather than to sexual experiences in early childhood. In his system Erikson stresses the "intrusive" features of the phallic-locomotor stage, such as aggressiveness, competition, curiosity, and the pleasure of conquest.

Relationships to others revolve around the Oedipus complex, defined as sexual love for the parent of the opposite sex accompanied by hatred for the parent of the same sex. In the case of the boy the transition is relatively simple, for the pre-oedipal object, the mother, continues to be the preferred parent. The girl, however, has to undergo a complicated switch in her affections from mother to father. The particular form which the Oedipus complex takes is said by Fenichel to be a product of family influence.

Other theorists offer a variety of explanations. Adler emphasizes pampering by the mother and the child's subsequent lust for power over her. Jung considers the Oedipus to be really a possession complex, with the mother seen as the source of protection, nourishment, and love. For Rank it represents an unsuccessful attempt to overcome the birth trauma. He also stresses the importance of the family situation and the child's struggle for individuality. Likewise family attachments are pointed up by Horney, based mainly on two conditions: sexual stimulation by the parents and anxiety aroused by conflict between dependency needs and hostile impulses toward the mother and father. Fromm minimizes the sexual tie and prefers to ascribe the difficulties between father and son to the effects of authoritarian patriarchal society. Sullivan's interpretation is in terms of familiarity and strangeness between parent and child, and Thompson also emphasizes interpersonal relationships beyond the erotic reactions.

In the orthodox framework the heir of the Oedipus complex is the superego. Psychosexual frustrations are said to cause a regression from object choice to identification, so that sexual longing for the object is replaced by an asexual alteration within the ego. The child identifies with his own idealized version of the parents, and being on good or bad terms with his superego becomes as important as being on good or bad terms with the parents previously was. Whereas the ego holds an executive position mediating between id, superego, and outside world, the superego functions center about moral demands and thereby represent the incorporated standards of society.

Rank traces the growth of the superego genetically from inhibited sadism, with the real nucleus being the strict mother as sadistically conceived by the child. Fromm attempts to distinguish authoritarian from humanistic conscience, the relative strengths of which depend upon the individual's experiences. The authoritarian conscience is described as the voice of internalized external authority, corresponding to Freud's superego. In contrast the humanistic is the voice of the person himself, the expression of man's self-interest and integrity.

With respect to mechanisms, Fenichel draws a distinction between successful defenses, which bring a cessation of the blocked impulses, and unsuccessful defenses, which necessitate a continuing repetition of the warding-off process. Included in the former are various types of sublimation, involving the desexualized expression of impulses via an artificial route. Among the latter are the previously discussed mechanisms of denial, projection, introjection, and regression, along with repression, reaction formation, undoing, isolation, and displacement. Sullivan adds his concepts of selective inattention and disassociation; and Fromm offers three mechanisms of escape from the feeling of isolation engendered by our society: sado-masochism, destructiveness, and automaton conformity.

NOTES

1. *Anal vs. Urethral Training.* Fenichel's explanation of a closer association of pride with urethral than with anal training, based on more frequent use of shame by parents in punishing failures of the former, is open to question. We wonder, first of all, whether shame is actually employed more often in connection with wetting, since anal incontinence probably provokes stronger reactions of disgust in most parents. Even granted a significant difference in favor of the child's being more proud of his control over urination, an alternative explanation might be in terms of the greater frequency of the latter, so that parental rewards for accomplishment occur more often and continually reinforce the feeling of pride.

2. *Origins of Ambition.* Obviously not all ambition can be traced back to the fight against shame over urethral incontinence, as Fenichel (74) himself points out. A more common explanation derives from the child's identification with the broadly ambitious goals set for him by his parents. How much of ambition can be attributed specifically to urethral training remains a matter for empirical research. It should be possible to differentiate children

according to types of sphincter training and then follow the later acquisition of personality traits like ambition.

3. *Evidence for Increased Interest in the Genitals.* Isaacs (149) observed 31 English children (mostly boys, ages two to six) in nursery school over a three-year period. Exhibitionism and voyeurism, as well as sadism, were common at ages three and four. She noted persistent curiosity about the anatomy of the opposite sex, and boys made repeated approaches toward women in both playful and serious attempts to examine the genitals. Hattendorf (135) secured information from mothers concerning the sex questions their children had asked. Second in frequency to questions by children aged two to five about the origin of babies were those relating to physical sex differences. While we may contest the unsystematic collection of data in the former study and the gross distortions and unreliability probably involved in mothers' recall in the latter, the actual fact of increased interest in the genitals by children at this age level can be commonly observed in their behavior.

4. *Relationship of Castration Anxiety to Oral and Anal Disturbances.* According to orthodox theory (74), castration anxiety has its forerunners in oral and anal anxieties over loss of breast and feces, respectively. Likewise castration fear can be regressively supplanted by oral or anal fears. Supportive evidence for these predicted associations was obtained in a study by Blum (34) which dealt in part with intercorrelations of certain psychosexual dimensions. Using the Blacky Pictures (35), a projective technique oriented toward psychoanalytic theory, the author found that disturbance in the area of castration anxiety was positively correlated with disturbance in orality ($r_t = .35$, $P < .05$) and in anality ($r_t = .36$, $P < .02$) for a group of 119 male college students.

5. *Universality of the Castration Complex.* There has been some controversy over the frequency of castration anxiety in the population. Sears (258) attacks what he calls Freud's "overgeneralization" by citing a couple of studies. In the dubious Hattendorf research referred to above, the mothers reported only 3 questions out of 137 which suggested that boys thought the girl's lack of a penis was the result of injury. Likewise Conn (54), using a doll-play technique with children from four to twelve years of age, noted that only 17 out of the 50 children who reacted to sex differences seemed shocked or disturbed by them. Of the total group of 200

three-fourths reported having seen the genitals of the opposite
sex. Levy (190) has criticized Conn's conclusions that shock is
not universal on the ground that inadequate recall for the older
children was not taken into account. But the issue of universality
itself is really irrelevant. It does not matter whether or not we
can find some slight evidence of castration anxiety in every last
man. Doubtless there is some sort of continuum. More important
problems relate first to measurement of the anxiety (through projective tests, doll play in children, etc.) in order to separate groups
with large and small amounts, and then to investigations of both
antecedent conditions and consequences for personality development.

6. *Studies on Masturbation.* Sears (258) has surveyed the earlier
research on masturbation. He describes Willoughby's (287) summary of the literature (1937), in which only 5 per cent of men
and 18 per cent of women could recall having masturbated before
ten years of age. In another study, Levy (190) had reported that,
on questioning the mothers of 49 boys, it was found that genital
manipulation had been observed in 53 per cent by the age of three
years. Sears reconciles the two divergent findings by saying that
masturbation was probably not defined similarly, since it was more
likely to represent habitual activity in Willoughby's summary.

In addition to these studies reported by Sears, there is one by
Huschka (148) presenting data on 320 problem children referred
by a general pediatrics clinic for psychiatric consultation. As part
of a routine intake history parents were asked whether the child
had been known to masturbate, if so at what age the masturbation
had first occurred, and finally what measures, if any, were used in
dealing with the situation. Forty-five per cent (142) of the children, whose ages ranged from one to fourteen years, were reported
to have masturbated; and 54 per cent of this subgroup were known
to have first done so before the age of five. Of the 142 children, in
73 per cent the problem was dealt with destructively. Direct
threats, predominantly physical, were employed most frequently;
and specifically their most common form was threat of genital injury. In the majority of cases it was the mother figure who scolded
the child. Huschka makes the pertinent observation that all such
studies represent understatements, since they involve only those
cases in which the parents had not forgotten the child's masturbation and how it was handled, and who felt secure enough to tell

what happened. She concludes by raising a number of provocative questions relating to incidence of masturbation threats in non-problem children; significance of the parental source of threat; the relationship between parental background and response to the child's masturbation; and the correlation of harsh treatment with the occurrence of anxiety and neurotic symptoms in children. Above all she stresses the positive implications of the findings for the psychoanalytic formulation of castration anxiety.

7. *Primary Penis Envy.* The most satisfactory avenue to determining whether penis envy in the little girl contributes significantly to "masculine protest" behavior in the adult woman would be a longitudinal approach. On the basis of such techniques as direct observation, doll play, and projective tests, it should be possible to separate young girls who exhibit strong signs of jealousy of the male genitals from those who do not. The Hattendorf type of approach (see Note 3) does not seem worth while as a source of information; in fact, Sears (258) comments that Hattendorf's data contained no evidence that girls envied the penis or wished to be boys. Later assessment in adulthood (*e.g.*, by Masculinity-Femininity scales) of the extent of active masculine strivings in the two female groups would serve to check the hypothesis of primary penis envy. Another area for study might be the systematic investigation of attitudes toward physical sex differences in those deviant cultures (*e.g.*, Tchambuli, Okinawan) where males normally play passive rather than aggressive roles [*cf.* Mead (202) and Moloney and Biddle (210)].

8. *Complications in the Girl's Oedipus Complex.* Corroborative evidence for the theoretical statement of stronger pre-oedipal attachments in the case of the girl was obtained in the previously cited study on college students by Blum (see Note 4). On two of the inquiry items for the oedipal dimension of the Blacky Pictures, significantly more females than males chose pre-oedipal rather than oedipal responses. In addition, fewer females received total scores indicating oedipal involvement. Another finding supports the notion that the presence of siblings, who presumably absorb some of the mother's attention, is related to the extent to which the little girl does turn away from mother to father. Sibling rivalry was found to be positively correlated with oedipal intensity in females ($r_t = .37, P < .05$).

9. *The Oedipus Controversy.* In the past there has been much

debate over whether the Oedipus complex is or is not universal. The facts themselves, as many neo-Freudians rightfully point out, suggest that both existence and form of the Oedipus are culture-bound. Fenichel reflects this position when he states that the complex is undoubtedly a product of family influence. The time seems ripe, therefore, to cease disproving Freud's outdated conception of an innate basis and to proceed instead to investigate, as recommended in the case of castration anxiety, the kinds of antecedent conditions and subsequent effects. The wide variety of theoretical positions concerning the development of oedipal conflicts certainly provides ample opportunity for the formulation of testable hypotheses.

10. *Studies on Identification.* This key concept has received considerable attention for many years in both the psychoanalytic literature and in the field of social psychology, especially. Until recently, however, studies have been few and far between. A growing research interest in the problem is reflected by the symposium on "Learning Theory and Identification" held at the 1951 meetings of the American Psychological Association, and the extensive programs along the same lines currently being carried out by Sears, Mowrer, and others. The existing evidence bears on such diverse topics as sex differences in identification, correlates of disturbed identification, and the relationship to other therapy variables of a patient's identification with his psychotherapist. England (67) and Blum (34), for example, have both presented data substantiating the familiar observation that boys tend to identify with their fathers and girls with their mothers. The latter also has found, according to theoretical expectation, that the identification process in females seems to be more confused and less clear-cut than in the case of males. Laden and Raush (183) noted a tendency for those high-school senior boys with little or no conflict on Blacky dimensions relevant to identification to perceive their own interests as more similar to their fathers'. In addition, this less conflicted group scored higher on the McClelland-Atkinson (197) need achievement index. Schrier (256), utilizing a series of ratings by patients, therapists, and judges, discovered that degree of patient identification with therapist correlated positively with amount of rapport between the two as well as with therapeutic success.

Systematic research on identification will have to start from a

clear definition of the concept itself. There are at least two controversial issues involved: the levels of awareness through which the
process operates, and the extent to which it serves adaptive rather
than defensive functions. Concerning the first, psychoanalytic
writers have generally considered identification to be an unconscious process, as distinguished from conscious imitation. Schilder
(255) and Knight (178), though, prefer to include the more conscious components along with the deeper ones. With reference to
the second issue, Alexander (12, p. 117) says that "identification
operates in the healthy growth of the ego and in the learning
process by which the ego acquires functional efficiency." Under
traumatic conditions, he adds, it serves as a defense. Balint (16)
stresses the defensive operation of identification in early life when
the environment is perceived as alien. The organism then seeks
to internalize the alien in order to render it harmless. Anna Freud's
(83) concept of "identification with the aggressor," in which the
fearful child transforms himself into a powerful individual by
introjecting the aggressive characteristics of the threatening person, similarly belongs in the defensive category. The double-edged
meaning of the term is further pointed up by Fenichel's statement
that identification, a regressive mechanism, is part of the positive
solution of the Oedipus complex.

Mowrer (213) and his associates (184, 55) have employed the
terms "developmental" and "defensive" identification, the former
referring to the child's attempts to imitate his parents and the latter
to "identification with the aggressor." With respect to the relationship between identification and object choice, Mowrer takes issue
with the orthodox position by maintaining that identification "precedes and, later, dictates object choice."

11. *"Fatherly" versus "Motherly" Superegos.* Fenichel's statement that the fatherly superego is generally decisive for both sexes
is contradicted by data obtained in the Blacky Pictures research
(34). Male college students did tend to attribute fatherly characteristics to the superego, but females, for the most part, ascribed
motherly ones. Perhaps this departure from Fenichel's opinion
may be a reflection of the increasing influence of the mother in
American life, in contrast to the patriarchal European society in
which psychoanalysis grew up. The related theoretical observation that the superego in both sexes contains mixed parental elements was indirectly supported by the fact that there were 31 per

cent of the males who did present motherly superegos and 29 per
cent of the females with fatherly ones.

12. *Sex Differences in Guilt.* The above study also revealed sex
differences in the degree and type of guilt feelings. Significantly
more females than males showed strong evidence of internalized
guilt, whereas males typically chose externalized alternatives. The
latter finding agrees with the theoretical contention that males
suffer more from anxiety over the possibility of external harm.

13. *The Mechanisms of Defense: Unexplored Fixtures in Theory
and Practice.* Current emphasis on the importance of mechanisms
of defense is equaled only by the paucity of knowledge concerning them. There have been scattered studies, referred to in this
and earlier chapters, bearing on individual mechanisms, but by
and large many major questions remain unanswered. To enumer-
ate a few: (1) ignorance of the chronological sequence in which
defenses tend to be acquired and utilized; (2) problems relating
to the consistency of use of mechanisms by the individual; (3)
interrelationships of the mechanisms themselves; (4) cultural
similarities and differences; (5) influence of social class upon
defense preferences; and (6) the nebulous area of conditions under which it is "good or bad" for the individual to employ defenses
at all, or any one defense in particular.

Recently Goldstein (117) has attempted to explore (2) and
(3) in the above list. Modifying the Blacky Pictures technique
to include a defense preference inquiry, he obtained the choices
of 104 male and female college students according to their rank-
ing of repression, projection, reaction formation, and regression
on each of eight psychoanalytic areas of conflict. The analysis of
consistency of individual preferences revealed a significantly
large minority ("general defenders") who tended to employ the
same hierarchy of defenses regardless of conflict area, whereas
the majority ("specific defenders") made specific choices for each
of the areas. The two groups of defenders continued to respond in
much the same fashion on a retest administration one month later,
indicating stability of choice over time. Some suggestive evidence,
based on the spontaneous stories which the subjects also wrote
for each cartoon, pointed to the general defenders as possibly a
more neurotic group.

With respect to relationships among the four mechanisms,
Goldstein discovered a mutual affinity between preferences for

repression and reaction formation on the one hand, and for projection and regression on the other. Whenever reaction formation was chosen first, repression tended to be second, and so on. This dichotomy was interpreted to be congruent with the theoretical description of the former pair as more advanced and the latter as more primitive mechanisms. In another research program at the University of Michigan, Miller and Swanson are currently investigating the effects of social class upon defense preferences.

14. *Can the Child Sublimate?* Sterba's illustration of the child who sublimates anal impulses by modeling clay appears to contradict Fenichel's position that genitality is a necessary condition for sublimation. However, the latter's reply would probably be that so-called "sublimations" in children and adolescents are merely partial processes which resemble the more complete adult sublimations. He does describe "forerunners" of sublimations which can be seen in children's play.

15. *Research on Sublimation.* It is no accident that the mechanism of sublimation remains virtually neglected from a research standpoint. The elusive nature of the concept itself makes any operational definition exceedingly tenuous. Its differentiation from displacement and reaction formation hinges upon the experimenter's ability to detect the absence of countercathexis. For example, overtly similar behavior may reflect the operation of either sublimation or reaction formation, depending upon the state of energy discharge. A further complication is provided by the fact that the term sublimation, according to the theory, does not designate a specific mechanism, but rather a class of mechanisms. The most widely quoted study in the literature stands as a solitary monument of how not to approach the problem. Taylor (281) in 1933 "disproved" sublimation by showing that 40 young, unmarried men of outstanding intellect and character all habitually obtained some sort of direct genital gratification. The inappropriateness of this investigation has already been pointed out in detail by others [see Sears (258), A. Freud (84)]. Sublimation is in no way linked theoretically with absence of genitality. Fenichel, as we have seen, goes so far as to say that only those individuals who have mastered the genital stage are able to sublimate. In any case, the impulses eligible for sublimation are considered to be the infantile, pregenital ones.

16. *Repression Experiments.* Repression is the one psychoana-

lytic mechanism which has received widespread attention from researchers. There have been literally dozens of studies reported in the literature. Except for a handful of recent experiments, the field has been amply surveyed by Rapaport (238), Sears (258), Zeller (293), and Korner (180), among others. Typically these earlier studies dealt with the phenomenon of repression proper (afterexpulsion) and utilized a variety of approaches to the recall of pleasant versus unpleasant experiences, incomplete versus completed tasks, and the like. Their irrelevance to the theoretical concept has already been forcefully hammered home by the several reviewers and need not be reiterated here. Instead we shall attempt first to spell out the criteria which ought to be met by a satisfactory operational definition of repression, and secondly to apply these criteria to the most recent, and possibly more sophisticated, studies.

Repression proper refers to the pushing back into unconsciousness of painful material that was once conscious. "Painful material" pertains to emotionally charged ideas which have become attached to basic, underlying impulses (*e.g.*, sex or aggression). The conscious expression of these conflict-laden ideas poses a threat to the ego in the form of severe anxiety or guilt. Therefore the ideas themselves are warded off, in an unconscious process, at the price of a continuing counterpressure. Although checked at a level below awareness, they keep striving actively for expression in direct or derivative ways. Once the painful aspects are removed, as in psychotherapeutic working through, the ideas can then become accessible to consciousness. Thus an operational definition should allow for the following elements: (1) disturbing ideas related to conflict-provoking impulses; (2) unconscious processes whereby the ideas are removed from awareness; (3) continued striving for some sort of expression while in check; and (4) renewed availability for conscious expression under benign conditions.

Of the recent studies the one by Keet (166) has probably stimulated the greatest interest. Though the experiment is aimed at comparing the relative efficacy of interpretive versus expressive techniques of psychotherapy, the operations center about the concept of repression. Keet used the Jung word-association test to pick out, for each subject, a word having some reference to an area of disturbance. Then a learning experience, in which the subject was likely to fail to recall the word, was carried out. Following the failure, subjects (30 in all) were individually given 25 minutes of therapy by Keet, who used an expressive technique on one-half the group and combined expressive and interpretive techniques on the other. At the conclusion of the experimental therapy each subject was again placed in a learning situation similar to the original one, except that the reaction word was substituted for the failed stimulus word. Considering recall of the reaction word as a criterion of successful therapy, he found that the combined expressive and interpretive methods proved consistently superior to the expressive alone.

Judging Keet's approach to repression in terms of the four elements outlined above, we are impressed most by the ingenious way he manipulated (4). Certainly his experimental conditions for restoring lost associations closely approximate the theoretical model. The second element was also taken care of satisfactorily. Some evidence for (3) can be inferred from the qualitative account of the subjects' tenseness and irritability on not being able to remember the key words. The first element—stimulus content —seems more appropriately handled than in earlier investigations but possibly still leaves something to be desired. The design tended to place an unduly heavy burden on the emotional significance of a single word, which is reflected in the fact that he had to eliminate a number of subjects from the experiment for failure to perform in the required fashion. The elusive, indecisive nature of the task is borne out by Keet's statement, in a personal communication, that he had to practice on many subjects before he could get the repression phase to work often enough. Similarly at least two other attempts, by graduate students in psychology at the University of Michigan and Stanford, have failed to duplicate the prerequisite conditions.

Zeller (294) performed two related experiments on repression proper. Using seminonsense syllables, he set up experimental and control groups on the basis of different interpolated material between original and subsequent learning tasks. The experimental groups were made to undergo a severe failure experience, while trying to reproduce patterns of tapping, between the first and second retention series. Between the second and third series the same circumstances were altered to provide a feeling of success. The control groups took part in neutral tapping tasks both times.

Experiments I and II differed mainly in the elaborateness of control measures. The results indicated that induced failure serves to reduce the ability to recall previously learned material, whereas induced success increases it. From our criterion standpoint, these studies are less satisfactory than Keet's. Allowance is made for elements (2) and (4), but not for (1) and (3). The most serious criticism pertains to the originally meaningless content, which achieves significance only by virtue of its association with an unrelated failure situation.

Another recent study, by Korner (180), utilized a novel approach to the concept of repression. He presented several groups of subjects with 18 stimulus sentences and asked them to write an additional three or four sentences on each one and also to provide every story with a three-word title. The experimental subjects, in individual sessions, were made to believe that six among their 18 titles indicated lack of balance in their personalities; six showed good balance; and the remaining six were not designated either way. Next they had to learn the 18 titles to one perfect recall. Four days later the subjects were requested to recall as many of the titles as they could. Significantly more of the negatively connoted titles (117 as compared with 81 positive and 90 undesignated) were forgotten. In control groups, where the implied threat to the security of the individual was omitted, no differential forgetting took place. Korner, however, falls down on several of the criterion counts—(1), (3), and (4). The stimulus content again assumes meaning only in terms of an artificially associated threat; there was no opportunity to observe continued striving for expression; and no attempt was made to restore the lost material to consciousness.

Belmont and Birch (22) make the very sound observation that studies on repression tend to ignore the fact that repression is only one of several possible mechanisms which a person may employ to cope with ego threat (see Goldstein experiment described in Note 13). If isolation, for example, is a more characteristic defense for him, he will probably fall into the wastebasket category of negative cases. The authors suggest that the smallness of the obtained absolute differences, though statistically significant as in the Korner research, may reflect this failure to "re-individualize the repression hypothesis." In their own study 55 subjects learned a list of 15 nonsense syllables. Five of the fifteen syllables were associated with a painful shock throughout the learning session. Then 24 hours later the subjects were tested for retention by recall, relearning, and recognition methods. The results showed that the group as a whole learned the shock syllables at a faster rate than they learned the neutral material, but approximately one-third of the group learned the shock syllables more slowly. Investigation of these two subgroups revealed significant differences between them in a number of further breakdowns of the data. Belmont and Birch conclude that the findings support their original contention. From the point of view of suitable operational criteria, the experiment, like Korner's, is deficient on (1), (3), and (4).

Two additional studies have utilized more of a perceptual approach to repression. Rosenstock (248) flashed eight sentences on a screen at different steps of illumination and asked subjects to write down what they had seen. Four sentences dealt with "repressible" material—sexual and aggressive impulses directed at parents—as opposed to four neutral control sentences. He found that the repressible sentences were more difficult to see than the neutral ones and were more frequently distorted. Women tended to repress aggressive material, whereas men repressed the sexual. This experiment is noteworthy for its adequate handling of the first element, meaningful content. The second also operates, but (3) is not observable and (4) is completely omitted.

The other perceptual research, by Clapp (52), was intended primarily to test the hypothesis that a shift in response would occur from a deeper level of awareness to one closer to consciousness. However, repression was one of the key constructs used in defining the problem. Clapp attempted to synthesize in his design the results of perception experiments performed by Bruner and Postman (43, 44), McGinnies (198), Howes and Solomon (146), McCleary and Lazarus (196) *et al.* with psychoanalytic theory. From the former group he borrowed the concepts of "selective vigilance" and "perceptual defense" and from the latter the notions of repressed strivings and ego defense. Accordingly he predicted that, when "more" and "less" emotional stimuli are presented in pairs at two levels of unconscious awareness, there will be a relative shift in the judgment of perceptual clarity. Since the human organism was shown to be capable of perceptual discrimination at levels well below conscious awareness, he reasoned that traumatic material, which theoretically continues to strive for expression, would be responded to more readily at deeper levels. At close to conscious awareness, on the other hand, the threatening stimuli would tend to be perceived by the ego and subsequently pushed away from expression.

In the actual experiment he selected three pairs of Blacky Pictures, two pairs each containing a relatively more and less traumatic stimulus situation (Pair I: Masturbation Guilt vs. Oral Sadism; Pair III: Oedipal Intensity vs. Sibling Rivalry) and one control pair with no outstanding difference in affect (Pair II: Identification vs. Ego Ideal). These pairs were presented to groups of subjects tachistoscopically at three very fast speeds and three slower ones at which the stimuli were not quite recognizable consciously. Subjects were asked simply to record which picture in each pair (shown one after the other) seemed the "clearer" or "closer to meaning something." The experimental groups on Pair I showed a relative shift in choice, from Masturbation Guilt seen as significantly clearer at the levels farther from consciousness (the exposure times varying around $\frac{1}{20}$ second) to Oral Sadism seen as significantly clearer at the levels closer to conscious recognition (around $\frac{1}{6}$ second). The controls on Pair I did not show the shift. Pair II, the control set of pictures, did not shift for the experimental group, again as predicted, and did for the controls. Pair III revealed equivocal results based on similar shifts in both experimental and control situations. Clapp's study probably best fulfills the first three criteria for an operational definition of repression, but neglects (4).

17. *Anal Components in Handwriting.* A study of male college students by McNeil and Blum (200) lends support to the theoretical contention that handwriting can serve as a medium of anal expression. They found significant relationships between disturbance on the dimension of Anal Retentiveness, as measured by the Blacky Pictures, and deviation on 8 out of 17 handwriting variables, including an over-all sign of atypicality.

18. *Reaction Formation.* This concept somehow poses a particular problem for nonanalytically oriented students of personality. Their response often is a hopeless disdain for the psychoanalytic "flip-flop hypothesis." If a result is contrary to what was expected, the magical explanation in terms of reaction formation can always be invoked. However, this feeling is in fact not justified.

It is perfectly permissible and often necessary, in light of our currently limited knowledge about personality, to make contingent predictions—in other words, to state in advance that an individual will behave in either of two opposite extreme fashions but not anywhere between them. If the mechanism accurately describes a kind of behavior, then it behooves us to make allowances for its operation in our experimental designs, rather than to oversimplify data by ignoring relevant factors. Of course, the individual who does abuse the concept in a *post hoc* explanatory manner must be considered equally at fault.

The research literature on reaction formation, apart from the Goldstein finding reported in Note 13, contains only a reference to Mowrer's (212) experiment with rats. Incidental to an investigation of habit regression, he noted that the animals seemed to be in a state of conflict or ambivalence between the impulse to approach and press a pedal in order to escape a grill shock, and the opposite impulse to run away to avoid an additional shock from the pedal itself. As a consequence, they were "running away from the pedal because they wanted to go toward and touch it."

19. *Selective Inattention and Disassociation.* Here Sullivan is undertaking a worth-while task in trying to set up a continuum of attention or levels of awareness, which presumably can be investigated research-wise. However, in their current descriptive form, the terms "selective inattention" and "disassociation" seem merely to be synonymous with preconscious and deeply repressed material, respectively.

20. *The Chronology of Fromm's Mechanisms.* Fromm does not specify the age levels for which the three mechanisms are appropriate. They seem to apply generally to later childhood as well as to adulthood, so that they are included in this chapter along with the other mechanisms mainly for convenience.

CHAPTER 6   *The Latency Period (Age Five*
to Prepuberty)

Once the hectic events of the phallic period have subsided, the child, according to orthodox theory, takes a long breathing spell and consolidates his position. Now, armed by a stronger ego and a growing superego, he turns to new fields—school, playmates, books, and other objects in the real world. The turbulent sexual interests are presumed to be quiescent (we may wish to question this point later), and behavior tends to be dominated by partial sublimations and reaction formations.

ORTHODOX VIEW

Ego and Superego Formation

Anna Freud describes developments in this period as follows (83, pp. 157–158):

The latency-period sets in, with a physiologically conditioned decline in the strength of the instincts, and a truce is called in the defensive warfare waged by the ego. It now has leisure to devote itself to other tasks and it acquires fresh contents, knowledge and capacities. At the same time it becomes stronger in relation to the outside world; it is less helpless and submissive and does not regard that world as quite so omnipotent as heretofore. Its whole attitude to external objects gradually changes as it surmounts the Oedipus situation. Complete dependence on the parents ceases and identification begins to take the place of object-love. More and more the principles held up to the child by his parents and teachers—their wishes, requirements, and ideals—are introjected.

127

In his inner life the outside world no longer makes itself felt solely in the form of objective anxiety. He has set up within his ego a permanent institution, in which are embodied the demands of those about him and which we call the superego. Simultaneously with this development a change takes place in the infantile anxiety. Fear of the outside world looms less large and gradually gives place to fear of the new representatives of the old power—to superego anxiety, anxiety of conscience and the sense of guilt. This means that the ego of the latency-period has acquired a new ally in the struggle to master the instinctual processes. Anxiety of conscience prompts the defence against instinct in the latency-period, just as it was prompted by objective anxiety in the early infantile period. As before, it is difficult to determine how much of the control over instinct acquired during the latency-period is to be attributed to the ego itself and how much to the powerful influence of the superego.

Thus, in latency the ego is relatively strong and can relax its efforts to tame the instinctual processes. The intellectual work performed by the ego becomes incomparably more solid, more reliable, and much more closely connected with action (see Note 1).

Hartmann, Kris, and Loewenstein (133) discuss the changes taking place in the superego at this time. At first the newly formed superego is exposed to many conflicting demands. It tends to be overly rigid and, rather than compromise, it yields. Early in latency obsessional symptoms are said to be very frequent. As the period progresses, there is a gradual adjustment in superego functions, due partly to the growth of intellectual comprehension and educational or religious indoctrination, but also partly to the fact that the function of the superego is less in danger and therefore needs less protection.

Similarly Bornstein (39) in a recent paper suggests that there are really two major phases in the latency period—the first from five and one-half to eight years, and the second from eight until about ten years. The element common to both is the strictness of the superego in its evaluation of incestuous wishes. The ego in the earlier phase, still buffeted by impulses, is threatened by the new and foreign superego, which functions in a harsh and rigid manner. Later, however, the ego is exposed to less severe conflicts as a result of diminished sexual demands and a more pliable superego. The organism then devotes greater attention to coping with reality.

Psychosexual Development

The latency period is characterized by a relative drop in the infantile sexual interests and the emergence of new interests, activities, and attitudes. The energy for these new interests is still derived from the sexual but operates extensively through partial sublimations and reaction formations. Psychosexual development in latency is referred to as "aim-inhibited." Both Sterba and Helene Deutsch make the point that the apparent quiescence is often not real, however, and masturbation, oedipal strivings, and pregenital regressions continue to some extent. The de-emphasis in sexuality is, therefore, relative and not absolute (see Note 2). Bornstein (39) describes these pregenital regressions as more typical of the first latency stage. In the second the temptation to masturbate is not completely overcome, but the child is so opposed to the temptation, as well as to the occasional break-through, that he must deny or repress both.

Relationships with Others

During latency the libidinal desires for the parental love object are replaced by sublimated expressions of affection—tenderness, devotion, and respect. Proximity to the love object is still sought, however. Hostile reactions tend to drop out, and there are beginnings of reaching out toward others in the environment for friendly relations. Bornstein (39) prefers to think of these new attitudes as belonging more specifically to the second latency phase. She states that the average eight-year-old is ready to be influenced by the children around him and by adults other than his parents. Since he is able to compare them with other adults, his belief in the omnipotence of his parents subsides. The earlier phase, however, is said to be characterized by a heightened ambivalence, which is expressed in behavior by alternating obedience and rebellion, followed by self-reproach.

According to Anna Freud (83), interests, in the case of boys, are concentrated on things which have an actual, objective existence. Some boys love to read about discoveries and adventures or to study numbers and proportions or to devour descriptions of strange animals and objects, while others confine their attention to machinery, from the simplest to the most complicated form. The point which these two types usually have in common is that the object in which they are interested must be a concrete one, not the product of fantasy like the fairy tales enjoyed in childhood. There are two possible explanations for this concrete thinking: (1) children in latency dare not indulge in abstract thought because of the danger of rearousing sexual conflicts; and (2) there is no need to do so, since the ego is now relatively strong and not in imminent danger (see Note 3).

Mechanisms

No new mechanisms are introduced at this age level. As mentioned above, partial sublimations and reaction formations are generally held to be the major operating defenses of the latency period. Consistent with her position, Bornstein (39) treats earlier and later defensive reactions. The former phase is complicated by the intermingling of two different sets of defenses, against genital and against pregenital impulses. As a defense against genital impulses, the ego temporarily regresses to pregenitality, since the latter impulses appear less dangerous. However, the pregenital drives themselves are sufficiently threatening to elicit extensive reaction formations. During the second latency period there is less need to defend and the ego is concerned primarily with maintaining its newly acquired equilibrium.

NEO-FREUDIAN VIEWS

Thompson

Thompson questions whether the child's interest in his sexual organs actually dies out during the so-called "latency period." She says that with an expanded relationship to his playmates and awareness of the disapproval of parents, the child tends to share his interests and experiences with those of his own age and to keep his ideas to himself where his parents are concerned. Insofar as the latency period is real, it is a product of our civilization. It probably appears not only because the child's sexual interests are disapproved and repressed, but because at this period the world becomes much larger. He goes to school, and the process of becoming part of a group of contemporaries absorbs his interest (see Note 4).

Sullivan

Sullivan refers to latency as the "juvenile era." It begins with the growth of a need to interact with other children in the same age range. The child shifts from contentment in an environment of authoritarian adults and more or less personalized toys and pets to an environment of persons significantly like him. If playmates are available, his integrations with them show new meaningfulness. If there are no playmates, the child's reverie processes create imaginary playmates. A new tendency toward cooperation comes into being, and along with this ability to play with other children goes the learning of competition and compromise.

School experiences assume very great significance. Whether they acquire painful proportions or not depends upon the child's previous upbringing. The one who has to resort to inappropriate magic from childhood—like tears, tantrums, or telling mama—will have a very hard time because his peers do not yet possess much sympathy. School also brings new experiences in adjusting to authority. In dealing with teachers the techniques previously used with parents are often ineffective. The interpersonal relationships between teacher and pupil may affect the growth of personality in either a good or bad direction. Where the parents have been extremely puritanical and rigid, school experiences may expand the self in a very constructive fashion. On the other hand, the child from a happy home who is subjected to a harsh, cruel teacher may be affected adversely. The unpleasant school situation may force him into regressive reveries about his younger days at home.

Fears of ostracism by others are prominent in the juvenile era. Also, at this time the personification of the self is greatly affected by one's reputation. Children tend to be classified as popular, average, or unpopular. Another new phenomenon is the introduction of the chum—the very desirable person who somehow is conducive to the satisfaction of needs and the avoidance of anxiety (see Note 5).

SUMMARY

During the latency period, says Anna Freud, the ego becomes much stronger in relation to the outside world. Along with a decline in strength of the instincts, the ego has a new ally, the superego, in its struggle to master impulses. The superego tends to be overly rigid at first but gradually adjusts and grows more pliable. There is said to be a relative drop in infantile sexual interests. Energy for the new activities, interests, and attitudes still derives from the sexual but operates mainly through the mechanisms of partial sublimation and reaction formation. Thompson doubts whether sexual latency even takes place. She maintains that the child, because of his expanded relationships, tends to share his thoughts and actions with those his own age.

Libidinal desires for the parental love object are replaced by sublimated expressions of affection. Hostile reactions seem to drop out and there are beginnings of reaching out toward others in the environment for friendly relations. Sullivan, coining the term "juvenile era," stresses the importance of school experiences and the need to interact with other children in the same age range. One's reputation becomes crucial and fears of ostracism by others are prominent. The introduction of the chum is another characteristic of this period.

NOTES

1. *Explanations for the Newly Acquired Ego Strength.* Anna Freud presents the orthodox position in terms of a "physiologically conditioned decline in the strength of the instincts, and a truce . . . in the defensive warfare waged by the ego." Therefore the ego, which also becomes stronger in relation to the outside world, can relax its efforts to tame instinctual processes. In light of evidence which seriously questions any physiological decline in sexual impulses (see Note 2), it seems plausible to view the expanded ego functioning of this period as due primarily to the greatly increased scope of social behavior. If the child's broadened environment no longer dictates urgent exercise of ego defenses, then we have a more parsimonious explanation for the development of constructive ego activities.

2. *Evidence Concerning Sexual Latency in Our Own Culture.* There has been a growing trend, both within and outside psychoanalytic circles, to doubt the existence of sexual latency. Many observations can be cited to support this view. Sears (258) quotes studies by Campbell (49), Achilles (2), Davis (57), and Hamilton (128) as illustrations that sexual interests continue to figure prominently between the ages of five and ten. More recently Kinsey *et al.* (168) have presented data indicating sizable frequencies of masturbation, orgasm, and general sex play during these years. Alpert (14), reporting on her extensive observations of children, describes the six-year-old as showing active and frank sexual curiosity, with mutual explorations common. Masturbation, however, occurs less at age six than at five. The seven-year-old comes closest to being sexually quiescent, but Alpert feels it is more accurate to say that sexual impulses are disguised. Between eight and eleven there is evidence of strong homosexual and heterosexual interest, often sadistic in expression. Heterosexual behavior becomes progressively more provocative until pu-

berty, at which time the teasing becomes transformed into a shy and warm attachment.

Two explorations of latency via projective techniques have been conducted recently. Hilgeman (140), using the Blacky Pictures (35) with six- and nine-year-olds of both sexes, found all her groups showing strong disturbance in oral sadism, anality, and sibling rivalry. Also, six-year-old boys were more oral-dependent than nine-year-old boys, and scores of the girls at six were stronger on oral and anal dimensions than were those at age nine. Castration anxiety was marked in boys at both ages, as was penis envy in girls. Gurin's (124) study, in which the Michigan Picture Test (134) was administered to two groups, one aged eight to nine and a half and the other twelve to fifteen and a half, did reveal significantly more psychosexual expressions in stories told by the adolescent group.

In summary, the relative de-emphasis in sexuality to which Sterba and Deutsch allude can probably be described more precisely as an increased emphasis on nonsexual behavior rather than any sharp decrease in underlying sexual concern.

3. *Concrete versus Abstract Thinking.* It has been commonly observed that the capacity for abstract thinking increases markedly during this age level [see Biber, Murphy, Woodcock, and Black (31), for example]. The seeming contradiction between this fact and Anna Freud's contention that concrete thinking dominates the latency period can probably be reconciled on the basis of differing definitions of abstract thought. In the former case the concept connotes symbolic, higher level, problem-solving ability, whereas for Anna Freud it seems to refer to emotionally laden fantasy production. The two opposing hypotheses which she offers as possible explanations for the absence of fantasy thinking certainly do not narrow the field appreciably.

4. *Cultural Variations.* Thompson's point, concerning the culture-bound quality of any latency characteristics which do exist, is substantiated by anthropological observations like those of Malinowski (201). The latter, in his study of the Trobriand Islanders, found no evidence for a decline in sexual interests. Instead sex play became increasingly direct and its control by the culture more highly formalized.

5. *Sullivan's Account of the "Juvenile Era."* Sullivan makes one of his best contributions here. His detailed description of the so-

cialization process helps to fill a vital gap and should serve to stimulate further investigations of this age. The relative neglect of these five years of later childhood by other psychoanalytic writers is attested to by the brevity of this chapter in comparison with the preceding ones. The new label also makes sense inasmuch as the evidence cited above (see Note 2) points to "latency period" as a misnomer.

CHAPTER 7 *Prepuberty and Adolescence*

If there has been relative peace and quiet in the latency period, it comes to an abrupt end with the onset of puberty. Attainment of sexual maturity brings in its wake a wave of disturbance, not only in the sexual area but also in the broader realm of social behavior. According to psychoanalytic theory, the adolescent, flooded by his own resurgent impulses, must regroup the defensive forces of his ego in an attempt to meet this new onslaught.

ORTHODOX VIEWS

Psychosexual Development

The interval between latency and puberty—known as "prepuberty" or "preadolescence"—is preparatory to physical sexual maturity. There are no qualitative changes, says Anna Freud, but the quantity of instinctual energy has increased (see Note 1). The increase is not confined to the sexual life. There is more libido at the id's disposal and it cathects indiscriminately any impulses which are at hand. In her own words (83, p. 159):

Aggressive impulses are intensified to the point of complete unruliness, hunger becomes voracity and the naughtiness of the latency-period turns into the criminal behaviour of adolescence. Oral and anal interests, long submerged, come to the surface again. Habits of cleanliness, laboriously acquired during the latency-period, give place to pleasure in dirt and disorder, and instead of modesty and sympathy we find exhibitionistic tendencies,

136

brutality and cruelty to animals. The reaction-formations, which seemed to be firmly established in the structure of the ego, threaten to fall to pieces. At the same time, old tendencies which had disappeared come into consciousness. The Oedipus wishes are fulfilled in the form of phantasies and day-dreams, in which they have undergone but little distortion; in boys ideas of castration and in girls penis-envy once more become the centre of interest. There are very few new elements in the invading forces. Their onslaught merely brings once more to the surface the familiar content of the early infantile sexuality of little children. [See Note 2.]

Deutsch (58) presents a different account of prepuberty in girls. She characterizes it as a period of greatest freedom from infantile sexuality and from aggression. The increased activity is interpreted, not as a manifestation of aggression, but rather as an intensive process of adaptation to reality and mastery of the environment, which precedes the passivity of puberty. Spiegel (267), in a review of psychoanalytic contributions to adolescence, questions these conclusions on the basis of Deutsch's own materials. He points out that it is difficult to reconcile the supposed freedom from infantile sexuality with evidences of strong interest in the function of the sexual organs, the preoccupation with prostitution fantasies, and sado-masochistic interpretations of intercourse. Also the prepubertal girl is described as being full of rage and hatred as well as of dependent, clinging feelings toward the mother.

With the arrival of bodily sexual maturity (puberty proper), there is, according to Anna Freud, a further change of a qualitative character (see Note 3). Previously the heightening of instinctual cathexis was general and undifferentiated; now libido, especially in males, is concentrated specifically on genital feelings, aims, and ideas. Pregenital tendencies are relegated to the background, which results in an apparent improvement in behavior. The boorish aggressiveness of preadolescence gives way to the more refined genital masculinity. What seems to be a spontaneous cure of pregenitality is largely deceptive, though. The temporary triumph of genitality over early fixations recedes in adult life, when the pressure of the instincts sinks to its normal level and all the old anxieties and conflicts reappear unchanged.

Heterosexual outlets, however, are limited by the fact that society strongly opposes sexual intercourse during adolescence (see Note 4). According to Fenichel, the conflicts between drives and anxieties are felt consciously by present-day adolescents principally in the form of conflicts around masturbation. The heightened genital strivings sooner or later find expression in masturbatory activity, unless the infantile repressions have been too intense. The fears and guilt feelings originally connected with the accompanying oedipal fantasies are displaced to the masturbation. Adolescents react to these fears and guilt feelings by taking sides with the drive and fighting with anxiety and the parents, or they may more frequently side with the anxiety and the parents and try to fight off instinctual temptations. Often they do both (see Note 5).

For the boy, sexual developments in puberty are said to be a reawakening and continuation of infantile sexuality. He maintains his interest in the penis, whereas for the girl there is a change of direction. During adolescence she becomes aware of her vagina as a source of pleasure, while previously she had been interested solely in her clitoris and the desire to be boyish. At puberty the feminine function and its passive role must be accepted. Where strong penis envy exists, this switch is seriously impeded. The first menstruation, says Spiegel (267), may play an important role in the process, either by supporting the feminine tendencies with all the fantasies concerning passive-masochistic gratification, pregnancy, and childbirth; or, on the contrary, leading to a rejection of femininity by increasing penis envy and the castration complex (see Note 6). Buxbaum (46) reports that, unconsciously, the first menstruation is experienced as an injury to the genitals, as a castration, and as a punishment for masturbation. Deutsch (58) also emphasizes the double sexual role of mother and lover which the girl must ultimately integrate.

Sex differences in narcissism at puberty, originally formulated by Harnick, are summarized in Spiegel's review. The male is said to retain the narcissistic estimation of his own penis to a great extent throughout his life, while the woman, on reaching maturity at puberty, tends to prize the beauty of her face and figure. The basis for this female libidinal shift from the genitals to the body as a whole is found in the wave of repression, occurring at puberty, which relates especially to sexuality associated with the clitoris. The male undergoes a similar but less extreme shift in setting up ideals of bodily strength and manliness.

Ego and Superego Formation

With the advent of preadolescence, as we have seen, the balanced relationship or truce between the ego and the id in latency is disrupted. Physiological forces stimulate the instinctual processes and upset the balance. The ego, already strengthened and consolidated, struggles desperately to regain the equilibrium by using all the defenses in its repertory. The conflict is translated readily into behavior. While the id is winning out, there is an increase in fantasy, lapses into pregenital sexual gratification, and aggressive or even criminal actions. While the ego is ahead, there are various forms of anxiety, neurotic symptoms, and inhibitions.

In adolescence there are two extremes in which the conflict may possibly end. Either the id, now grown strong, may overcome the ego, in which case no trace will be left of the previous character of the individual and the entrance into adult life will be marked by a "riot of uninhibited gratification of instinct," in Anna Freud's words. Or the ego may be victorious, in which case the character of the individual during the latency period will remain permanently. When this happens, the id impulses of the adolescent are confined within the narrow limits prescribed for the instinctual life of the child. No use can be made of the increased libido and there has to be a constant expenditure on countercathexes, defense mechanisms, and symptoms. The ego generally remains rigid and inflexible throughout life. As a result of these conflicting forces, adolescent personality characteristically manifests such contradictory traits as altruism and selfishness, gregariousness and solitariness, indulgence and asceticism.

The factors which determine whether the outcome will be a one-sided or a happier solution are threefold: (1) the strength of the id impulses, which is conditioned by the physiological process at puberty; (2) the ego's tolerance or intolerance of instinct, which depends on the character formed during the latency period; and (3) the nature and efficacy of the defense mechanisms at the ego's command (see Note 7).

The ego also alienates itself from the superego during adolescence. Since the superego is still intimately related to the parents, it is itself treated as a suspicious incestuous object. The principal effect of this break between ego and superego is to increase the danger which threatens from the instincts. The individual tends to become asocial, since the former alliance of ego and superego is at an end. The defensive measures prompted by superego anxiety become inoperative and the ego is thrown back to the level of pure instinctual anxiety, accompanied by its primitive protective measures (see Note 8). Conditions are then ripe for the development of what Fenichel describes as an "impulsive character." At the other extreme is Spiegel's (267) commentary on the growing stress which society places upon superego formation during adolescence. This tendency to maximize compliance may be responsible for the frequent appearance of the pseudo-mature adolescent who, although he complies with the serious demands of present-day society, is nevertheless emotionally very close to blind revolt against these demands. The revolutionary type of adolescent, he adds, does not seem to be found so frequently nowadays.

Bernfeld (26, 27, 29, 30), in a series of papers, has attempted to classify reactions of adolescents to the libidinal changes of puberty and also to the shifting ego-superego relations. With respect to the former, he distinguishes two types: the neurotic and the simple or uncomplicated. The neurotic group tries to deny the pubertal changes and to live as if nothing new has occurred. Anxiety and defense against anxiety characterize their behavior. The simple group, on the other hand, maintains the ideal of being grown up and consequently assumes a positive, welcoming attitude to the signs of sexual maturity. On the ego-superego variables Bernfeld differentiates the adolescent who is extremely compliant to the wishes of the environment, the one who is extremely rebellious, and the one who is mixed in his reactions. Wittels (288) suggests a chronological type of breakdown of adolescent phases into a second phallic period, a second latency, and finally a mature ego stage.

Relationships with Others

In the preadolescent phase libido is again directed toward the love objects of childhood. Incestuous oedipal fantasies are prominent. The adolescent ego's first task is to revoke these tendencies at all cost. Typically, the young person isolates himself and behaves like a stranger with members of his own family (see Note 9). He substitutes new attachments to replace the parental ties. Sometimes the individual becomes attracted to young people of his own age, in which case the relationship takes the form of passionate friendship or of actually being in love; sometimes the attachment is to an older person, whom he takes as his leader—clearly a substitute for the abandoned parents. While they last, these love relations are passionate and exclusive, but they are of short duration. Persons are selected as objects and abandoned without any consideration for their feelings, and others are chosen in their place. The abandoned objects are quickly and completely forgotten, but the form of the relation to them is preserved down to the minutest detail and is generally reproduced, with an exactness which almost suggests obsession, in the relation to the new object. Spiegel makes the point that the reanimation of the Oedipus complex often does not appear in clear form, especially after adolescence has been under way for some time. Parent substitutes who have less and less in common with the original parent images are chosen with increasing frequency as maturation continues.

According to Anna Freud, these fleeting love fixations are not really object relations, but rather identifications of the most primitive kind. The fickleness characteristic of puberty does not indicate any inner change in the love or convictions of the individual, but instead a loss of personality as a consequence of a change in identification. Fenichel says that in many ways objects are used as mere instruments to relieve inner tensions, as good or bad examples, as proofs of one's own abilities, or as reassurances. Objects are easily abandoned if they lose their reassuring significance.

Anna Freud goes on to state that the adolescent regresses in his libidinal life from object love to narcissism. He avoids complete collapse by convulsive efforts to make contact with external objects once more, even though by a series of narcissistic identifications.

Following this wave of narcissism, orthodox theory describes a normal, temporary phase of homosexual object choices (see Note 10). Fenichel elaborates this topic by maintaining that homosexual preferences are due to social factors as well as a narcissistic orientation. Adolescents prefer to meet in homosexual gatherings so as to avoid the exciting presence of the other sex and at the same time avoid being alone. In this way they hope to find the reassurance they are looking for. However, the friendships that were formed in the hope of avoiding sexual object relationships often assume a sexual character themselves.

In her discussion of the girl's development Deutsch (58) says that object choice changes from homosexual in preadolescence to bisexual in early puberty and to heterosexual in later puberty. The homosexual relationship at times shows a sado-masochistic quality. There are typical crushes on some older girl, as well as very close contacts with another girl of the same age. The bisexuality of early adolescence is emphasized in frequently occurring love triangles. Along with the growing sexual desires come numerous fantasies, the most common concerning pregnancy and prostitution and, to a lesser extent, rape.

Psychologically, there is the appearance of narcissism, which is one of the important parts of the feminine core, along with passivity and masochism. The development of passivity is aided by the fact that women cannot be active and aggressive because of the double standard. Also, the trauma associated with the lack of an active organ, the penis, leads the girl to seek passive means of sexual gratification. Since activity and aggression cannot be expressed toward the outside world, they are turned against the self in a masochistic fashion. Narcissism, the intensification of self-love, serves as a defense against the masochistic urges.

Mechanisms

Prepubertal Defenses. In an effort to regain the equilibrium of the latency period, the prepuberty ego indiscriminately calls upon all the defense mechanisms at its command. Even the breakthroughs of pregenital tendencies, while representing a failure in defense, are considered by Lander (185) to serve as regressive protection against delinquency. Greenacre (122) describes a specific defense of this period—the "prepuberty trauma," in which the young girl provokes or cooperates in a sexual act with an adult. By shifting her feelings of guilt to the adult, she can keep the experience in consciousness and use it as a "real defense" against the demands of puberty. Spiegel (267) cites this illustration as evidence for the fact that external reality may be used primarily for defensive purposes.

Asceticism. A common mechanism in adolescence is the repudiation of all instinctual impulses, so-called "asceticism." The individual mistrusts enjoyment in general, and the safest policy for him is to counter his urgent desires with more stringent prohibitions, similar to those of strict parents in early training. The mistrust of instinctual wishes has a tendency to spread, extending even to the ordinary physical needs.

Examples are adolescents who avoid the society of those of their own age, decline to join in any entertainment, and refuse to have anything to do with plays, music, or dancing. More extreme forms of asceticism are exposures to unnecessary health risks, like wearing inadequate clothing, giving up food pleasures, rising very early in the morning, and so on.

Anna Freud (83) differentiates asceticism from repression on two grounds: (1) Repression deals with a specific instinctual relationship and is concerned with the nature and quality of the instinct. Anal-sadistic tendencies may be repressed and oral ones gratified. Asceticism, on the other hand, is concerned with the quantity of the instinct, and all instinctual impulses are regarded as dangerous. (2) In repression there is some form of substitute expression, such as a hysterical symptom, whereas asceticism can be altered only by a sudden switch to instinctual excesses. Generally, asceticism is a more primitive and less complex process.

Intellectualization. A second mechanism in adolescence is intellectualization. The aim of asceticism is to keep the id within limits simply by imposing prohibitions. The aim of intellectualization is to link up instinctual processes closely with ideational contents in order to render them accessible to consciousness and amenable to control. This mechanism has its origin in the increased effectiveness of intellectual functioning. Interests change from the concrete ones of latency to abstractions (see Note 11). There are all sorts of abstract discussions on such topics as marriage, political philosophy, religion, professions, and so on. However, the superiority of intellectual performance at this time makes very little imprint on the adolescent's actual behavior. Despite his lofty views he remains preoccupied by his own mundane personality problems. The intellectualization is not reality oriented, but rather serves as a defense against instincts. Instead of an ascetic flight from instinct, there is a turning toward it, but only in thought. Anna Freud describes the situation as follows (83, pp. 177–178):

The abstract intellectual discussions and speculations in which young people delight are not genuine attempts at solving the tasks set by reality. Their mental activity is rather an indication of a tense alertness for the instinctual processes and the translation into abstract thought of that which they perceive. The philosophy of life which they construct—it may be their demand for revolution in the outside world—is really their response to the perception of the new instinctual demands of their own id, which threaten to revolutionize their whole lives. Their ideals of friendship and undying loyalty are simply a reflection of the disquietude of the ego when it perceived the evanescence of its new and passionate object-relations. The longing for guidance and support in the often hopeless battle against their own powerful instincts may be transformed into ingenious arguments about man's inability to arrive at independent political decisions. We see then that instinctual processes are translated into terms of intellect. But the reason why attention is thus focussed on the instincts is that an attempt is being made to lay hold of and master them on a different psychic level.

Creativity as a Defense. Spiegel (267) summarizes the writings of several psychoanalytic authors who interpret adolescent creativity as a defense against impulses aroused by the reenactment of the oedipal conflict. The most common form of creative endeavor at this time is the diary, which contains in addition to actual events all sorts of reflections, plans, and recollections. Poetry and other literary efforts have also been studied in this connection. Bernfeld states that the incestuous libidinal drives are deflected to other permissible objects, fantasies, values, and ideas, which he calls "also-objects." Creativity in this form is approved by the ego ideal. Rank points out that dramas written in adolescence concern themselves primarily with problems of incest. The frequent sudden cessation of creative activity toward the end of adolescence is accounted for by the inability to master the incest conflict.

The transformation of defensive into true creativity comes about when the adolescent sacrifices his private needs to the demands of communicability, thus finding his way back from fantasy to reality. The motive for renunciation of gratification derived from private daydreams, as recorded in diaries, is to be found in the ambitious strivings of the adolescent for fame and power gained from impressing a wide audience. The hero of these literary products represents the author's ego ideal, for whom he pleads in order to obtain sympathy, recognition, and love.

RANKIAN VIEW: HANKINS

Blanchard (32) describes Rankian theories of adolescence, as expounded in a paper by Hankins. According to the latter, the period of adolescence brings new developments in the child's continuing struggle for independence and sense of self. The sexual drives appear as generic forces within the individual which offer a threat to this recently increased self-assertiveness and self-differentiation. The adolescent fears and resists his sexual impulses because they might dominate him and force him to renounce his capacity to act as a total self. The reconciliation, provided by our culture, between sexual drives and individual self-expression is in a love relationship with another person. However, the adolescent is reluctant to enter such a relationship because he would have to give up total personal control and to accept partial control from the other person.

Hankins states that the normal outcome of adolescence is an acceptance of the fact that new experiences and relationships enrich the personality, despite some element of self-sacrifice. She criticizes Anna Freud's explanation of adolescent asceticism on the grounds that it serves mainly to promote individuality by denying sexuality or keeping it under strict control. Also sexual promiscuity is to be viewed, not as an uninhibited effort for instinctual gratification, but rather as an attempt to preserve the individual self. This kind of transitory relationship can be used to dominate the other person through his sexual needs, while at the same time refusing to yield any part of the self.

NEO-FREUDIAN VIEWS: SULLIVAN

In the preadolescent era, according to Sullivan, the capacity to love matures. Love exists only when the satisfactions and security of the loved one are as important as one's own satisfactions and security. Since boys feel more at ease with each other than with girls at this time, the capacity to love first involves a member of the same sex, the chum. When this happens, there is a great increase in the consensual validation of symbols. The preadolescent learns to see himself through the other's eyes, so that there is a consensual validation of one's own personal worth. In Sullivan's words (277, pp. 20–21):

In this period there begins the illumination of a real world community. As soon as one finds that all this vast artistic and somewhat validated structure to which one refers as one's mind, one's thoughts, one's personality, is really open to some comparing of notes, to some checking and counter-checking, one begins to feel human in a sense in which one has not previously felt human. One becomes more fully human in that one begins to appreciate the common humanity of people—there comes a new sympathy for the other fellow, whether he be present to the senses or mediated by rumors in the geography, or the like. In other words, the feeling of humanity is one of the aspects of the expansion of personality which comes in adolescence. Learning at this stage begins to assume its true aspect of implementing the person in securing satisfactions and maintaining his security in interpersonal relations through the rest of life.

Preadolescence, for most people in our culture, is the period closest to untroubled human life (see Note 12). From that time on life's problems reduce them to "inferior caricatures of what they might have been." Difficulties in adolescence center around the maturation of the "genital lust mechanism." Sex finally comes into its own, but conflicts concerning sex are a function of two cultural factors: (1) premarital sexual experience is frowned upon; and (2) early marriage is discouraged, so that the gap between the adolescent awakening of lust and the proper circumstances for marriage is progressively being widened.

Lust cannot be dissociated easily when the sexual impulses collide with the self-system. In most people it cannot be dissociated at all; in some it can, but only at grave risk to effective living. Generally, sexual feelings operate again and again to threaten security and produce anxiety. One method which may or may not work is sublimation, or as Sullivan phrases it, the sublimatory reformulation of interpersonal relations. He describes sublimation as follows (277, p. 62): "A motive which is involved in painful conflict is combined with a social (culturally provided) technique of life which disguises its most conflict-provoking aspect and usually provides some representation for the opposing motive in the conflict." An illustration is the young woman with fantasies of prostitution who devotes her time to philanthropic work with fallen women in the city slums. Mullahy (216) claims that Sullivan's use of the term "sublimation" is much broader than the orthodox, since it can refer to any tendency system or drive (see Note 13).

If adolescence can be successfully negotiated, the person emerges with self-respect adequate to almost any situation. Along with this self-respect goes respect for others and a freedom of personal initiative which allows him to adapt his personal characteristics to the social order.

SUMMARY

Anna Freud describes the prepuberty phase as one in which impulses once again break through, accompanied by aggression, pregenital symptoms, and oedipal fantasies. Deutsch, on the other hand, says that for girls this is the period of greatest freedom from infantile sexuality and aggression. At the onset of puberty, according to orthodox theory, libido becomes concentrated specifically on genital feelings, aims, and ideas, with an apparent improvement in behavior. Heterosexual outlets, however, are limited by society, so that conflicts around masturbation are common. The adolescent girl is said to become aware of the vagina as a source of pleasure while previously she had been interested solely in the clitoris and the desire to be boyish. At this time she faces the problem of accepting the feminine function and its passive role. Narcissism is high-lighted in both sexes during adolescence.

Conflict between the ego and the id is characteristic. Two possible extremes can result: if the id wins out there is a "riot of uninhibited gratification of instinct," and if the ego is victorious impulses are confined within narrow limits and there has to be constant expenditure of energy on countercathexes, defense mechanisms, and symptoms. The ego also alienates itself from the superego in this period, which further increases the danger from instincts and tends to make the individual asocial.

In the area of relationships to others, the adolescent has to fight off the oedipal fantasies stirred up again during prepuberty. He substitutes new attachments to replace parental ties. These love relations, whether to a person of his own age or a parental substitute, are passionate and exclusive but typically of short duration. Others are selected as objects and then abandoned without any consideration for their feelings. Fleeting love fixations of this sort, says Anna Freud, are highly narcissistic and really represent primitive forms of identification. Following this wave of narcissism is a normal, temporary phase of homosexual relationships. In the case of the girl Deutsch states that there is a change in object choice from homosexual in prepuberty to bisexual in early puberty to heterosexual in later puberty. Significant elements in the feminine core are said to be narcissism, passivity, and masochism.

In prepuberty the ego has to call indiscriminately upon all the defense mechanisms at its command. During adolescence two frequent mechanisms are asceticism, the repudiation of all instinctual wishes, and intellectualization, the linking of instinctual processes to ideational contents. Adolescent creativity, such as the diary, is also interpreted as a form of defense.

The Rankian view of adolescence stresses the continuing struggle for independence and sense of self. The individual fears and resists his sexual impulses because they might dominate him and force him to renounce his capacity to act as a total self. Sullivan describes prepuberty as the most untroubled phase of human life, during which the capacity to love matures. Difficulties in adolescence occur in relation to the "genital lust mechanism." Sex becomes conflict-laden because premarital sexual experience is frowned upon and early marriage is discouraged. If adolescence can be successfully negotiated through the use of sublimation, Sullivan adds, then the person emerges with self-respect adequate to almost any situation.

NOTES

1. *Energy Complications Once More.* Anna Freud's reference to the increased quantity of instinctual energy in prepuberty seems to be at variance with the orthodox notion of a closed system containing a fixed amount of energy. Perhaps she intends to convey an increase in the amount of energy actively mobilized at this time. In any case, the psychic energy concept, with all its attendant confusions and limitations, stands as something less than a cure-all for what ails personality theory.

2. *The Problem of Individual and Class Differences.* A difficulty inherent in many psychoanalytic formulations is the unknown extent to which they apply to the population at large. A prime example here is Anna Freud's description of the unruly, boorish behavior of the preadolescent. The issue of how many preadolescents conform to this picture is not treated, so the reader is left with the impression that such characteristics are at least typical. Doubtless there are wide individual differences. The crucial effects, in this connection, of social class membership have been sharply delineated by sociologists. Allison Davis (56), for example, describes adolescent aggression as an approved, socially rewarded form of behavior in the lower classes. Until adequate

normative evidence becomes available, judgments concerning frequency should probably be reserved.

3. *Onset of Physical Changes in Adolescence*. Kinsey *et al.* (168) state that the onset of adolescent physical changes in boys is more or less abrupt, usually occurring between eleven and fourteen years of age. In girls adolescent development is said to be more gradual, spread over a longer period of time, and does not reach its peak until a good many years after boys are sexually mature. Stolz and Stolz (273) describe three phases of adolescent growth: prepubertal, pubertal, and postpubertal. The first phase takes place sometime before age thirteen in boys and before eleven in girls. Its duration for boys is approximately a year and a quarter and for girls slightly shorter. The pubertal phase, which contains the most noticeable growth spurt, occurs between thirteen and fifteen for males and between eleven and fourteen for females. The third phase in the girl lasts for a year and a half and is somewhat shorter in the case of the boy. The legal definition of puberty, according to Webster's Dictionary, is usually given as fourteen for boys and twelve for girls.

4. *Sexual Activities*. Surveys of the sexual habits of adolescents confirm the widespread use of masturbatory and homosexual outlets. Kinsey *et al.* (168) report the incidence of masturbation in boys by age fifteen to be 82 per cent. For the period of preadolescence 60 per cent of the boys recalled some homosexual activity, with the average initial contact occurring at 9.2 years, in comparison with 40 per cent who recalled heterosexual activity, beginning typically at 8.8 years. Between the ages of twelve and fifteen the reported frequency of homosexual play ranged from 20 to 29 per cent, of heterosexual play from 16 to 23 per cent. Willoughby's (287) survey of the literature in 1937 revealed adolescent masturbation to be more characteristic for boys than for girls. Concerning homosexuality he inferred that many individuals were so inclined, but for the most part their homosexual activity was a function of restricted heterosexual companionship. In a study of normal and psychotic women Landis and his coworkers (186) noted that masturbation and emotional attachments to other women were frequent in adolescence.

The forms of expression of sexuality are, of course, culturally determined. Malinowski (201) and Mead (204) have described primitive cultures in which adolescents have much more sexual freedom than in our own. In the latter connection Mead stresses the inconsistency of American customs with respect to hetero-sexual activity. "Dating" now begins as early as the prepubertal period and follows the rules of the game, especially in the middle classes, according to social rather than sexual motives. Later, when sexual urges become dominant, their permitted expression in ado-lescence is distorted in such a way as to hinder future sexual ad-justment in marriage. Cattell (51) points out the differences be-tween Western culture, in which the lack of structure and sign-posts confuse the adolescent in his new role, and the comfortingly clear expectations and initiation rites among the Arunta, An-damanese, and Kwoma.

5. *Adolescent Fantasy.* Symonds (279) administered 42 pic-tures, similar in type to those in the Thematic Apperception Test series, to 20 normal adolescent boys and 20 girls. They were asked to make up stories about each one as a "test of creative imagina-tion." The resulting 1,680 stories revealed, among others, a fre-quently occurring theme of "Oedipus longing and conflict." In addition, almost everyone in the group gave at least three stories revolving about aggression and love. Other characteristic themes concerned depression, anxiety, ambition, guilt, independence, in-jury, popularity, appearance, and dominance. While this study cannot itself be considered definitive, on the basis of the limited sample of subjects and the absence of comparative data for other age groups, it offers a fruitful method for further explorations of fantasy.

6. *The First Menstruation.* Mead (204) emphasizes the signifi-cance in primitive cultures of the first menstruation (menarche) as a sharp dividing line between childhood and womanhood. She goes on to describe in detail the variety of customs which have arisen. The puritanical Manus women have an important, festive ceremony for the adolescent girl at menarche, but all later men-struations are concealed with great secrecy. Among the Arapesh, the girl's first menstruation, which takes place several years after she has been betrothed, is also an occasion for ceremony. Her brothers come and build her a menstrual hut, placing it beyond the edge of the village to keep the village safe from the dangerous supernatural strength attached to menstruating women. In con-trast the peoples of Iatmul, Tchambuli, Mundugumor, and Samoa place little or no social stress on menarche.

Apart from anthropological sources, there are two well-controlled studies by Stone and Barker (274, 275), who compared the interests and attitudes of pre- and postmenarcheal girls. The latter group showed greater heterosexual interests and activities, regardless of chronological age; indulged in daydreaming more frequently; avoided vigorous physical exercise; and showed more concern over their physical appearance. A similar investigation in boys was conducted by Sollenberger (262), who separated more and less mature boys on the basis of amount of male sex hormone content in their urine. The sexually mature group proved to be more interested in heterosexual activities, strenuous competitive sports, and personal appearance.

7. *Factors Determining Outcome of the Adolescent Struggle.* A fourth factor affecting adolescent development, in addition to impulse strength, ego tolerance, and efficacy of defenses, is omitted by Anna Freud. This relates to the degree and type of stress provided by the environment. Presumably two equally equipped adolescents, from the point of view of the three listed attributes, will react differently if one becomes subjected to a malevolent social climate and the other does not.

8. *Explanations of Asocial Behavior.* An alternative way of looking at asocial behavior, other than the ego-superego split, is in terms of the adolescent's marginal position. Being no longer a child and not yet a man, he is placed in a very tenuous situation by society. One conceivable reaction to this anomalous role is social withdrawal.

9. *Adolescent Revolt against Parents.* Dollard *et al.* (59) interpret the adolescent's commonly observed rebelliousness, directed against his parents and authority figures in general, as a response to frustration. The source of the frustration lies in the situation described in Note 8. However, according to this group of authors, aggressive reactions are most typical of early adolescence, since substitute satisfactions tend to be worked out gradually by trial and error. Placing the focus of aggression in early adolescence is in disagreement with Tryon's (283) observation that the period of greatest resistance to adults is middle adolescence, when growth is most accelerated. Thus our knowledge of adolescent relationships, if we can generalize from this particular form, seems to be deficient in the facts of actual behavior, to say nothing of underlying reasons.

A few isolated studies have been done in this area, but even the surface has hardly been scratched. Kitay (169) found that the majority of children between eleven and fourteen, responding to a questionnaire, felt that their parents understood them, whereas from age fifteen on there was a much greater feeling of being misunderstood. Stott (276), averaging ratings on several personality tests, noted poorer adjustment in those adolescents who criticized their parents most. Another suggestion of the connection between disturbance and rebelliousness comes from Watson's study, reported by Cattell (51), in which those individuals with radical antiauthority views turned out to have been punished more frequently and more severely by their parents.

10. *Homosexual Behavior.* See Note 4 for a summary of existing data on homosexuality during adolescence.

11. *Interests and Attitudes.* This general area is one which has received considerable attention from investigators, though not specifically on the concrete-abstract dimension stressed by Anna Freud. Beginning with the preadolescent period, we have available a foreign study by Zillig (295) [summarized by Cattell (51)], who used recorded spontaneous conversations of a large number of boys and girls ranging from nine to twelve years of age. The group manifested a boastful and fantastic tone, wishful thinking, and a lack of modesty and ethics. Boys talked mainly about physical strength and daring exploits, whereas girls were concerned with appearance, possessions, and social prominence. In connection with this research, it is interesting to note the congruence with Anna Freud's description of pre-adolescent behavior, which was based largely on observations of children in Austria. The need for more extensive cross-cultural checks again makes itself felt at this point.

The early adolescent, as portrayed by Tryon (283), Zeligs (292), Jones (156), James and Moore (153), and others, indulges in like-sex club or gang activities. These cliques, formed slightly earlier in the case of girls, emphasize in-group secrets, slang, loyalties, and by and large, tend to suppress individuality. Twelve-year-old boys behave in an active, aggressive, competitive, boisterous manner, whereas girls of the same age are generally neat, docile, and prim, though some tomboyishness is acceptable. Interests in boys emphasize political and social questions, personal development, and possessions and pleasures; in girls family welfare. With respect to superego functioning, Buck (45) notes that twelve- or thirteen-year-olds consider about 50 per cent more activities to be morally wrong than do twenty-year-olds.

The period of middle adolescence, according to Tryon (283), features the striving for social conformity. Boys of fifteen become less boisterous and more interested in social poise. Early maturing girls at this age stress sophistication; others attach importance to being "good fellows." Parties are especially attractive. Using the Strong Vocational Interest Blank, Taylor (280) found relatively greater stability of interests during the later rather than the earlier years of mid-adolescence. Subsequently, around the ages of seventeen and eighteen, Tryon reports boys to be concerned with social maturity, athletics, and leadership, whereas girls are absorbed with feminine ideals and security. James and Moore (153), analyzing leisure activities by keeping diaries, noted increasingly heterosexual and social interests at these ages. Symonds (278) characterizes the older adolescent boy as intrigued primarily by an urge toward success, and the girl as being more passive, receptive, and interested in people.

12. *Conflicting Views on Preadolescence.* Sullivan's description of preadolescence as the period closest to untroubled human life is in sharp contrast to Anna Freud's. The latter, as we have seen, stresses unruliness, brutality, exhibitionism, and pregenital breakthroughs. Deutsch's portrayal of the preadolescent girl as showing the greatest freedom from infantile sexuality and aggression corresponds to Sullivan's, whereas Spiegel's reinterpretation of Deutsch's data follows Anna Freud. These discrepancies point to the necessity for systematic, reliable observations of behavior.

13. *The "Sublimatory Reformulation of Interpersonal Relations."* The merit, if any, in Sullivan's attempt to redefine sublimation obviously requires greater substantiation than Mullahy provides. Broader coverage alone is frequently not a virtue.

CHAPTER 8

Adult Character Structure

The experiences of the first two decades of life all contribute to the gradual emergence in the individual of characteristic ways of thinking, feeling, and behaving. Every adult man or woman comes to acquire a particular constellation of traits, a unique style of living. However, psychoanalytic theories of adult personality, apart from those dealing with pathology, tend to stress common patterns. The various theoretical views presented in this chapter, therefore, are concerned mainly with "types" of character structure.

ORTHODOX POSITION

Definition and Classification of "Character"

Fenichel (74) describes character as "the ego's habitual modes of adjustment to the external world, the id and the superego, and the characteristic types of combining these modes with one another." (See Note 1.) This youngest branch of psychoanalysis, so-called "ego psychology," had its origins in two factors: first the growing awareness in psychotherapy of the necessity to analyze the patient's resistances and ego defenses; and second, the greater prominence of defenses in the clinical picture of the neuroses. The historical development, remarks Fenichel, is easy to understand, since psychoanalysis began with the study of unconscious phenomena, alien to the ego, and proceeded only gradually to consider character or the customary mode of behavior.

Character, however, has a broader scope than the defense

mechanisms, for it includes the positive, organizing functions of the ego. Through the defense mechanisms the ego protects the organism from external and internal stimuli by blocking reactions. But the ego also serves to sift and organize stimuli and impulses. Some are permitted direct expression, others indirect. Hartmann (131), enumerating ego functions, includes reality testing, the control of motility and perception, action and thinking, inhibition and delay of discharge, anticipatory signaling of danger, and a synthetic or organizing function.

Instinctual demands are always bound up in the character structure, according to Fenichel. The organization, direction, and sifting of impulses, which must be made consonant with demands of the external world, constitute the attitudes of the ego. Likewise the superego is decisive in forming character, for the individual sets up habitual patterns based on what he considers good or bad. In the latter connection the adoption and modification of ideals in later life are also of importance. The other source of influence, the external world, is crucial in the sense that man's character is said to be socially determined. In Fenichel's words (74, p. 464):

The environment enforces specific frustrations, blocks certain modes of reaction to these frustrations, and facilitates others; it suggests certain ways of dealing with the conflicts between instinctual demands and fears of further frustrations; it even creates desires by setting up and forming specific ideals. Different societies, stressing different values and applying different educational measures, create different anomalies. Our present unstable society seems to be characterized by conflicts between ideals of individual independence (created during the rise of capitalism and still effective) and regressive longings for passive dependence (created by the helplessness of the individual with respect to security and gratifications as well as by active educational measures which are the outcome of the social necessity of authoritative influences).

The relative constancy of character is presumed to depend on three facets: partly on the hereditary constitution of the ego, partly on the nature of the instincts against which the defense is directed, and mainly on the special attitude forced on the individual by the external world.

Fenichel classifies character traits into two broad categories —sublimation and reactive. In the sublimation category the original instinctual energy is discharged freely as a result of an alteration in aim. The "genital character" belongs here. The conditions underlying the formation of sublimation traits are felt to be obscure. In general such traits are fostered by the absence of fixations, plus favorable environmental conditions for providing substitute channels of expression.

Instinctual energy in the case of the reactive category is constantly held in check by countercathexes. Attitudes are concerned with avoidance (phobic) or opposition (reaction formation). Fatigue, inhibition, rigidity, and inefficiency are common. The flexibility of the person is limited, for he is capable neither of full satisfaction nor of sublimation. Some persons develop a defensive attitude only in certain situations; others have to protect themselves continually. The latter are said to employ "character defenses," which are unspecific and maintained indiscriminately toward everyone. For example, they may always be either impudent or polite, empty of emotions or ever ready to blame others. Reactions to conflict in the area of self-esteem manifest themselves in arrogant behavior to hide deep inferiority feelings; ambitious behavior to cover inadequacy; and so on. The development of reactive traits is said to be fostered by early psychosexual fixations.

Reich (239), a pioneer in the field of character analysis, describes reactive traits in terms of "character armor." A chronic alteration in the ego serves to protect against external and internal dangers. The armor, originally forged as a result of the conflict between instinctual demands and the frustrating outer world, gets its strength and reason for existence from continuing actual conflicts between these same opposing forces. Character grows out of the attempted solution of the Oedipus complex, with the subsequent hardening of the ego being accounted for by three processes: (1) identification with the main person who represents frustrating reality, (2) aggression turned inward as an inhibitory force, and (3) formation by the ego of reactive attitudes toward the sexual impulses. Thus, the armor serves to strengthen the ego by alleviating the pressure from repressed libidinal impulses. At the same time, though, it operates to insulate the person from external stimuli and renders him less susceptible to education (see Note 2).

Character Types

Orthodox psychoanalytic literature contains descriptions of a wide variety of types—oral, anal, urethral, phallic, genital, compulsive, hysterical, phobic, cyclic, schizoid, and others. However, organization of these types into a meaningful classification has remained elusive. Fenichel expresses his own discontent in the following words (74, p. 527):

The differentiation of individual character traits into those of the sublimation types and reactive ones is not of much value in judging personalities, since every person shows traits of both kinds. And still it seems the relatively most useful approach to distinguish personalities in whom the sublimation type of traits prevails from those that are predominantly reactive. It had become customary to distinguish genital from pregenital characters; however, although the traits of anal or oral characters consist of both sublimations and reaction formations, pregenital traits become predominant only in cases in which countercathexes suppress still operative pregenital impulses; in other words, pregenital characters, as a rule, are also reactive characters, whereas the attainment of genital primacy is the best basis for the successful sublimation of the remaining pregenital energies.

One source of confusion lies in the attempt to distinguish the more or less "normal" types from those which are primarily "neurotic." The problem becomes especially acute when, as in this text, the area of psychopathology has been excluded from consideration. A solution suggested by common practice is to designate arbitrarily the various pregenital types and the genital type as falling within the normal range and hence eligible for detailed discussion here. The psychoanalysts, in addition to Freud, who contributed heavily to the original formulation of these characterizations were Abraham (1), Jones (155), Glover (111), and Reich (239).

The Oral Character. The oral character is one whose habitual mode of adjustment contains strong elements of oral fixations produced in early childhood. He is extremely dependent on others for the maintenance of his self-esteem. External supplies are all-important to him, and he yearns for them passively. The mouth serves an especially significant function. When he feels depressed, he eats to overcome the emotion. Oral preoccupations, in addition to food, frequently revolve around drinking, smoking, and kissing. As a consequence of the infantile association in the feeding situation, love is equated with food. Conflicted longings for love and narcissistic supplies may even generate physiological effects, such as the increased secretion of gastric juices observed in peptic ulcer cases.

Fenichel (74) links oral overindulgence in infancy to a later feeling of optimism and self-assurance, provided that the external environment does not threaten the individual's security. Early oral deprivation is said to determine a pessimistic or sadistic attitude. Persons in whom the oral-sadistic component is marked are aggressive and biting in their relationships. They continually demand supplies in a vampirelike fashion and affix themselves by "suction."

The passive-dependent, receptive orientation to life brings with it a number of other related personality characteristics. All positive or negative emphasis on taking and receiving is said to indicate an oral origin. Marked generosity and niggardliness both stem from oral eroticism. Generous persons sometimes betray their original stinginess, just as stingy ones occasionally resort to exceptional generosity. Gifts assume unusual importance. The particular form of behavior depends upon the ratio between sublimation and reaction formation in the handling of oral drives.

Some individuals manifest their dependent needs directly

and insatiably by begging or even demanding to be cared for. According to Fenichel, the demanding tone prevails in persons who are incapable of getting sufficient reassurance, so that every real gift makes them long for more. The begging tone occurs in persons who actually are satisfied when taken care of, and who willingly sacrifice ambition and comfort in order to buy the necessary affection. Others tend to overcompensate for their unconscious passive longings by behaving in an extremely active and masculine fashion, under the pretense of being entirely independent. Alexander (9) describes the latter constellation as typical of the ulcer personality.

Another common form of behavior in oral characters is identification with the object by whom they want to be fed. Certain individuals always act like nursing mothers, showering everyone with presents and help. The attitude has the magical significance of "As I shower you with love, I want to be showered." Under favorable circumstances, this may serve a truly altruistic function. More often, it tends to be annoying. In contrast, some identify with a frustrating rather than a giving mother. Here the behavior is completely selfish and stingy, implying "Because I was not given what I wanted, I shall not give other people what they want." Additional oral traits described by Fenichel include curiosity (as a displacement of "hunger"), volubility, restlessness, haste, and a tendency toward obstinate silence (see Note 3).

The Anal Character. Traits associated with anal fixations were Freud's (98) first insights in the area of character structure. Personality features are said to grow out of the conflicts around toilet training, since the child, as we have seen earlier, has opportunities to please or defile his parents and also to gain physiological pleasure from elimination and retention. The predominant adult anal traits are known as the three "P's" —parsimony, petulance, and pedantry, or, as phrased more commonly, frugality, obstinacy, and orderliness. Fenichel (74) describes frugality as a continuation of the habit of anal retentiveness, sometimes motivated by the fear of losing, sometimes more by erogenous pleasure. Based on the equating of feces with money (see Chapter 4), attitudes toward money become irrational, as were the original anal instinctual wishes. No longer viewed as an objectively useful thing, money is retained and hoarded or sometimes carelessly thrown away. Similar attitudes exist toward time, so that the anal character may be punctual to the fraction of a minute or grossly unreliable.

Obstinacy is a passive type of aggression, stemming from the child's refusal to produce when his parents were intent upon his doing so. After a while this "magical" superiority or feeling of power is replaced by a "moral" superiority in which the superego plays a decisive part. Stubbornness in the behavior of adults is explained as an attempt to use other persons as instruments in the struggle with the superego. By provoking people to be unjust, such individuals strive for a feeling of moral superiority which serves to increase self-esteem and to counterbalance pressure from the superego. The stubborn person considers himself to have been unfairly treated and often elicits affection forcibly by making his antagonist feel sorry afterward. Thus, says Fenichel, obstinacy, which originally is the combative method of the weak, later becomes a habitual method of struggle for maintaining or restoring self-esteem. Excessive orderliness arises from compliance and obedience to parental demands. Tidiness, punctuality, meticulousness, and propriety are all said to signify a displacement of compliance with the environmental requirements in regard to defecation.

The mechanism of reaction formation is frequently apparent in anal traits, for the scrupulously clean and orderly individual may at certain times be astonishingly messy and disorganized. Another example is painting, which in some cases represents a reaction formation to the unconscious desire for anal smearing. The artist who is not sublimating effectively often fails in his work or becomes inhibited in his ability to paint. Other anal characteristics manifest themselves as displacements to speech and thinking in the irrational modes of retaining or expelling words and thoughts. All anal traits are said to contain a sadistic element, in accordance with the original ambivalent object relations of the anal stage (see Note 4).

The Urethral Character. The outstanding personality features of the urethral character are ambition and competitiveness, both of which are presumed to be reactions against shame. As mentioned in Chapter 5, the child who wets his pants is often made an object of ridicule and shame. In response to this feeling he later develops ambitious desires in order to prove that there is no longer any need for him to be ashamed. Another contributing element is the original competition with respect to urination, *e.g.*, who can direct a longer stream (see Note 5).

Fenichel (74) also discusses the various displacements and secondary conflicts created by urethral ambition. The latter may be condensed with trends derived from earlier oral sources or, under the influence of the castration complex, may be displaced to the anal field. This is especially characteristic in girls because of the futility of urethral competition. Too, the reassurances which ambition and success provide against the idea of being castrated may be turned into prohibitions if they acquire, in connection with the Oedipus complex, the unconscious meaning of killing the father.

The Phallic Character. The phallic character behaves in a reckless, resolute, and self-assured fashion, mainly as a wishfulfilling reaction to castration anxiety. The overvaluation of the penis and its confusion with the whole body, typical of the early phallic stage, are reflected by intense vanity, exhibitionism, and sensitiveness. These individuals usually anticipate an expected assault by attacking first. They appear aggressive and provocative, not so much from what they say or do, but rather in their manner of speaking and acting. Wounded pride, according to Reich (239), often results in either cold reserve, deep depression, or lively aggression. The resentment of subordination and the tendency to dominate

others are both grounded in fear. Overtly courageous behavior, as exhibited by the motorcycle daredevil, is said to
represent an overcompensation.

Basically the phallic character is extremely oral-dependent,
and his narcissistic orientation precludes the establishment
of mature relationships with others. The male, driven to attempts to demonstrate his masculinity, is nevertheless con-
temptuous and hostile toward women. The phallic female,
motivated by strong penis envy, assumes the masculine role
and strives for superiority over men. Narcissism is again a
central characteristic (see Note 6).

The Genital Character. Fenichel (74) himself states that
the normal "genital" character is an ideal concept. However,
the achievement of genital primacy is presumed to bring a
decisive advance in character formation. The ability to attain
full satisfaction through genital orgasm makes the physiological regulation of sexuality possible and thus puts an end to
the damming up of instinctual energies, with its unfortunate
effects on the person's behavior. It also makes for the full development of love and the overcoming of ambivalence. Furthermore, the capacity to discharge great quantities of excitement means the end of reaction formations and an increase
in the ability to sublimate. Emotions, instead of being warded
off, are used constructively by the ego as part of the total
personality. The formation of traits of the sublimation type
thus becomes possible. Pregenital impulses are mostly sublimated, but some are also incorporated into the forepleasure
mechanisms of the sexual act.

THE EARLY DEVIANTS

Adler

Adler (3, 4, 5, 6), like the orthodox theorists, emphasizes
the importance of early childhood for the molding of character. An individual's pattern or "style of life" is said to be
determined, at least in nuclear form, by the time he is five
years old. Underlying attitudes remain unchanged, though

their expression in later life is often quite different. However, Adler departs radically from the Freudian position in his explanations of personality development.

In place of the sexual component, he stresses universal feelings of inferiority. The child, by virtue of his small size and helplessness, inevitably considers himself inferior to the adult figures in his environment. Parents who neglect, ridicule, or lack tenderness in their dealings with the child often accentuate his feeling of being subordinate. The mother plays an especially crucial part in this process, for by treating him lightly or by pampering and overprotecting him she hinders the acquisition of social skills. The family constellation also serves to intensify inferiority feelings: the only child, having been treated with abnormal importance, devotes the rest of his life to a futile search to regain his youthful position; the oldest child, a displaced only child, is often so discouraged by his fall from power that he does not recover effective use of his capabilities; the second child lives under the shadow of an older sibling whom he seeks to overtake; and the youngest may shrink from competition with the others. In addition, there are organ inferiorities, either morphological or functional, which reinforce the picture.

To relieve his inferiority feelings the individual strives to be strong and powerful. In the quest for superiority as "the complete man," he avails himself of "guiding fictions" which serve as frames of reference or modes of organizing experience conducive to the attainment of goals. These goals, in their broadest sense, stand for security and adaptation. The outcome of the striving for superiority may be successful, provided that the guiding principles are modifiable in terms of the demands of reality. Very often, though, the attempted compensations relate to goals which are impractical and lead ultimately to neurosis. The search for power, underlying determinant of man's actions and development, results in the adoption of a unified way of responding to the environment. Character, then, refers to the individual's unified manner of meeting situations along the path to his goal.

In addition to the direct struggle for power, another avenue of approach is sometimes utilized. This is the flight into illness, through which a person can dominate by acting helpless and forcing others to adjust to his demands. The organ inferiorities also lead to two types of reaction. In the first, another organ is substituted for the inferior one as in the case of the blind individual who develops an especially acute sense of hearing. The second reaction is to concentrate on the inferior organ long enough to overcome its inadequacy. The stutterer who eventually becomes an orator is given as an illustration. The opportunity to make advantageous use of inferiority feelings is emphasized in the extreme by Adler when he asserts that even genius can be interpreted as an expression of the urge to compensate for an individual defect.

Western civilization establishes the male as the symbol of power. Masculinity is considered superior and femininity inferior. Therefore, everyone seeks to achieve a more masculine ideal—the so-called "masculine protest." This behavior is most marked in women but applies also to men, especially those in weak positions. Sexual activity is always to be understood in terms of its relation to the style of life, which in turn is based on the early childhood prototype. The child with a sociable prototype will later respond with loyalty to the partner in the love situation; the one who must struggle for superiority will eventually use sexuality in order to rule. Love is but one of life's three great problems, the remaining two being attitudes toward fellow men and toward one's job. Of the three the attitude toward others is central (see Note 7).

Jung

Jung's (151, 158) theory of character is also expressed in nonsexual terms. He states that there are four basic psychological functions: thinking, feeling, sensation, and intuition. Everyone possesses all four functions in varying degrees, but on the basis of natural inherited disposition and environment each person tends to emphasize one particular function. Thinking refers to active, logical, directed thought, so that this type of individual meets every situation in a cool, detached, rational fashion. His feelings are relatively undeveloped, since feeling interferes with logical thinking. Feeling, which is essentially subjective and value-laden, is to be distinguished from emotion because it is a more rational and less intense activity. In the feeling type of person, thinking is relegated to an inferior role. Sensation and intuition, on the other hand, are both irrational functions. The former is said to apply to perceptions at the present moment, and the latter to the future. The sensation type, weak in intuition, is quick to perceive everything given through the senses, as well as all bodily innervations; whereas the intuitive type, inferior in sensation, is intensely alive to all the possibilities of a situation.

According to Jung, the conscious aspects of men are usually thinking and sensation, whereas feeling and intuition are repressed. In women, feeling and intuition are dominant, with thinking and sensation repressed. The repressed feminine side of man is called his "anima," of woman her "animus." The well-rounded individual has a balance or equilibrium between his conscious and repressed characteristics. A related concept is the "persona," which refers to the role played by the individual in society. In the course of his life he learns to behave in accord with what is expected of him. Each profession, for example, has a characteristic mask which the member tends to wear. The persona is not a part of the true character but is firmly attached to it and acts as a sort of protection of the inner man.

The four basic functions are further classified into two general attitude types: extraverted and introverted. These are two ways of looking at the world, two modes of experience. In the former there is an outward movement of interest toward the object; in the latter a movement of interest away from the object toward the self. Everyone possesses both tendencies, but again one is usually dominant. The ideal relationship is a rhythmic alternation of the two, which seldom occurs in actuality. The personality features of these two broad types are summarized below (see Note 8).

The Extravert. The extravert lives according to external necessity. His interest and attention are centered on his immediate local environment. He concentrates on persons and things and behaves in agreement with the demands of the community. His capacities are limited, for he "tries to do or to make just what his milieu momentarily needs and expects from him, and abstains from every innovation that is not entirely obvious, or that in any way exceeds the expectation of those around him." The relation of the unconscious to the conscious is compensatory. A consciously extraverted person is unconsciously introverted. Unconscious tendencies may be stripped of their compensatory quality because of repressing forces in the collective unconscious, and then open conflict with consciousness ensues. Either the person no longer knows what he really wants and has no interests, or he desires too much at once and cannot be satisfied. The unconscious attitude of the extravert is said to verge often on the cruel and brutal.

The Introvert. The introvert, on the other hand, is defensive against the external world and sets up an artificial "subjectification" of consciousness. He tends to equate the ego with the whole personality. Unconsciously, however, external objects are reinforced through the compensatory mechanism, and the individual becomes a slave to them. He becomes enmeshed in practical difficulties. The illusion of superiority created by the ego is shattered, so that the introvert's desire to dominate and control ends in a pitiful craving to be loved. In time he learns to fear other persons and things and shrinks from the external objects which he imbues with magical powers.

Rank

Rank's (237) character theory centers about his concept of "will," described as "a positive guiding organization and integration of self which utilizes creatively as well as inhibits and controls the instinctual drives." Originally the process of willing is said to arise as "an inner primarily negative opposing force against a compulsion." The compulsion may be due to external factors such as parental commands or the internal demands of sexuality. These inevitable obstacles and restraints met by the child cause him to resist and thereby exercise his "counterwill." A second step in the development of the will is directed toward the attainment of particular things, desiring what others have, not in the sense of envy but rather merging one's own will with the will of the group. Comparisons with others are continually being made. The third step occurs when a person no longer measures himself by other's standards and, in a truly positive fashion, can take responsibility for his own willing. Prohibitions in childhood lead the individual to mistrust his will as evil, so that the adult possesses a will whose contents are in part good, or approved by parents and society, and in part bad, or disapproved. The resistance to authority, the bad aspect, is the counterwill.

In addition to will, personality is characterized by impulses and emotions. Impulses seek immediate gratification through motor discharge. When blocked or dammed up, they produce emotions. Will differs from emotion in that it "is an impulse, positively and actively placed in the service of the ego, and not a blocked impulse." The ego, in a sense, is the autonomous representative of the will. Sexuality exists not only for procreation and pleasure but as an outlet for emotion and an instrument of will. While sex is the only "natural" method for reducing conflicts of will, it often serves as a negative influence by threatening to dominate the individual and force him under the will of another person in order to satisfy the craving. Differences between men and women lie in their reactions to sex. Men are unable to accept the fact of being mortal, so that sex, which signifies mortality to them, provokes fear. Dictated by selfish ego needs, they strive instead to control and create. Women, on the other hand, accept sex as a means of immortality through procreation and tend to fear the more powerful wills of men.

As we have seen in earlier chapters, Rank also stresses the importance of separation for the development of the individual. The original traumatic physical separation from the mother at birth is followed by various forms of psychological dependence and loss of the feeling of "wholeness." In order to achieve independence and make his ego "real," the individual must initiate separations as expressions of his own will, rather than experience them passively and traumatically according to the will of others. There are three stages in this process of becoming free: the first occurs when he himself wills what he was formerly compelled to will by external or internal demands; the second witnesses an inner conflict between the will and counterwill, in which the person begins to form ideals and standards possibly different from those sanctioned socially; and the third is characterized by an integrated, harmonious solution which results in high-level creativity. Corresponding to these stages are the three character types appearing below.

The Average Man. The average or normal person is one who has surrendered his will and accepted the will of the group. Culturally accepted reality becomes his own "truth." He tends to keep his fantasies, whose contents are viewed as evil, to himself, and consequently develops guilt feelings toward others. Knowledge of self is illusory, since the role he must pretend to play turns out to be in reality only himself and not a role at all. Compliance with the will of the group need not, however, be a passive submission, for it can also be a healthy, active alignment. On the other hand, the average man is not automatically in good mental health either, because he may be conforming out of fear of disapproval. In general, the normal individual is subjected to fewer conflicts and has fewer opportunities to be creative.

The Neurotic. The neurotic cannot conform to the will of the group and yet is not free to assert his own will. He cannot make a positive identification with the group and cannot stand alone, for he becomes plagued by feelings of inferiority and guilt. He has to fight both external and internal pressures and winds up by being at war with himself and society. Fantasies must be repressed or hidden from himself as well as from others, not so much because of their content but as expressions of his own evil will. Guilt feelings, therefore, are directed toward himself.

The Creative Man. The creative individual, like the artist, has succeeded in fully accepting and affirming himself. He is in harmony with his powers and ideals. In Rank's words, there "is formed neither a compromise, nor merely a summation, but a newly created whole, the strong personality with its autonomous will, which represents the highest creation of the integration of will and spirit." Ideals are formed, not merely from what is given, but from self-chosen factors consciously sought after. In the accomplishment of his will he goes "beyond the limits set by nature," since the sex instinct is forced into the service of the will. In a sense he finds his own "truth," which he then proposes to make general or real in his productions. Thus, his fantasies are necessarily revealed to the world. Guilt exists toward others as well as toward himself but serves as a stimulus for further creative work. So, while the creative man sets his own ideals, he is still able to live in the world without coming into conflict with it (see Note 9).

MORE RECENT VIEWS

Horney

Character structure, according to Horney (142, 144), develops from the sum total of childhood experiences. With some the process may stop by age five, with others it stops in adolescence, with still others around thirty, and with a few people development goes on until old age. However, there are no causal connections between libidinal manifestations in childhood and later personality traits, as postulated by orthodox theory. In Horney's words (142, pp. 61–62):

In the case of greediness or possessiveness, one would think of those character structures which in the psychoanalytical literature are described as "oral" or "anal," but instead of relating these traits to the "oral" or "anal" sphere, one would understand them as a response to the sum total of experiences in the early environment. As a result of these experiences the individual acquires, in both cases, a deep feeling of helplessness toward a world conceived as potentially hostile, a lack of spontaneous self-assertion and a disbelief in his own capacity to create or master something of his own accord. . . .

Thus, the difference in point of view may be expressed in this way: a person does not have tight lips because of the tenseness of his sphincter, but both are tight because his character trends tend toward one goal—to hold on to what he has and never give away anything, be it money, love or any kind of spontaneous feeling.

Horney's account of the dynamics of character formation is presented within the context of neurosis, but presumably many of the same forces operate, less pathologically, in the normal individual. Of primary importance are strivings for safety, conditioned by an underlying "basic anxiety." The latter arises in connection with repressed hostility, in turn a result of childhood experiences of rejection and disapproval. In seeking to escape from the feeling of anxiety, the child acquires lasting characteristics which become part of his personality—so-called "neurotic trends." One attempted solution to conflict lies in the creation of an "idealized image," whereby the person substitutes an illusory sense of power and superiority for his actual weakness and lack of confidence. Another is through "externalization," a more general kind of projection in which all inner feelings tend to be experienced as outside of the self.

The main directions which the child can take in coping with the environment are moving *toward* people, *against* them, or *away from* them. When moving toward people he accepts his own helplessness and, in spite of his fears, tries to win the affection of others. When moving against people he takes for granted the hostility around him and determines to fight. When moving away he wants neither to belong nor to fight, but to keep apart. In the elaboration of these forces Horney (144) describes three character types or basic attitudes.

The Compliant Type. The individual who "moves toward"

others shows a marked need for affection and approval. His compulsive desires for intimacy and belonging create an intense yearning for a partner. Love is all-important, and even sexual intercourse is valued more as proof of being wanted. The compliant person feels weak and helpless, tends to subordinate himself to others, and generally behaves in a very dependent fashion. Self-esteem is regulated mainly by what others think of him. Any kind of aggressive action must be inhibited, so that he can never afford to be critical or assertive. When there is occasion for placing blame, he always prefers to accuse himself. On the positive side, this type of individual is often sensitive to the needs of others and, within the limits of his emotional understanding, is able to provide sympathy and help in return for being liked. At the unconscious level he has deeply repressed tendencies toward power and aggression and actually feels a callous lack of interest in people. These tendencies must, of course, be kept down at all costs in order to preserve a sense of unity and to avoid the possibility of arousing hostility from others.

The Aggressive Type. The "moving against" type assumes that everyone else is hostile and refuses to admit they are not. Life is a struggle for survival; so his primary need is to control others. He tries to excel in any way, to outsmart and to belittle them. Sometimes the attitude is quite apparent, but more often it is covered by a veneer of suave politeness, fair-mindedness, and good fellowship. This front, however, has some genuine components, for it may contain a certain amount of benevolence as long as there is no question that he is in command. Arguments are especially important. He often provokes them in order to demonstrate his alertness and keenness. In general, he is a bad loser and prefers to blame others. He considers himself strong, honest, and realistic and, in fact, functions efficiently and resourcefully in business situations as a result of careful planning and assertiveness. The softer side of his nature must be violently rejected, since it threatens his whole manner of living. Love plays a negligible role for this person.

The Detached Type. The individual who "moves away" from people is always intent on keeping an emotional distance between himself and others. Closeness creates anxiety; so he develops a compelling need to be self-sufficient. Competition, prestige, and success are to be avoided, inasmuch as they interfere with the strong desire for privacy. He dislikes sharing experiences and is very sensitive to anything that resembles coercion. There is a tendency to suppress all feeling and, in particular, to shy away from attachments which threaten to become indispensable. An intense need to feel superior arises in order to justify being isolated. Sexual relationships for this kind of person are sometimes not possible; at best they are enjoyed if transitory. In general, the detachment serves as a defense against contradictory strivings for affection and for aggressive domination. In mild form it can function positively to preserve integrity and a feeling of serenity. Also the attitude can foster original thinking to some extent and contribute to the expression of creative abilities (see Note 10).

Fromm

Fromm (107) defines character as "the relatively permanent form in which human energy is canalized in the process of assimilation and socialization." In childhood it is molded by the family, which serves as the "psychic agency" of society. The child, in adjusting himself to the family situation, acquires a character whose core is common to most members of his social class and culture. On this common core or "social character" are superimposed variations of the individualized character, which are due to specific parental influences.

In Fromm's opinion character types, then, are the product of the interaction of child and parent, which begins from the first moment of life. He disputes the orthodox notion that the types are a result of alterations in libido (see Note 11). The anal character, for example, has nothing to do with libido. Constipation is not a cause of character formation, but rather an expression of it. The important feature is a home atmosphere which is ungiving, anxious, and suspicious, so that the child is impressed with a "feeling of scarcity" and wants to hang onto what he has. The stingy person is not stingy because he hangs onto feces; he hangs onto everything, including his feces. The type of parent who withholds tends to have a meticulous attitude toward toilet training.

Fromm distinguishes the following five character types:

The Receptive Orientation. The receptive character believes that everything he needs or wants must come from an outside source. He leans passively on authority for knowledge and help, and on people in general for support. Love to him means being loved, not the active process of loving; so he becomes extremely sensitive to any withdrawal of affection or attention. Passivity is linked with the inability to say "no" to requests from others, and to the never-ending search for a "magic helper." The fear of losing love prevents him from being able to choose between two friends if the situation requires a choice, since picking one might result in a withdrawal of love by the other. This type of person has great fondness for food and drink, activities which he utilizes to overcome anxiety and depression. The mouth is an especially prominent feature, often the most expressive one. By and large, his outlook is optimistic and friendly, except when sources of supply are threatened. He is often warm and helpful to others, but underneath lies the need to secure their favor.

The Exploitative Orientation. The exploitative person tries to take everything from people by force or cunning. In the realm of love and affection he feels attracted only to individuals whom he can take away from someone else. Similarly he steals ideas from others and proclaims them as his own. The lack of originality in many gifted persons, says Fromm, can be attributed to this character orientation. The attitude also extends to material things, an extreme example being the kleptomaniac, who enjoys objects only if he can steal them even though he has plenty of money. A prominent feature is the biting mouth, typified in sarcastic, "biting" remarks about people. Suspicion, cynicism, envy, and jealousy are all characteristic. In general, he overrates what others have and does his utmost to procure them for himself.

The Hoarding Orientation. The hoarder bases his security on saving and keeping what he has. Spending is felt to be a threat and arouses anxiety. He surrounds himself by a protective wall and aims to bring in as much as possible while letting virtually nothing out. The miserliness extends to feelings and thoughts as well as money and material things. Even love is viewed as a means of possessing the loved one. Pedantic orderliness, compulsive cleanliness, obsessive punctuality, and obstinacy characterize his behavior. The mouth tends to be tight-lipped, and his gestures express the withdrawn attitude. Suspicion and a fear of intimacy are usual accompaniments.

The Marketing Orientation. People in this category regard their personalities as commodities to be bought and sold. They mold themselves to fit whatever qualities are in demand by others. They have no stable and genuine character, no real experience of being able to guide their own destiny. Feelings of emptiness and anxiety are basic. The marketing orientation also affects thinking. The latter assumes the function of grasping things quickly so as to be able to manipulate them successfully. This leads to superficiality rather than penetrating to the essence of phenomena. Such persons must remain free of all individuality in order to fill in roles which are currently most salable on the market.

The Productive Orientation. According to Fromm, the four previous orientations are all nonproductive. Productiveness is defined as "man's ability to use his powers and to realize the potentialities inherent in him." It implies developing one's powers, such as creativity and love, and making full use of them. Such an individual does not have to become a great scientist or artist. He simply can think independently, respects himself and others, enjoys sensuous pleasures without anxiety, and delights in the works of nature and art. In short, he enjoys living. Nonproductive elements may still persist, but they are transformed. Stubbornness, for example, becomes steadfastness, and exploitativeness becomes ability to take initiative (see Note 12).

Kardiner

Kardiner (164, 165), a pioneer in the application of psychoanalytic principles to the fields of sociology and anthropology, offers a somewhat different approach to the study of character. For him character represents the special variation of each individual to the series of cultural norms encompassed in the "basic personality structure" of his particular society. This basic personality structure, described as the personality configuration shared by the bulk of the society's members as a result of common early experiences, is said to provide the matrix in which character traits develop. The same underlying structure may be reflected in many different forms of behavior. For example, in Alorese society distrust is a permanent feature of basic personality, but this distrust may show itself in any number of character traits.

The formulation of basic personality type proceeds from the following four postulates: (1) an individual's early experiences exert a lasting effect upon personality; (2) similar experiences tend to produce similar personality configurations in the individuals who are subjected to them; (3) child-rearing practices are culturally patterned and tend to be similar, though never identical, for various families within the society; and (4) child rearing differs from one society to another. Since members of a given society share many early experiences, they also have many personality elements in common. Between societies there are often very different experiences, so that their personality norms also differ.

The vehicles through which specific influences are brought to bear on the growing individual are the institutions, or practices and customs of the society. These are separated into the primary institutions (family organization, feeding, weaning, anal training, basic disciplines, sexual taboos, subsistence techniques, etc.) and the secondary institutions (religion, folklore, rituals, taboo systems, and techniques of thinking). The reality systems taught to the child are derived partly from projective systems, such as religion, and partly from empirical sources, such as science. The incompatibility of these two approaches, both learned, is resolved differently by each individual. Some are able to tolerate them both; others find it necessary to discard either one or the other. The interaction between individual and institution is not a one-way process, however. The basic personality type, once established, determines the reactions of the individual to other established institutions with which he comes into contact. Changes in certain institutions thus result in changes in basic personality structure which, in turn, lead to the modification or reinterpretation of existing institutions (see Note 13).

By way of illustrating character formation, Kardiner suggests an alternative explanation for the origin of the traits of orderliness, obstinacy, and stinginess. The latter are said to be acquired through conflicts between parents and child in the course of training for cleanliness. Rigid discipline in teaching sphincter control may be met with complete compliance (orderliness) or a refractory attitude (obstinacy). Stinginess is to be understood in terms of a general concern over retention or anxiety at a loss of something valuable, not as a function of anal eroticism.

Alexander

A leader in the field of psychosomatic medicine, Alexander (9) proposes a scheme for classifying emotional reactions of the individual to the environment, analogous to three physiological life processes. These are the functions of "intaking" of substance and energy from the environment, partially "retaining" it during the process of growth, and "elimination" of the end products of metabolism, of substances for the purpose of propagation, and the constant production of thermal and mechanical energy. The psychological correlates are the wish to receive or take, the wish to give or eliminate, and the wish to retain (see Note 14).

An individual's character can thus be distinguished from

a "vector analysis" of the relative participation of these three elementary attitudes in his dealings with other people. Alexander has applied this formulation most extensively to gastrointestinal disorders but voices the belief that they will be found to have general significance. The upper end of the gastrointestinal tract, corresponding to its normal function, is described as well fitted to express the receptive or taking tendencies, whereas the lower end of the tract is more suitable for the expression of giving and retentive tendencies. The gastric type of person (*e.g.*, peptic ulcer case) emphasizes receiving and taking; the colitis type giving and aggressive elimination; and the constipation type retaining.

Both the intaking and eliminating tendencies may assume either more constructive or more destructive connotations: intaking being reflected in passive receiving as well as aggressive taking; and elimination in positive giving or sadistic expelling. The content of male and female sexuality is also said to be clarified by this approach. In pregenital sexuality the three elements appear unmixed, whereas in later organizations of sexual life male and female strivings may be thought of as mixtures of the three in varying proportions (see Note 15).

Erikson

Though Erikson (69, 70, 71) does not discuss character per se, he offers the relevant concepts of zones and modes (discussed earlier) and "ego identity." The latter is defined as a kind of "creative polarity of what one feels one is and of what others take one to be." Ego identity connotes more than the mere fact of existence, which is conveyed by "personal identity," for it refers to the subjective awareness of an inner sameness and continuity matched by the sameness and continuity of one's meaning for others. In other words, the individual who has achieved ego identity feels that he belongs to his group, that his past has meaning in terms of his future, and vice versa. He "knows where he is going." Both conscious and unconscious factors play a part, though ego identity is often described as less of a conscious process than self-esteem.

The development of a sense of ego identity grows out of the various identifications experienced in childhood, not as a summation but as an integration of available roles. The culmination occurs in late adolescence. The youth who is not sure of his identity shies away from interpersonal intimacy, but the surer he becomes of himself, the more he seeks it in the forms of friendship, combat, leadership, love, and inspiration. Ego identity engenders a new love of one's parents, free of the wish that they should have been different, and an acceptance of the fact that one's life is one's own responsibility. It also implies integrity and a "sense of comradeship with men and women of distant times and of different pursuits, who have created orders and objects and sayings conveying human dignity and love." The absence or loss of ego identity, as in the psychoneurotic, is accompanied by despair and an unconscious fear of death. The despair is often hidden behind feelings of disgust and displeasure with particular institutions and people but in reality signifies the individual's contempt for himself (see Note 16).

SUMMARY

In the orthodox system character is defined as "the ego's habitual modes of adjustment to the external world, the id and the superego, and the characteristic types of combining these modes with one another." It includes in addition to defense mechanisms the positive, organizing functions of the ego. Fenichel classifies character traits into two broad categories: sublimation and reactive. In the former the original instinctual energy is discharged freely as a result of an alteration in aim. The genital character belongs here. In the latter instinctual energy is constantly held in check by countercathexes. The various reactive types are the oral, anal, urethral, and phallic, in which psychosexual fixations predominate.

Among the early deviants, Adler also stresses the importance of early childhood for the molding of character but places his emphasis upon universal feelings of inferiority. The latter are accompanied by a compensatory struggle for power and "masculine protest" behavior. Jung focuses upon four basic psychological functions: thinking, feeling, sensation, and intuition. The conscious aspects of men are said to be thinking and sensation, whereas feeling and intuition are repressed. The opposite is true of women. The four functions are further classified into two general ways of looking at the world, extraverted and introverted. In addition each individual plays a prescribed role in society—the concept of "persona." Rank's characterology hinges upon his theory of will. The average man, the neurotic, and the creative man each correspond to stages in the development of will.

Neo-Freudian theorists like Horney and Fromm discount any causal connections between libidinal manifestations in childhood and later personality traits. Instead they stress the sum total of parent-child interactions in the early environment. Horney distinguishes the compliant type who "moves toward" people; the aggressive type who "moves against"; and the detached who "moves away" from others. Fromm speaks of the "social character," a core common to most members of a social class, on which are superimposed individual variations due to specific parental influences. His typology includes five different orientations: receptive, exploitative, hoarding, marketing, and productive. In applying psychoanalytic principles to the field of anthropology, Kardiner evolved the formulation of "basic personality structure," which refers to the personality configuration shared by the bulk of a society's members as a result of common early experiences. The vehicles through which the specific influences are brought to bear on the growing individual are the institutions, or practices and customs of the society.

A somewhat different approach to character structure is offered by Alexander, who points out the psychological correlates of the physiological life process of intaking, retaining, and elimination. An individual's character is said to reflect the relative participation of these three elementary attitudes in his dealings with other people. Erikson on his part emphasizes the concept of "ego identity," by which a person feels that he belongs to his group and knows where he is going. The development of this feeling arises from an integration of the various identifications experienced in childhood, culminating in late adolescence.

NOTES

1. *Definitions of Character.* The confusions inherent in various attempts to define character become self-evident from the following sample of quotations:

Fenichel (74): "This description of *character* is nearly identical with that previously given for the *ego*."

Abraham (1): "the sum of a person's reactions toward his social environment."

Hartmann (131): "Another set of functions which we attribute to the ego is what we call a person's character."

Beaglehole (19): "Character structure may be thought of as an organization of the needs and emotions within each person that fits him to respond adaptively to the major social values of the group."

From the above we gather only that character is somehow a function of the ego, related in some way to the social environment. Even the gross point of whether it is synonymous with all ego functioning (Fenichel) or simply one among a long list of functions (Hartmann) remains controversial. In view of this hazy state of affairs it appears futile to question the distinction between character and the equally vague concept of personality. Academic psychology's offering clouds the issue still further by way of MacKinnon's (199) two alternative definitions of character: (1) the ethical or moral aspect of personality; and (2) the conative aspect of personality without any ethical or moral evaluation.

2. *Reich's Heresy.* For the sake of the record it should be pointed out that Wilhelm Reich and his followers have been excommunicated from the orthodox psychoanalytic movement since 1933. Following his highly esteemed early contributions, he lapsed

into the extreme position that sexuality, as expressed in the orgasm, is all-important in understanding the ills of the individual and society.

3. *Studies on Orality.* The effects of various types of early oral experience upon later character structure has been a popular topic of discussion for some time. Prevailing views in this area are often translated into action in the form of child-rearing practices. However, the scattered anthropological and experimental evidence bearing on such issues as breast versus bottle feeding, length of breast feeding, self-demand versus scheduled feeding, form and age of weaning, etc., lacks definitive stature, as Orlansky (224) emphasizes in his summary of the literature. The frequent error in these studies, pointed out by various authors (131, 207, 224), lies in the attempt to relate specific feeding practices in a direct, causal, one-to-one fashion to subsequent personality traits. Oversimplifications of this sort obviously neglect the influence of such important factors as parental attitudes, cultural values, and the general interdependence of developmental phenomena.

Two recent researches have sought to explore psychoanalytic formulations of oral character structure. Goldman (115, 116), working in England, conducted a study in two parts, the first dealing with an attempt to verify descriptions of oral traits and the second relating these traits to age of weaning. During the former phase she obtained self-ratings from 115 men and women on 19 trait scales. These ratings were then subjected to a kind of factor analysis, which revealed a bipolar type factor containing negative traits (*e.g.*, pessimism, passivity, oral aggression) and positive traits (*e.g.*, optimism, nurturance, sociability). Type scores on this factor, interpreted by Goldman as strikingly similar to the theoretical description, were utilized in the second phase in comparison with weaning information, provided by mothers of the same subjects. Oral pessimism was found to be significantly associated ($r =$ .27) with early weaning (defined as not later than four months of age), and oral optimism ($r = .31$) with late weaning (five months or later). In her discussion of these results Goldman is wisely cautious. She stresses that a causal relationship has not been established by the data and also that the low magnitude of correlation suggests the operation of important unknown factors.

Another project designed to study orality has been undertaken by Blum and Miller (38). In the initial phase hypotheses deduced from statements in the psychoanalytic literature were tested by a variety of conventional psychological methods. The latter included teacher ratings, time sampling, sociometrics, and experimental situations, all of which were done on 18 children in a third-grade university elementary-school class. The operational definition of orality consisted of nonpurposive mouth movements recorded by observers. Correlations computed between ranks on this criterion measure and ranks on the series of hypothetical variables revealed varying degrees of association. The results lent strong support to hypotheses dealing with: (1) extreme interest in food and (2) social isolation; fair support to (3) need for liking and approval, (4) concern over giving and receiving, and (5) low boredom tolerance; no support to (6) depressive tendencies, (7) need to be ingratiating, and (8) inability to divide loyalties; while remaining equivocal were (9) dependency and (10) suggestibility.

A follow-up study (37) of 26 children was next conducted in the fourth grade of a public school having a less permissive atmosphere. The hypotheses relating orality to variables 2, 3, and 4 were again confirmed; those on variables 1, 5, 7, 8, and 10 were unconfirmed, in addition to three added hypotheses based on the oral character's inability to say "no," his desire for a magic helper, and low frustration tolerance. However, the unforeseen disruptions of procedure occasioned by the differences in social atmosphere led the authors to question the replication value of the experiment. Subsequent research has been aimed at the refinement of techniques for the large-scale selection of oral and nonoral children, so that the ultimate goal of extensive exploration of antecedent conditions in early childhood can be pursued.

4. *Studies on Anality.* Note 8 in Chapter 4 has already summarized anthropological observations concerning toilet-training practices and also the limited experimental work relating these practices to childhood development. Fragmentary evidence linking anality to adult personality stems from anthropological, clinical, and experimental sources. Miller and Hutt (207) point out the tentative nature of existing cultural data bearing on this topic. In both Tanala (163) and Japan (118) premature anal training is said to be reflected in the character structure of adult members of the culture. The Tanalan shows unusual personal cleanliness, compulsivity, and a desire for ritual. High values are attached to

property and hoarding is common. The Japanese also stresses neatness, perfectionism, and ritual. Furthermore, extreme shaming used during sphincter training is presumed to contribute to the later status needs. The Yurok (68, 70), on the other hand, commonly possess typical "anal" traits of compulsivity, retention, suspiciousness, and so forth, but observation reveals no undue emphasis on anal training in their childhood.

Clinical sources in this area, while not to be ignored, do not provide us with any more than statements to be accepted on faith. Fenichel (74), for example, asserts that the "psychoanalysis of stubborn persons provides abundant proof that stubbornness is connected with anal sensations and gives an anal-erogenous pleasure." Neo-Freudian analysts like Fromm, however, are equally forceful in attributing such traits to the general home atmosphere and the interaction of child and parent.

Experimental studies have been conducted by Hamilton (128) and Sears (257). The former found a somewhat higher incidence of stinginess, sadism, masochism, etc., in a group of 59 men and women who recalled some form of childhood anal eroticism than in a control group with no such recollections. The dubious validity of the recall task, combined with the inadequacy of the trait ratings, minimizes the significance of the results, as Sears (258) suggests in his review. The latter in his own research obtained low positive correlations, in the predicted direction, among the three traits of stinginess, obstinacy, and orderliness. The ratings were made by 37 members of a college fraternity on one another, with halo effect held constant in the data analysis. This study made no attempt to tie the traits back to childhood training, however.

5. *Urethral Ambition.* See Note 2 in Chapter 5.

6. *Penis Envy and Narcissism.* The association of narcissism with penis envy in women is supported by the Blacky Pictures (34) correlation of .34 ($P < .05$) between these two test dimensions.

7. *Pros and Cons of Adler's Views.* Thompson (282) presents a cogent analysis of the main strengths and weaknesses of Adler's position. On the positive side she lists his awareness of cultural factors, the increased attention he paid to parent-child relationships, and his pioneering in the area of ego psychology. The most frequently voiced criticisms emphasize the superficial and excessively ambitious nature of his theoretical system, oversimplifica-

tion of the problem of neurosis, and a seeming neglect of unconscious factors. Direct evidence of Adler's influence can be found in the views of Horney, Fromm, and Sullivan.

8. *The Typology Issue.* The various criticisms of type theories of personality like Jung's extraversion-introversion system have been summarized by MacKinnon (199). He points out that types are crude pictures of personality—easily drawn, invariably overlapping, and difficult to prove or disprove. Several psychoanalytic writers, including Fenichel, Rank, Horney, and Fromm, have qualified their own typologies as representing oversimplifications. Studies on the dichotomous typologies in particular have been attacked on the grounds of having been conducted by partisan investigators, with the selection of subjects not specified, the experimental procedures unclear, and the statistical treatment of data inadequate. Also, personality inventories designed to measure types (*e.g.*, the flock of extraversion-introversion tests which Jung's work inspired in the late 1920's) usually turned out to have unimodal rather than bimodal distributions.

9. *Rank's Contributions.* Apart from certain widely accepted emphases in therapy technique, Rank has also left his mark on the theoretical formulations of Horney, Fromm, and Sullivan. Though often presented in a confusing and obscure fashion, his views on the development of individuality and creativity seem to have stimulated a great deal of subsequent theorizing.

10. *Fuzzy Spots in Horney's Theory.* The distinction between the normal and the neurotic seems to be handled very superficially by Horney (144). Both individuals can possess all three character attitudes, but the difference is ascribed simply to the fact that the normal is capable of giving in to others, of fighting, and of keeping to himself, whereas the neurotic is not flexible in his exercise of these same attitudes. Positive values are said to accompany each attitude: in moving toward people the person tries to establish a friendly relationship to his world; in moving against people he equips himself for survival in a competitive society; and in moving away he seeks to attain a certain integrity and serenity. However, when these forces operate in a neurotic framework they somehow become "compulsive, rigid, indiscriminate, and mutually exclusive."

Mullahy (216) calls attention to the logical inconsistency in Horney's formulation of basic anxiety or conflict as it relates to the three attitudes. The basic anxiety is attributed to incompatibility among the attitudes, yet the latter are also said to represent major attempts at solution of the basic conflict. From this illustration of confused causality, Mullahy concludes with the statement that Horney has "not yet sufficiently clarified her fundamental concepts."

11. *Fenichel's Reply to Fromm.* Fenichel objects to the discarding of Freud's instinct concepts in the following passage (74, p. 588):

"Our comments make it plain that the insight into the formative power of social forces upon individual minds does not require any change in Freud's concepts of instincts, as certain authors [Fromm, Horney, Kardiner] believe. The instinctual needs are the raw material formed by the social influences; and it is the task of a psychoanalytic sociology to study the details of this shaping. . . . It is experience, that is, the cultural conditions, that transforms potentialities into realities, that shapes the real mental structure of man by forcing his instinctual demands into certain directions, by favoring some of them and blocking others, and even by turning parts of them against the rest." Certainly such an interactionist point of view—character as a function both of basic drives and environmental influences—must be considered more acceptable than either explanation by itself. The crucial, unanswered question, however, pertains to the relative significance of each for the process of character formation.

12. *Overlap in the Various Type Theories.* By now the reader has probably noted that the personality descriptions offered by the several theorists show certain marked similarities to one another. The following series of equations should serve to document this point:

1. Orthodox oral-passive = Horney's compliant = Fromm's receptive
2. Orthodox oral-sadistic = Horney's aggressive = Fromm's exploitative
3. Orthodox anal = Fromm's hoarding
4. Orthodox genital = Rank's creative artist = Fromm's productive
5. Jung's extravert = Rank's average = Fromm's marketing
6. Jung's introvert = Horney's detached

What can we infer from this obviously extensive overlapping? The rosiest of all possible inferences might be that these descriptions have considerable validity, since a number of independent observers have arrived at similar categorizations. At the opposite extreme one might be inclined to ascribe the agreement simply to a pervasive borrowing habit. The truth probably lies, as it usually does, between these two poles. However, it seems legitimate to voice some dissatisfaction with the large amount of paraphrasing and renaming and the small number of cross references and acknowledgments.

13. *Kardiner's Concept of Basic Personality.* The most commonly expressed criticism of Kardiner's approach and the attempts of others to describe "national character" is the charge of gross oversimplification of complex phenomena. Jahoda (152), for example, considers the concept of BPS appropriate only for small, uniform, self-contained cultures, and not at all feasible for contemporary American society. Thompson (282) goes even further in stating that Kardiner's work sometimes gives the impression that he is trying to make the data fit the theory.

By 1945 Kardiner and his associates (164) had applied their technique of analysis to 10 cultures. The most widely quoted investigation was done on data gathered by DuBois (62) for the people of Alor in the Dutch East Indies. Independent interpretations of Rorschach material by Oberholzer were found to be in essential agreement with the deduced basic personality configuration. Next Kardiner showed from life-history data that individual deviations from Alorese personality norms could be explained in terms of atypical early experiences. Studies of this sort, though, are more suggestive than definitive, for they lack the precision of a tightly designed experiment. More recently, Kardiner and Ovesey (165) have presented 25 psychoanalytic case studies of the American Negro, along with projective test materials. Smith (261), in reviewing this work, considers the term "basic personality structure" to be partly misleading, since the mode of handling nuclear personality conflicts varied from case to case. In addition he objects to the unsystematic analysis and conceptualization of the case materials as well as the relatively ineffective use of Rorschach and Thematic Apperception Test findings.

14. *Alexander's Types.* Alexander (13) claims no originality in the differentiation of intaking, eliminating, and retaining. He ac-

knowledges that they are fundamental to the original concepts of the pregenital tendencies of oral, anal, and urethral eroticism but considers his own contribution to lie in their consistent application to cases of gastrointestinal disturbance. Fenichel (74) criticizes Alexander's formulation as not being dynamic. The former states that it is by no means the case that one of the three attitudes necessarily prevails. The decisive factors are not the existence or strength of the attitudes, but rather their relation to anxiety, guilt, and defenses, all of which play a part in conflict.

15. *Alexander's Position among the Schools of Psychoanalysis.* Despite his start as a member of the orthodox school, it is apparent that Alexander has veered toward the neo-Freudians in his views. His position may be inferred as somewhere between the two from his following statements (11, pp. 330, 333):

"The most recent emphasis on the cultural factors in personality development in general, and in the causation of psychoneurosis in particular, comes from a group of critics of Freud, to whom occasional reference is made as 'neo-Freudians,' represented by authors such as Horney, Kardiner, Fromm, and others. That sometimes I also seem to be included in this group comes from the fact that I, too, recognize the need for reevaluation of cultural factors in personality development and share the views of this group concerning certain gaps in traditional psychoanalytic formulations." [p. 330.]

"This leads us back to the error into which the so-called 'neo-Freudians' fall when they underestimate the specific influence of the parental personalities and overstress the cultural factor—an error to which I have referred as the ethnological bias." [p. 333.]

16. *Ego Identity versus Self-esteem.* Erikson (71) attempts to distinguish his concept of ego identity from the orthodox one of self-esteem. He admits that the two are very close, except that self-esteem is a more conscious thing whereas ego identity is something both conscious and unconscious. The proportion of conscious and unconscious elements in the concept of self-esteem or narcissism is a moot point, as it is in the case of ego identity; so we must accept on faith Erikson's statement that his own concept connotes more of the unconscious.

CHAPTER 9 *Post-mortem*

By rights the last chapter in a book dealing with, in this instance, the eight ages of man should be read softly, accompanied by a few fading strains of organ music. However, our mission in this concluding note is neither to bury nor to praise, but instead to sum up and exhort.

In the Preface we began with the premise that psychoanalytic formulations contain the seeds of an ultimately sound theory of personality. Two preliminary steps toward maturation were suggested: first, the organization of diverse theoretical positions around the common framework of personality development by age levels; and second, the evaluation of existing evidence relevant to these positions. The expository sections of the text have sought to accomplish the former, the notes sections the latter.

If one may venture a guess as to the reader's (and author's) state of mind upon finishing this effort, the most appropriate word is probably "confused." It seems as though a large number of psychoanalysts through many years of observing patients, discussing cases, and borrowing from their own unconscious ideas have contributed to a massive, vague, yet potent personality theory. Encompassed are many controversial issues and many sharp disagreements. As if this were not enough, we have complicated the picture still further by introducing a curious assortment of bits of evidence. Obviously none of these factors makes for a feeling of closure.

But perhaps some degree of comfort can be gained by looking to the future rather than the past. The scientist typically achieves contentment first by selecting what for him is a meaningful area in which to work; next he sets up hypotheses which he considers to be worth investigating; and finally he puts them to the test. His security and peace of mind derive at least in part from the knowledge that he can apply methods adequate to his task, even though the final answers may be a long way off.

We can reason similarly with respect to psychoanalysis. The importance of its domain has been clearly established. Its assertions continue to enjoy wide application. If these assertions can be viewed, not as indestructible facts, but as hypotheses subject to verification or disproof, we have the makings of a theory. From the preceding pages there is ample justification for the belief that psychoanalytic concepts *can* be put to independent test in settings other than the traditional couch. Herein lies the exhortation. A combined and concerted research approach—through the experimental laboratory, the interview situation, the projective technique, the field study, etc.—holds real promise for the development of a sound theory of personality. With such an approach we can hope to chart, not the "future of an illusion," but the future of a science.

Bibliography

1. ABRAHAM, K., 1927. *Selected Papers on Psychoanalysis.* Hogarth, London.
2. ACHILLES, P. S., 1923. *The Effectiveness of Certain Social Hygiene Literature.* American Social Hygiene Association, New York.
3. ADLER, A., 1917. *The Neurotic Constitution,* trans. by B. Glueck and J. E. Lind. Moffatt, New York.
4. ADLER, A., 1917. *A Study of Organ Inferiority and Its Psychical Compensation,* trans. by S. E. Jelliffe. Nervous and Mental Disease Monograph Series, No. 24, New York.
5. ADLER, A., 1927. *Understanding Human Nature,* trans. by W. B. Wolfe. Greenberg, New York.
6. ADLER, A., 1938. *Social Interest: A Challenge to Mankind,* trans. by J. Linton and R. Vaughan. Faber, London.
7. ADORNO, T. W., FRENKEL-BRUNSWIK, ELSE, LEVINSON, D. J., and SANFORD, R. N., 1950. *The Authoritarian Personality.* Harper, New York.
8. AICHHORN, A., 1936. *Wayward Youth.* Putnam & Co., Ltd., London.
9. ALEXANDER, F., 1934. Psychologic factors in gastrointestinal disturbances. *Psychoanal. Quart.,* 3: 501–588.
10. ALEXANDER, F., 1942. *Our Age of Unreason.* Lippincott, Philadelphia.
11. ALEXANDER, F., 1948. Educative influence of personality factors in the environment. In H. A. Murray and C. Kluckhohn (eds.), *Personality in Nature, Society, and Culture,* pp. 325–339. Knopf, New York.
12. ALEXANDER, F., 1949. *Fundamentals of Psychoanalysis.* Norton, New York.
13. ALEXANDER, F., 1950. *Psychosomatic Medicine: Its Principles and Applications.* Norton, New York.
14. ALPERT, AUGUSTA, 1941. The latency period. *Amer. J. Orthopsychiat.,* 11: 126–133.
15. ARONSON, M. L., 1950. A study of the Freudian theory of paranoia by means of a group of psychological tests. Ph.D. thesis, Univ. of Michigan.

16. BALINT, ALICE, 1943. On identification. *Int. J. of Psycho-Anal.,* 24: 97–107.

17. BARKER, R. G., DEMBO, TAMARA, and LEWIN, K., 1943. Frustration and regression. In R. G. Barker, J. S. Kounin, and H. F. Wright (eds.), *Child Behavior and Development,* pp. 441–458. McGraw-Hill, New York.

18. BATESON, G., and MEAD, MARGARET, 1942. *Balinese Culture, A Photographic Analysis.* New York Academy of Sciences, New York.

19. BEAGLEHOLE, E., 1944. Character structure. *Psychiatry,* 7: 145–162.

20. BELLAK, L., 1944. The concept of projection. *Psychiatry,* 7: 353–370.

21. BELLAK, L., and EKSTEIN, R., 1946. The extension of basic scientific laws to psychoanalysis and to psychology. *Psychoanal. Rev.,* 23: 306–313.

22. BELMONT, LILLIAN, and BIRCH, H. G., 1951. Re-individualizing the repression hypothesis. *J. abnorm. soc. Psychol.,* 46: 226–235.

23. BENEDEK, THERESE, 1938. Adaptation to reality in early infancy. *Psychoanal. Quart.,* 7: 200–215.

24. BENEDICT, RUTH, 1949. Child-rearing in certain European countries. *Amer. J. Orthopsychiat.,* 19: 342–350.

25. BENJAMIN, J. D., 1950. Methodological considerations in the validation and elaboration of psychoanalytical personality theory. *Amer. J. Orthopsychiat.,* 20: 139–156.

26. BERNFELD, S., 1923. Über eine typische Form der männlichen Pubertät. *Imago. Lpz.,* IX.

27. BERNFELD, S., 1924. *Vom dichterischen Schaffen der Jugend.* Verlag, Vienna.

28. BERNFELD, S., 1929. *The Psychology of the Infant.* Brentano, New York.

29. BERNFELD, S., 1935. Über die einfache männliche Pubertät. *Z. psa. Pädagogik,* IX.

30. BERNFELD, S., 1938. Types of adolescence. *Psychoanal. Quart.,* 7: 243–253.

31. BIBER, BARBARA, MURPHY, LOIS B., WOODCOCK, LOUISE P., and BLACK, IRMA S., 1942. *Children in School: a Study of a Seven-year-old Group.* Dutton, New York.

32. BLANCHARD, PHYLLIS, 1944. Adolescent experience in relation to personality and behavior. In J. McV. Hunt (ed.), *Personality and the Behavior Disorders,* Vol. II, pp. 691–713. Ronald, New York.

33. BLANTON, M. G., 1917. The behavior of the human infant during the first thirty days of life. *Psychol. Rev.,* 24: 456–483.

34. BLUM, G. S., 1949. A study of the psychoanalytic theory of psychosexual development. *Genet. Psychol. Monogr.,* 39: 3–99.

35. BLUM, G. S., 1950. *The Blacky Pictures: A Technique for the Exploration of Personality Dynamics.* Psychological Corporation, New York.

36. BLUM, G. S., and HUNT, H. F., 1952. The validity of the Blacky Pictures. *Psychol. Bull.*, 49: 238–250.
37. BLUM, G. S., and MILLER, D. R., 1951. Exploring the psychoanalytic theory of the "oral character": a follow-up study. *Amer. Psychol.*, 6: 339–340 (abstract).
38. BLUM, G. S., and MILLER, D. R., 1952. Exploring the psychoanalytic theory of the "oral character." *J. Personal.*, 20: 287–304.
39. BORNSTEIN, BERTA, 1951. On latency. *Psychoanal. Study of the Child*, 6: 279–285.
40. BOWLBY, J., 1951. *Maternal Care and Mental Health.* World Health Organization, Geneva.
41. BRONFENBRENNER, U., 1951. Toward an integrated theory of personality. In R. R. Blake and G. V. Ramsey (eds.), *Perception: An Approach to Personality.* Ronald, New York.
42. BROWN, J. F., 1940. *The Psychodynamics of Abnormal Behavior.* McGraw-Hill, New York.
43. BRUNER, J. S., and POSTMAN, L. J., 1947. Emotional selectivity in perception and reaction. *J. Personal.*, 16: 69–77.
44. BRUNER, J. S., and POSTMAN, L. J., 1949. Perception, cognition, and behavior. *J. Personal.*, 18: 14–31.
45. BUCK, W., 1936. A measurement of changes of attitudes and interests of university students over a ten-year period. *J. abnorm. soc. Psychol.*, 31: 12–19.
46. BUXBAUM, EDITH, 1933. Angstäusserungen von Schulmädchen im Pubertätsalter. *Z. psa. Pädagogik*, VII.
47. CAMERON, N., 1938. Reasoning, regression and communication in schizophrenics. *Psychol. Monogr.*, 50, No. 1.
48. CAMERON, N., 1938. A study of thinking in senile deterioration and schizophrenic disorganization. *Amer. J. Psychol.*, 51: 650–664.
49. CAMPBELL, ELISE H., 1939. The social-sex development of children. *Genet. Psychol. Monogr.*, Vol. 21, No. 4.
50. CARMICHAEL, L., 1946. The onset and early development of behavior. In L. Carmichael (ed.), *Manual of Child Psychology*, pp. 43–166. Wiley, New York.
51. CATTELL, R. B., 1950. *Personality.* McGraw-Hill, New York.
52. CLAPP, C. D., 1951. Two levels of unconscious awareness. Ph.D. thesis, Univ. of Michigan.
53. CONKLIN, E. S., 1920. The foster-child fantasy. *Amer. J. Psychol.*, 31: 59–76.
54. CONN, J. H., 1940. Children's reactions to the discovery of genital differences. *Amer. J. Orthopsychiat.*, 10: 747–754.
55. COURTNEY, P. D., 1949. Identification and learning: a theoretical analysis. Ph.D. thesis, Harvard Univ.
56. DAVIS, A., 1947. Socialization and adolescent personality. In T. M. Newcomb and E. L. Hartley (eds.), *Readings in Social Psychology*, pp. 139–150. Holt, New York.

57. DAVIS, K. B., 1929. *Factors in the Sex Life of Twenty-two Hundred Women.* Harper, New York.
58. DEUTSCH, HELENE, 1944. *The Psychology of Women,* Vol. I. Grune & Stratton, New York.
59. DOLLARD, J., DOOB, L. W., MILLER, N. E., and SEARS, R. R., 1939. *Frustration and Aggression.* Yale University Press, New Haven.
60. DOLLARD, J., and MILLER, N. E., 1950. *Personality and Psychotherapy.* McGraw-Hill, New York.
61. DREIKURS, R., 1950. *Fundamentals of Adlerian Psychology.* Greenberg, New York.
62. DU BOIS, CORA, 1944. *The People of Alor.* University of Minnesota Press, Minneapolis.
63. DU BOIS, P. H., and FORBES, T. W., 1934. Studies of catatonia: III. Bodily postures assumed while sleeping. *Psychiat. Quart.,* 8: 546–552.
64. DUNBAR, FLANDERS, 1944. Effect of the mother's emotional attitude on the infant. *Psychosom. Med.,* 6: 156–159.
65. EKSTEIN, R., 1949. Ideological warfare in the psychological sciences. *Psychoanal. Rev.,* 36: 144–151.
66. ELLIS, A., 1950. An introduction to the principles of scientific psychoanalysis. *Genet. Psychol. Monogr.,* 41: 147–212.
67. ENGLAND, A. O., 1947. Cultural milieu and parental identification. *Nervous Child,* 6: 301–305.
68. ERIKSON, E. H., 1945. Childhood and tradition in two American Indian tribes. *Psychoanal. Study of the Child,* 1: 319–350.
69. ERIKSON, E. H., 1946. Ego development and historical change. *Psychoanal. Study of the Child,* 2: 359–396.
70. ERIKSON, E. H., 1950. *Childhood and Society.* Norton, New York.
71. ERIKSON, E. H., 1950. Growth and crises of the healthy personality. In M. E. Senn (ed.), *The Healthy Personality,* pp. 91–146. Josiah Macy, Jr., Foundation, New York.
72. ESCALONA, SIBYLLE K., 1945. Feeding disturbances in very young children. *Amer. J. Orthopsychiat.,* 15: 76–80.
73. FEDERN, P., 1928. Narcissism in the structure of the ego. *Int. J. Psycho-Anal.,* 9: 401–419.
74. FENICHEL, O., 1945. *The Psychoanalytic Theory of Neurosis.* Norton, New York.
75. FERENCZI, S., 1916. *Contributions to Psychoanalysis.* Badger, Boston.
76. FERENCZI, S., 1926. *Further Contributions to the Theory and Technique of Psychoanalysis.* Hogarth, London.
77. FLÜGEL, J. C., 1921. *Psychoanalytic Study of the Family.* Hogarth, London.
78. FLÜGEL, J. C., 1942. Sublimation: its nature and conditions. *Brit. J. educ. Psychol.,* 12: 162–166.
79. FLÜGEL, J. C., 1947. *Man, Morals, and Society.* International Universities Press, New York.

80. FODOR, N., 1949. *The Search for the Beloved*. Hermitage, New York.
81. FRENCH, T. M., 1938. Defense and synthesis in the function of the ego. *Psychoanal. Quart.*, 7: 537–553.
82. FRENCH, T. M., 1944. Clinical approach to the dynamics of behavior. In J. McV. Hunt (ed.), *Personality and the Behavior Disorders*, Vol. I, pp. 255–268. Ronald, New York.
83. FREUD, ANNA, 1946. *The Ego and the Mechanisms of Defence*, trans. by C. Baines. International Universities Press, New York.
84. FREUD, ANNA, 1951. The contribution of psychoanalysis to genetic psychology. *Amer. J. Orthopsychiat.*, 21: 476–497.
85. FREUD, A., and BURLINGHAM, D. T., 1944. *Infants without Families*. International Universities Press, New York.
86. FREUD, S., 1922. *Group Psychology and the Analysis of the Ego*. Liveright, New York.
87. FREUD, S., 1927. *The Ego and the Id*. Hogarth, London.
88. FREUD, S., 1933. *New Introductory Lectures on Psychoanalysis*, trans. by J. H. Sprott. Norton, New York.
89. FREUD, S., 1936. *The Problem of Anxiety*. Norton, New York.
90. FREUD, S., 1938. *The Basic Writings of Sigmund Freud*. A. A. Brill (ed.). Random House, New York.
91. FREUD, S., 1938. Three contributions to the theory of sex. In A. A. Brill (ed.), *The Basic Writings of Sigmund Freud*, pp. 553–629. Modern Lib., New York.
92. FREUD, S., 1939. *Civilization and Its Discontents*, trans. by Joan Riviere. Hogarth, London.
93. FREUD, S., 1942. *Beyond the Pleasure Principle*. Hogarth, London.
94. FREUD, S., 1943. *A General Introduction to Psychoanalysis*. Garden City Publishing Company, Inc., Garden City, N.Y.
95. FREUD, S., 1948. The defence neuro-psychoses. In *Collected Papers*, Vol. I, pp. 59–75, trans. under supervision of Joan Riviere. Hogarth, London.
96. FREUD, S., 1948. The passing of the Oedipus complex. In *Collected Papers*, Vol. II, pp. 269–276, trans. under supervision of Joan Riviere. Hogarth, London.
97. FREUD, S., 1948. Instincts and their vicissitudes. In *Collected Papers*, Vol. IV, pp. 60–83, trans. under supervision of Joan Riviere. Hogarth, London.
98. FREUD, S., 1948. Character and anal eroticism. In *Collected Papers*, Vol. II, pp. 45–50, trans. under supervision of Joan Riviere. Hogarth, London.
99. FREUD, S., 1948. A child is being beaten. A contribution to the study of the origin of sexual perversions. In *Collected Papers*, Vol. II, pp. 172–201, trans. under supervision of Joan Riviere. Hogarth, London.
100. FREUD, S., 1948. On narcissism. In *Collected Papers*, Vol. IV, pp. 30–59, trans. under supervision of Joan Riviere. Hogarth, London.

101. FREUD, S., 1948. The unconscious. In *Collected Papers,* Vol. IV, pp. 98–136, trans. under supervision of Joan Riviere. Hogarth, London.
102. FREUD, S., 1948. Repression. In *Collected Papers,* Vol. IV, pp. 84–97, trans. under supervision of Joan Riviere. Hogarth, London.
103. FREUD, S., 1949. *An Outline of Psychoanalysis.* Norton, New York.
104. FRIEDMAN, S., 1950. An empirical study of the Oedipus complex. Unpublished study.
105. FRIES, MARGARET E., 1946. The child's ego development and the training of adults in his development. *Psychoanal. Study of the Child,* 2: 85–112.
106. FROMM, E., 1941. *Escape from Freedom.* Farrar & Rinehart, Inc., New York.
107. FROMM, E., 1947. *Man for Himself.* Rinehart, New York.
108. FROMM, E., 1948. The Oedipus complex and the Oedipus myth. In Ruth N. Anshen (ed.), *The Family: Its Function and Destiny,* Vol. V. Harper, New York.
109. GARDNER, G. E., 1931. Evidences of homosexuality in 120 unanalyzed cases with paranoid content. *Psychoanal. Rev.,* 18: 57–62.
110. GLIXMAN, A. F., 1948. An analysis of the use of the interruption-technique in experimental studies of "repression." *Psychol. Bull.,* 45: 491–506.
111. GLOVER, E., 1925. Notes on oral character formation. *Int. J. Psycho-Anal.,* 6: 131–154.
112. GLOVER, E., 1931. Sublimation, substitution, and social anxiety. *Int. J. Psycho-Anal.,* 12: 263–297.
113. GLOVER, E., 1945. Examination of the Klein system of child psychology. *Psychoanal. Study of the Child,* 2: 75–118.
114. GLOVER, E., 1949. *Psycho-analysis.* Staples, New York.
115. GOLDMAN, FRIEDA, 1948. Breastfeeding and character-formation. *J. Personal.,* 17: 83–103.
116. GOLDMAN, FRIEDA, 1950. Breastfeeding and character formation. II: The etiology of the oral character in psychoanalytic theory. *J. Personal.,* 19: 189–196.
117. GOLDSTEIN, S., 1952. A projective study of psychoanalytic mechanisms of defense. Ph.D. thesis, Univ. of Michigan.
118. GORER, G., 1943. Themes in Japanese culture. *Trans. N.Y. Acad. Sci.,* 2: 106–124.
119. GOULD, ROSALIND, 1942. Repression experimentally analyzed. *Character & Pers.,* 10: 259–288.
120. GREENACRE, PHYLLIS, 1941. The predisposition to anxiety. *Psychoanal. Quart.,* 10: 66–94, 610–638.
121. GREENACRE, PHYLLIS, 1945. The biological economy of birth. *Psychoanal. Study of the Child,* 1: 31–51.
122. GREENACRE, PHYLLIS, 1950. The prepuberty trauma in girls. *Psychoanal. Quart.,* 19: 298–317.
123. GRIFFITHS, RUTH, 1935. *A Study of Imagination in Early Child-*

hood and Its Function in Mental Development. Kegan Paul, Trench, Trubner & Co., London.

124. GURIN, MAIZIE G., 1952. Differences between latents and adolescents. Unpublished study.

125. HALL, D. E., and MOHR, G. J., 1933. Prenatal attitudes of primaparae: a contribution to the mental hygiene of pregnancy. *Ment. Hyg., N.Y.,* 17: 226–234.

126. HALVERSON, H. M., 1938. Infant sucking and tensional behavior. *J. genet. Psychol.,* 53: 365–430.

127. HALVERSON, H. M., 1940. Genital and sphincter behavior of the male infant. *J. genet. Psychol.,* 56: 95–136.

128. HAMILTON, G. V., 1929. A Research in Marriage. Boni, New York.

129. HARRIS, D. B., and HARRIS, E. S., 1946. A study of fetal movements in relation to mother's activity. *Hum. Biol.,* 18: 221–237.

130. HART, H., 1947. Displacement, guilt and pain. *Psychoanal. Rev.,* 34: 259–273.

131. HARTMANN, H., 1950. Comments on the psychoanalytic theory of the ego. *Psychoanal. Study of the Child,* 5: 74–96.

132. HARTMANN, H., and KRIS, E., 1945. The genetic approach in psychoanalysis. *Psychoanal. Study of the Child,* 1: 11–30.

133. HARTMANN, H., KRIS, E., and LOEWENSTEIN, R. M., 1947. Comments on the formation of psychic structure. *Psychoanal. Study of the Child,* 2: 11–38.

134. HARTWELL, S. W., HUTT, M. L., ANDREW, GWEN, and WALTON, R. E., 1951. The Michigan Picture Test: diagnostic and therapeutic possibilities of a new projective test in child guidance. *Amer. J. Orthopsychiat.,* 21: 124–137.

135. HATTENDORF, K. W., 1932. A study of the questions of young children concerning sex: a phase of an experimental approach to parent education. *J. soc. Psychol.,* 3: 37–65.

136. HEALY, W., BRONNER, AUGUSTA F., and BOWERS, ANNA MAY, 1930. *The Structure and Meaning of Psychoanalysis.* Knopf, New York.

137. HENDRICK, IVES, 1939. *Facts and Theories of Psychoanalysis.* Knopf, New York.

138. HILGARD, E. R., 1948. *Theories of Learning.* Appleton-Century-Crofts, New York.

139. HILGARD, E. R., 1949. Human motives and the concept of the self. *Amer. Psychol.,* 4: 374–382.

140. HILGEMAN, LOIS M., 1951. Developmental and sex variations in the Blacky Test. Ph.D. thesis, Ohio State Univ.

141. HORNEY, KAREN, 1937. *The Neurotic Personality of Our Time.* Norton, New York.

142. HORNEY, KAREN, 1939. *New Ways in Psychoanalysis.* Norton, New York.

143. HORNEY, KAREN, 1942. *Self Analysis.* Norton, New York.

144. HORNEY, KAREN, 1945. *Our Inner Conflicts.* Norton, New York.

145. HORNEY, KAREN, 1950. *Neurosis and Human Growth*. Norton, New York.

146. HOWES, D. H., and SOLOMON, R. L., 1950. A note on McGinnies' "Emotionality and perceptual defense." *Psychol. Rev.*, 57: 229–234.

147. HUSCHKA, MABEL, 1942. The child's response to coercive bowel training. *Psychosom. Med.*, 4: 301–328.

148. HUSCHKA, MABEL, 1944. The incidence and character of masturbation threats in a group of problem children. In S. S. Tomkins (ed.), *Contemporary Psychopathology*. Harvard University Press, Cambridge.

149. ISAACS, SUSAN, 1933. *Social Development in Young Children*. Routledge, London.

150. ISAACS, SUSAN, 1948. The nature and function of fantasy. *Int. J. Psycho-Anal.*, 29: 73–97.

151. JACOBI, JOLAN, 1943. *The Psychology of Jung*, trans. by K. W. Bash. Yale University Press, New Haven.

152. JAHODA, MARIE, 1950. Toward a social psychology of mental health. In M. E. Senn (ed.), *The Healthy Personality*, pp. 211–231. Josiah Macy, Jr., Foundation, New York.

153. JAMES, H. E. O., and MOORE, F. F., 1940. Adolescent leisure in a working-class district. *Occup. Psychol.*, 14: 132–145.

154. JERSILD, A. T., and HOLMES, F. B., 1935. *Children's Fears*. Child Development Monograph, No. 20. Teachers College, Columbia University, New York.

155. JONES, E., 1913. *Papers on Psychoanalysis*. Wood, New York.

156. JONES, H. E., 1943. *Development in Adolescence*. Appleton-Century-Crofts, New York.

157. JUNG, C. G., 1915. *The Theory of Psychoanalysis*. Nervous and Mental Disease Monograph Series, No. 19, New York.

158. JUNG, C. G., 1926. *Psychological Types or the Psychology of Individuation*, trans. by H. G. Baynes. Harcourt, Brace, New York.

159. JUNG, C. G., 1927. *The Psychology of the Unconscious*, trans. by Beatrice M. Hinkle. Dodd, Mead, New York.

160. JUNG, C. G., 1928. *Contributions to Analytical Psychology*, trans. by H. G. and C. F. Baynes. Harcourt, Brace, New York.

161. JUNG, C. G., 1928. *Two Essays on Analytical Psychology*, trans. by H. G. and C. F. Baynes. Dodd, Mead, New York.

162. JUNG, C. G., 1933. *Modern Man in Search of a Soul*, trans. by W. S. Dill and C. F. Baynes. Harcourt, Brace, New York.

163. KARDINER, A., 1939. *The Individual and His Society*. Columbia University Press, New York.

164. KARDINER, A., 1945. *The Psychological Frontiers of Society*. Columbia University Press, New York.

165. KARDINER, A., and OVESEY, L., 1951. *The Mark of Oppression: A Psycho-Social Study of the American Negro*. Norton, New York.

166. KEET, C. D., 1948. Two verbal techniques in a miniature counseling situation. *Psychol. Monogr.*, Vol. 62, No. 7.

167. KENWORTHY, MARION, 1927. The pre-natal and early post-natal phenomena of consciousness. In E. Dummer (ed.), *The Unconscious*. Knopf, New York.

168. KINSEY, A. C., POMEROY, W. B., and MARTIN, C. E., 1948. *Sexual Behavior in the Human Male*. Saunders, Philadelphia.

169. KITAY, P. M., 1940. A comparison of the sexes in their attitude and beliefs about women: a study of prestige groups. *Sociometry*, 3: 399–407.

170. KLEIN, HENRIETTA, and HORWITZ, W., 1949. Psychosexual factors in the paranoid phenomenon. *Amer. J. Psychiat.*, 105: 697–701.

171. KLEIN, HENRIETTE R., POTTER, H. W., and DYK, RUTH B., 1950. Anxiety in pregnancy and childbirth. *Psychosom. Med. Monogr.* Hoeber, New York.

172. KLEIN, MELANIE, 1932. *The Psychoanalysis of Children*. Hogarth, London.

173. KLEIN, MELANIE, 1935. A contribution to the psychogenesis of manic-depressive states. *Int. J. Psycho-Anal.*, 16: 145–174.

174. KLEIN, MELANIE, 1944. The early development of conscience in the child. In S. Lorand (ed.), *Psychoanalysis Today*, pp. 149–161. International Universities Press, New York.

175. KLEIN, MELANIE, 1948. *Contributions to Psychoanalysis, 1921–1945*. Hogarth, London.

176. KLEIN, MELANIE, and RIVIERE, JOAN, 1938. *Love, Hate and Reparation*. Hogarth, London.

177. KLEIN, MELANIE, HEIMANN, P., ISAACS, SUSAN, and RIVIERE, JOAN, 1952. *Developments in Psychoanalysis*. Hogarth, London.

178. KNIGHT, R. P., 1940. Introjection, projection, and identification. *Psychoanal. Quart.*, 9: 334–341.

179. KOCH, HELEN L., 1935. An analysis of certain forms of so-called "nervous habits" in young children. *J. genet. Psychol.*, 46: 139–170.

180. KORNER, I. N., 1950. Experimental investigation of some aspects of the problem of repression: repressive forgetting. Teachers College, Columbia University. Contributions to Education, No. 970. Columbia University, New York.

181. KRIS, E., 1951. Psychoanalytic propositions. In M. H. Marx (ed.), *Psychological Theory: Contemporary Readings*, pp. 332–349. Macmillan, New York.

182. KUNST, M. S., 1948. A study of thumb- and finger-sucking in infants. *Psychol. Monogr.*, Vol. 62, No. 3.

183. LADEN, ESTHER, and RAUSH, H. L., 1952. Identification and the adolescent boy's perception of his father. *J. abnorm. soc. Psychol.* (in press).

184. LAIR, W. S., 1949. Psychoanalytic theory of identification. Ph.D. thesis, Harvard Univ.

185. LANDER, J., 1942. The pubertal struggle against the instincts. *Amer. J. Orthopsychiat.*, 12: 456–461.

186. LANDIS, C., et al., 1940. *Sex in Development*. Hoeber, New York.

187. LEVY, D. M., 1928. Fingersucking and accessory movements in early infancy. *Amer. J. Psychiat.*, 7: 881–918.
188. LEVY, D. M., 1934. Experiments on the sucking reflex and social behavior of dogs. *Amer. J. Orthopsychiat.*, 4: 203–224.
189. LEVY, D. M., 1937. *Studies in Sibling Rivalry.* Research Monograph, No. 2, American Orthopsychiatric Association, New York.
190. LEVY, D. M., 1940. "Control-situation" studies of children's responses to the differences in genitalia. *Amer. J. Orthopsychiat.*, 10: 755–762.
191. LEVY, D. M., 1943. Maternal Overprotection. Columbia University Press, New York.
192. LEWIN, K., 1935. *A Dynamic Theory of Personality.* McGraw-Hill, New York.
193. LEWIN, K., 1937. Psychoanalytic and topological psychology. *Bull. Menninger Clin.*, 1: 202–211.
194. LICHTENBERG, P., 1949. Sublimation. *Persona*, 1: 2–9.
195. LORAND, S. (ed.), 1944. *Psychoanalysis Today.* International Universities Press, New York.
196. McCLEARY, R. A., and LAZARUS, R. S., 1949. Autonomic discrimination without awareness: an interim report. *J. Personal.*, 18: 171–179.
197. McCLELLAND, D. C., ATKINSON, J. W., CLARK, R. A., and LOWELL, E. L. The achievement motive. Unpublished ms.
198. McGINNIES, E. M., 1949. Emotionality and perceptual defense. *Psychol. Rev.*, 56: 244–251.
199. MACKINNON, D. W., 1944. The structure of personality. In J. McV. Hunt (ed.), *Personality and the Behavior Disorders*, Vol. I, pp. 3–48. Ronald, New York.
200. McNEIL, E. B., and BLUM, G. S., 1952. Handwriting and psychosexual dimensions of personality. *J. proj. techn.* (in press).
201. MALINOWSKI, B., 1927. *Sex and Repression in Savage Society.* Harcourt, Brace, New York.
202. MEAD, MARGARET, 1939. *From the South Seas.* Morrow, New York.
203. MEAD, MARGARET, 1947. Adolescence in primitive and in modern society. In T. M. Newcomb and E. L. Hartley (eds.), *Readings in Social Psychology.* Holt, New York.
204. MEAD, MARGARET, 1949. *Male and Female.* Morrow, New York.
205. MENNINGER, K., 1938. *Man against Himself.* Harcourt, Brace, New York.
206. MILLER, C., 1941. The paranoid syndrome. *Arch. Neurol. Psychiat.*, 45: 953–963.
207. MILLER, D. R., and HUTT, M. L., 1949. Value interiorization and personality development. *J. soc. Issues*, 5: 2–30.
208. MILLER, N. E., 1939. Experiments relating Freudian displacement to generalization of conditioning. *Psychol. Bull.*, 36: 516–517.
209. MILLER, N. E., and DOLLARD, J., 1941. *Social Learning and Imitation.* Yale University Press, New Haven.

210. MOLONEY, J. C., and BIDDLE, C. R., 1945. Psychiatric observations in Okinawa Shima. *Psychiatry,* 8: 391–402.

211. MONTAGU, A., 1950. Constitutional and prenatal factors in infant and child health. In M. Senn (ed.), *Symposium on the Healthy Personality,* pp. 148–175. Josiah Macy, Jr. Foundation, New York.

212. MOWRER, O. H., 1940. An experimental analogue of "repression" with incidental observations on "reaction-formation." *J. abnorm. soc. Psychol.,* 35: 56–87.

213. MOWRER, O. H., 1950. *Learning Theory and Personality Dynamics.* Ronald, New York.

214. MOWRER, O. H., and KLUCKHOHN, C., 1944. Dynamic theory of personality. In J. McV. Hunt (ed.), *Personality and the Behavior Disorders,* Vol. I, pp. 69–135. Ronald, New York.

215. MULLAHY, P., 1945. A theory of interpersonal relations and the evolution of personality. *Psychiat.,* 8: 177–206.

216. MULLAHY, P., 1948. *Oedipus Myth and Complex.* Hermitage, New York.

217. MURRAY, H. A., 1933. The effect of fear upon estimates of the maliciousness of other personalities. *J. soc. Psychol.,* 4: 310–329.

218. MURRAY, H. A., 1938. *Explorations in Personality.* Oxford, New York.

219. MURPHY, LOIS B., 1937. *Social Behavior and Child Personality.* Columbia University Press, New York.

220. NEWCOMB, T. M., 1950. *Social Psychology.* Dryden, New York.

221. NUNBERG, H., 1926. The sense of guilt and the need for punishment. *Int. J. Psycho-Anal.,* 7: 420–434.

222. O'KELLY, L. I., 1940. An experimental study of regression. I. Behavioral characteristics of the regressive response. *J. comp. Psychol.,* 30: 41–53.

223. O'KELLY, L. I., 1940. An experimental study of regression. II. Some motivational determinants of regression and perseveration. *J. comp. Psychol.,* 30: 55–95.

224. ORLANSKY, H., 1949. Infant care and personality. *Psychol. Bull.,* 46: 1–48.

225. PAGE, J., and WARKENTIN, J., 1938. Masculinity and paranoia. *J. abnorm. soc. Psychol.,* 33: 527–531.

226. PEARSON, G., 1931. Some early factors in the formation of personality. *Amer. J. Orthopsychiat.,* 1: 284–291.

227. PIAGET, J., 1920. *The Child's Concept of the World.* Harcourt, Brace, New York.

228. PIAGET, J., 1926. *The Language and Thought of the Child,* trans. by M. Worden. Kegan Paul, Trench, Trubner & Co., London.

229. PIAGET, J., 1937. *Factors Determining Human Behavior.* Harvard University Press, Cambridge.

230. PLATONOW, K. I., 1933. On the objective proof of the experimental personality age regression. *J. gen. Psychol.,* 9: 190–209.

231. PRATT, K. C., NELSON, A. K., and SUN, K. H., 1930. The behavior

of the newborn infant. *Ohio State Univ. Studies. Contributions in Psychology,* No. 10.

232. PUNER, HELEN W., 1947. *Freud, His Life and His Mind.* Howell, Soskin, New York.

233. RANK, O., 1914. *The Myth of the Birth of the Hero.* Nervous and Mental Disease Monographs, No. 18, New York.

234. RANK, O., 1929. *The Trauma of Birth.* Harcourt, Brace, New York.

235. RANK, O., 1932. *Modern Education,* trans. by Mabel E. Moxon. Knopf, New York.

236. RANK, O., 1932. *Art and Artist,* trans. by C. F. Atkinson. Knopf, New York.

237. RANK, O., 1945. *Will Therapy and Truth and Reality,* trans. by Jessie Taft. Knopf, New York.

238. RAPAPORT, D., 1942. *Emotions and Memory.* Williams & Wilkins, Baltimore.

239. REICH, W., 1945. *Character-analysis,* trans. by T. P. Wolfe. Orgone Institute, New York.

240. REIK, T., 1949. *Listening with the Third Ear.* Harcourt, Brace, New York.

241. REMMERS, H. H., 1950. A quantitative index of social psychological empathy. *Amer. J. Orthopsychiat.,* 20: 161–165.

242. RIBBLE, MARGARET A., 1943. *The Rights of Infants.* Columbia University Press, New York.

243. RIBBLE, MARGARET A., 1944. Infantile experience in relation to personality development. In J. McV. Hunt (ed.), *Personality and the Behavior Disorders,* Vol. 2, pp. 621–651. Ronald, New York.

244. RICHARDS, T. W., and NEWBERRY, H., 1938. Can performance on test items at six months postnatally be predicted on the basis of fetal activity? *Child Develpm.,* 9: 79–86.

245. ROBERTS, E., 1944. Thumb and finger sucking in relation to feeding in early infancy. *Amer. J. Dis. Child,* 68: 7–8.

246. ROHEIM, G., 1934. *The Riddle of the Sphinx.* Hogarth, London.

247. ROHEIM, G., 1943. Sublimation. *Psychoanal. Quart.,* 12: 338–352.

248. ROSENSTOCK, I. M., 1951. Perceptual aspects of repression. *J. abnorm. soc. Psychol.,* 46: 304–315.

249. ROSENZWEIG, S., 1938. The experimental study of repression. In H. A. Murray, *Explorations in Personality,* pp. 472–490. Oxford, New York.

250. ROSS, S., 1951. Sucking behavior in neonate dogs. *J. abnorm. soc. Psychol.,* 46: 142–149.

251. SACHS, H., 1929. One of the motive factors in the superego in women. *Int. J. Psycho-Anal.,* 10: 39–50.

252. SACHS, H., 1944. *Freud, Master and Friend.* Harvard University Press, Cambridge.

253. SARBIN, T. R., 1950. Mental age changes in experimental regression. *J. Personal.,* 19: 221–228.

254. SCHILDER, P., 1935. *The Image and Appearance of the Human*

Body. Psyche Monograph, No. 6, Kegan Paul, Trench, Trubner & Co., London.

255. SCHILDER, P., 1942. *Mind: Perception and Thoughts in Their Constructive Aspects.* Columbia University Press, New York.

256. SCHRIER, H., 1951. The significance of identification in short-term therapy. Ph.D. thesis, Univ. of Michigan.

257. SEARS, R. R., 1936. Experimental studies of projection: I. Attribution of traits. *J. soc. Psychol.,* 7: 151–163.

258. SEARS, R. R., 1943. *Survey of Objective Studies of Psychoanalytic Concepts.* Bulletin 51, Social Science Research Council, New York.

259. SEARS, R. R., and WISE, G. W., 1950. The relation of cup feeding in infancy to thumb-sucking and the oral drive. *Amer. J. Orthopsychiat.,* 20: 123–138.

260. SLOTKIN, J. S., 1952. *Personality Development.* Harper, New York.

261. SMITH, M. BREWSTER, 1952. Social psychology and group processes. In C. P. Stone and D. W. Taylor (eds.), *Annual Review of Psychology,* Vol. 3, pp. 175–204. Annual Reviews, Stanford.

262. SOLLENBERGER, R. T., 1940. Some relationships between the urinary excretion of male hormone by maturing boys and their expressed interests and attitudes. *J. Psychol.,* 9: 179–190.

263. SONTAG, L. W., 1941. The significance of fetal environmental differences. *Amer. J. Obstet. Gynec.,* 42: 996–1003.

264. SONTAG, L. W., 1944. Differences in modifiability of fetal behavior and physiology. *Psychosom. Med.,* 6: 151–154.

265. SONTAG, L. W., 1946. Some psychosomatic aspects of childhood. *Nervous Child,* 5: 296–304.

266. SPELT, D. K., 1948. The conditioning of the human fetus *in utero. J. exp. Psychol.,* 38: 338–346.

267. SPIEGEL, L. A., 1951. A review of contributions to a psychoanalytic theory of adolescence. *Psychoanal. Study of the Child,* 6: 375–393.

268. SPITZ, R. A., 1945. Hospitalism. *Psychoanal. Study of the Child,* 1: 53–74.

269. SPITZ, R. A., 1946. Hospitalism: A follow-up report. *Psychoanal. Study of the Child,* 2: 113–117.

270. SPITZ, R. A., 1946. Anaclitic depression. *Psychoanal. Study of the Child,* 2: 313–342.

271. STERBA, R., 1947. *Introduction to the Psychoanalytic Theory of the Libido.* Nervous and Mental Disease Monographs, No. 68, New York.

272. STOKE, S. M., 1940. An inquiry into the concept of identification. *J. gen. Psychol.,* 76: 163–189.

273. STOLZ, H. R., and STOLZ, L. M., 1944. Adolescent problems related to somatic variations. *Yearb. nat. Soc. Stud. Educ.,* 43: 80–99.

274. STONE, C. P., and BARKER, R. G., 1937. Aspects of personality and intelligence in post-menarcheal and pre-menarcheal girls of the same chronological ages. *J. comp. Psychol.,* 23: 439–455.

275. STONE, C. P., and BARKER, R. G., 1939. The attitudes and interests of pre-menarcheal and post-menarcheal girls. *J. genet. Psychol.*, 54: 27–71.
276. STOTT, L. H., 1940. Adolescents' dislikes regarding parental behavior and their significance. *J. genet. Psychol.*, 57: 393–414.
277. SULLIVAN, H. S., 1947. *Conceptions of Modern Psychiatry.* William Alanson White Psychiatric Foundation, Washington.
278. SYMONDS, P. M., 1937. Changes in sex differences in problems and interests of adolescence with increasing age. *J. genet. Psychol.*, 50: 83–89.
279. SYMONDS, P. M., 1949. *Adolescent Fantasy.* Columbia University Press, New York.
280. TAYLOR, K. VAN F., 1942. The reliability and permanence of vocational interests of adolescents. *J. exp. Educ.*, 11: 81–87.
281. TAYLOR, W. S., 1933. A critique of sublimation in males: a study of forty superior single men. *Genet. Psychol. Monogr.*, 13, No. 1.
282. THOMPSON, CLARA, 1950. *Psychoanalysis: Evolution and Development.* Hermitage, New York.
283. TRYON, CAROLINE M., 1944. The adolescent peer culture. *Yearb. nat. Soc. Stud. Educ.*, 43: 217–239.
284. WALLIN, P., and RILEY, ROSEMARY P., 1950. Reactions of mothers to pregnancy and adjustment of offspring in infancy. *Amer. J. Orthopsychiat.*, 20: 616–622.
285. WEISS, E., 1932. Regression and projection in the superego. *Int. J. Psycho-Anal.*, 13: 449–478.
286. WILE, I. S., and DAVIS, ROSE, 1941. The relation of birth to behavior. *Amer. J. Orthopsychiat.*, 11: 320–334.
287. WILLOUGHBY, R. R., 1937. Sexuality in the second decade. *Monogr. Soc. Res. Child Developm.*, 2, No. 10.
288. WITTELS, F., 1949. The ego of the adolescent. In K. R. Eissler (ed.), *Searchlights on Delinquency.* International Universities Press, New York.
289. WOLF, A., 1943. The dynamics of the selective inhibition of specific functions in infancy. *Psychosom. Med.*, 5: 27–38.
290. WRIGHT, B. P., 1940. Selfishness, guilt feelings, and social distance. Ph.D. thesis, Univ. Iowa.
291. YOUNG, P. C., 1940. Hypnotic regression—fact or artifact. *J. abnorm. soc. Psychol.*, 35: 273–278.
292. ZELIGS, R., 1945. Social factors annoying to children. *J. appl. Psychol.*, 29: 75–82.
293. ZELLER, A. F., 1950. An experimental analogue of repression. I. Historical summary. *Psychol. Bull.*, 47: 39–51.
294. ZELLER, A. F., 1950. An experimental analogue of repression. II. The effect of individual failure and success on memory measured by relearning. *J. exp. Psychol.*, 40: 411–422.
295. ZILLIG, M., 1938. Prollereien unter Schulkindern. *Z. pädag. Psychol.*, 39: 241–250, 263–270.

Name Index

A

Abraham, K., 38, 160, 182, 193
Achilles, P. S., 133, 193
Adler, A., 17, 90, 93, 112, 164, 165, 180, 185, 186, 193
Alexander, F., 118, 161, 178, 179, 181, 188, 189, 193
Alpert, A., 133, 193
Aronson, M. L., 58, 193
Atkinson, J. W., 117, 202

B

Balint, A., 118, 194
Barker, R. G., 59, 60, 153, 194, 205, 206
Beaglehole, E., 182, 194
Bellak, L., 58, 194
Belmont, L., 123, 124, 194
Bernfeld, S., 56, 140, 141, 145, 194
Biber, B., 134, 194
Biddle, C. R., 56, 116, 203
Birch, H. G., 123, 124, 194
Black, I. S., 134, 194
Blanchard, P., 146, 194
Blanton, M. G., 55, 194
Blum, G. S., 114, 116–118, 125, 183–185, 194, 195, 202
Bornstein, B., 128–130, 195
Bowers, A. M., 46, 99
Bowlby, J., 53, 195
Bronner, A. F., 46, 199
Bruner, J. S., 124, 195
Buck, W., 155, 195
Burlingham, D. T., 10, 197
Buxbaum, E., 138, 195

C

Cameron, N., 60, 195
Campbell, E. H., 133, 195

Carmichael, L., 9, 195
Cattell, R. B., 13, 152, 154, 195
Clapp, C. D., 124, 125, 195
Conn, J. H., 114, 115, 195
Courtney, P. D., 118, 195

D

Davis, A., 81, 150, 195
Davis, K. B., 133, 196
Davis, R., 13, 206
Dembo, T., 59, 60, 194
Deutsch, H., 129, 134, 137, 138, 142, 148, 149, 155, 196
Dollard, J., 153, 196
Drillien, M. C., 12
DuBois, C., 56, 188, 196
DuBois, P. H., 61, 196
Dyk, R. B., 10, 201

E

Ellis, A., 32, 196
England, A. O., 117, 196
Erikson, E. H., 41, 52, 71, 79, 90, 111, 179, 182, 185, 189, 196
Escalona, S. K., 57, 196

F

Fenichel, O., 14, 15, 18, 19, 22, 28–30, 34, 38, 49, 53, 62, 64, 71, 78, 81, 85–87, 90–92, 97, 99, 103–108, 111, 113, 114, 117, 118, 120, 138, 140, 142, 156–164, 180, 182, 185–187, 189, 196
Ferenczi, S., 35, 54, 66, 196
Fodor, N., 2, 3, 6, 7, 10, 197
Forbes, T. W., 61, 196
Freud, A., 10, 54, 58, 60, 75, 77, 80, 84, 106, 118, 120, 127, 130, 132–134, 136, 137, 139, 142,

Freud, A., 144, 146, 148–150, 153–
    155, 197
Freud, S., 3–8, 16–26, 29–32, 37, 40,
    44, 53, 55, 70, 86, 87, 92, 93,
    95–100, 105, 112, 114, 117, 160,
    161, 187, 197, 198
Fries, M. E., 57, 198
Fromm, E., 27, 28, 30, 32, 88, 95,
    100–102, 110, 112, 113, 126,
    174–176, 181, 185–187, 189,
    198

G

Gardner, G. E., 58, 198
Glover, E., 160, 198
Goldman, F., 183, 198
Goldstein, S., 119, 123, 126, 198
Gorer, G., 82, 184, 198
Greenacre, P., 1, 2, 5–10, 27, 30, 143,
    198

H

Hall, D. E., 9, 199
Halverson, H. M., 55, 199
Hamilton, G. V., 133, 185, 199
Hankins, D., 146
Harnick, J., 139
Harris, D. B., 8, 199
Harris, E. S., 8, 199
Hartmann, H., 34, 44, 82, 86, 128,
    157, 182, 183, 199
Hattendorf, K. W., 114, 116, 199
Healy, W., 46, 199
Hilgeman, L. M., 134, 199
Hirschl, D., 12
Horney, K., 89, 90, 94, 95, 111, 112,
    171, 172, 181, 186, 187, 189,
    199, 200
Horwitz, W., 58, 201
Howes, D. H., 124, 200
Huschka, M., 82, 83, 115, 200
Hutt, M. L., 57, 183, 184, 199, 202

I

Isaacs, S., 114, 200, 201

J

Jahoda, M., 188, 200
James, H. E. O., 154, 155, 200
Jones, E., 19, 160, 200
Jones, H. E., 154, 200

Jung, C. G., 16, 23, 24, 28, 29, 32,
    40, 52, 56, 93, 94, 112, 166, 167,
    181, 186, 187, 200

K

Kardiner, A., 56, 82, 177, 178, 181,
    184, 187–189, 200
Keet, C. D., 121–123, 200
Kenworthy, M., 8, 12, 201
Kinsey, A. C., 133, 151, 201
Kitay, P. M., 154, 201
Klein, H. R., 10, 58, 201
Klein, M., 36, 39, 44–48, 50–52, 54,
    201
Kluckhohn, C., 12, 203
Knight, R. P., 118, 201
Koch, H. L., 83, 201
Korner, I. N., 121, 123, 124, 201
Kris, E., 34, 44, 60, 82, 86, 128, 199,
    201
Kunst, M. S., 56, 201

L

Laden, E., 117, 201
Lair, W. S., 118, 201
Lander, J., 143, 201
Landis, C., 151, 201
Lazarus, R. S., 124, 202
Levy, D. M., 54, 115, 202
Lewin, K., 59, 60, 194, 202
Loewenstein, R. M., 34, 44, 82, 128,
    199

M

McCleary, R. A., 124, 202
McClelland, D. C., 117, 202
McGinnies, E. M., 124, 202
MacKinnon, D. W., 182, 186, 202
McNeil, E. B., 125, 202
Malinowski, B., 134, 151, 202
Mead, M., 56, 116, 151, 152, 202
Miller, C., 58, 202
Miller, D. R., 57, 120, 183, 184, 195,
    202
Milne, A. A., 76
Mohr, G. J., 9, 199
Moloney, J. C., 41, 56, 116, 203
Montagu, A., 8, 9, 11, 203
Moore, F. F., 154, 155, 200
Mowrer, O. H., 12, 117, 118, 126,
    203

Mullahy, P., 68, 148, 155, 186, 187, 203
Murphy, L. B., 134, 194

N

Nelson, A. K., 55, 203
Newberry, H., 10, 204

O

Oberholzer, E., 188
Orlansky, H., 53, 82, 183, 203
Ovesey, L., 188, 200

P

Page, J., 58, 203
Pearson, G., 12, 203
Piaget, J., 80, 81, 203
Platonow, K. I., 60, 203
Postman, L. J., 124, 195
Potter, H. W., 10, 201
Pratt, K. C., 55, 203

R

Rank, O., 2–8, 94, 100, 112, 145, 168, 169, 171, 181, 186, 187, 204
Rapaport, D., 121, 204
Raush, H. L., 117, 201
Reich, W., 158, 160, 163, 182, 204
Ribble, M. A., 53, 54, 204
Richards, T. W., 10, 204
Riley, R. P., 10, 206
Roberts, E., 55, 204
Rosenstock, I. M., 124, 204

S

Sarbin, T. R., 60, 204
Schilder, P., 118, 204, 205
Schrier, H., 117, 205
Sears, R. R., 55–59, 114–117, 120, 121, 133, 185, 205
Shirley, M., 12
Smith, M. B., 188, 205
Sollenberger, R. T., 153, 205
Solomon, R. L., 124, 200
Sontag, L. W., 2, 9–12, 205
Spelt, D. K., 9, 205

Spiegel, L. A., 137–141, 143, 145, 155, 205
Spitz, R. A., 53, 54, 205
Sterba, R., 14, 15, 104, 105, 120, 129, 134, 205
Stolz, H. R., 151, 205
Stolz, L. M., 151, 205
Stone, C. P., 153, 205, 206
Stott, L. H., 154, 206
Sullivan, H. S., 16, 17, 30, 36, 37, 45, 46, 51, 52, 54, 57, 67, 68, 70, 71, 73, 77–81, 84, 96, 109, 112, 113, 126, 131, 132, 134, 147, 148, 150, 155, 186, 206
Sun, K. H., 55, 203
Swanson, G. E., 120
Symonds, P. M., 152, 155, 206

T

Taylor, K., 154, 206
Taylor, W. S., 120, 206
Thompson, C., 16–19, 25, 30, 40, 70, 71, 83, 89, 96, 111, 112, 131, 134, 185, 188, 206
Tryon, C. M., 153–155, 206

W

Wallace, R. F., 2
Wallin, P., 10, 206
Warkentin, J., 58, 203
Wile, I. S., 13, 206
Willoughby, R. R., 115, 151, 206
Windle, W. F., 11
Wise, G. W., 55, 56, 205
Wittels, F., 141, 206
Wolf, A., 59, 206
Woodcock, L. P., 134, 194
Wright, B. P., 58, 206

Y

Young, P. C., 60, 206

Z

Zeligs, R., 154, 206
Zeller, A. F., 121, 122, 206
Zillig, M., 154, 206

Subject Index

A

Adolescence, 134, 147–150, 171
  aggression in, 153
  ego and superego in, 139–141
  ego identity in, 180, 182
  fantasies in, 152
  interests and attitudes in, 154, 155
  mechanisms in, 143–146
  physical changes in, 151
  psychosexual development in, 136–139
  relationships in, 141–143
  sexual activities in, 151
Afterexpulsion (see Repression)
Aggression, 16, 31, 36, 44, 51, 58, 73, 79, 111, 116, 118, 121, 124, 136, 137, 139, 148, 152, 159, 160, 162, 163, 173, 174, 179
  adolescent, 150, 153
  in females, 143
  identification with aggressor, 118
  in lower classes, 92, 150
  mutual, 90
  toward self, 18, 19, 29
  veiled, 87
  (See also Sadism)
Alorese, feeding practices among, 56
Ambition, 86, 158, 161
  in adolescent fantasies, 152
  origins of, 113, 114
  repressed, 90
  urethral, 185
Ambivalence, 52, 163
  anal, 72, 79
  definition of, 43
  and isolation, 108
  in latency period, 130
  oedipal, 92
  origins of, 44
  overcoming of, 164

Anal ambivalence, 72, 79
Anal anxieties, 73, 86
Anal character, 159, 161–163, 174, 180, 184, 185, 187
Anal components in handwriting, 125
Anal conflicts, 75
Anal eroticism and undoing, 108
Anal factors, 41, 83, 84, 100, 109, 114, 134, 136, 171, 178, 189
Anal phase, expulsive, 69, 70, 79
  retentive, 69, 70, 79, 85, 125, 161
Anal pleasure, 69–71, 79, 82, 85
Anal sadism, 69–72, 144
Anal versus urethral training, 113
Anima, 167
Animal research, value for personality theory of, 59
Animus, 167
Anxiety, 39, 41, 46, 49, 80, 89, 94, 97, 100, 112, 116, 121, 132, 138, 139, 141, 148, 152, 174–176, 178, 189
  adaptive, 81, 82
  anal, 73, 96
  anticipatory, 63, 78
  basic, 172, 186, 187
  and birth trauma, 3, 4, 8, 12
  castration (see Castration anxiety)
  content of childhood, 63
  depressive, 45, 50
  and fetal physiology, 9
  and guilt, 98, 128
  infantile, 50, 128
  and muscle tension, 81
  objective, 128
  persecutory, 50
  predisposition to, 1, 6–8
  and primary narcissism, 27, 30
  and self-dynamism, 68, 69, 79

211

Anxiety, superego, 128, 140
 unconscious readiness toward, 22
Arapesh, feeding practices among, 56
 reaction among, to first menstruation, 152
 to soiling, 57
Archetypes, explanation of, 24
 father, 24, 29
 mother, 24, 29
Asceticism, 140, 143, 146, 149
 and repression, 144
Autistic language, 67, 68, 78, 79
Autoeroticism, 26, 30, 38, 51, 85, 111
 (*See also* Self-love)
Automaton conformity, 110, 111, 113
Autonomy, 72
"Average man," 170, 187
Awareness, levels of, 14, 118, 121
 acceptance of concept of, 25
 early split into, 19
 research on, 124, 125

B

Basic personality structure, description of, 177, 181
 interaction in, 178, 181
 postulates of, 177
 research on, 188
Birth, 7, 11, 63
 accidental factors in, 4, 5, 8
 Caesarean section in, 12
 difficult, 5, 13
 duration of, 12
 and effects on later personality, evidence for, 12, 13
 problems of investigating, 13
 fear symbols, 6
 instrument delivery in, 13
 premature delivery in, 10, 12
 and primary narcissism, 27
 as prototype of later anxiety, 3, 6, 8
 as psychological shock, 3, 5
 and separation from mother, 3, 4, 8
 as sudden exposure to outside stimulation, 3
 visual impressions of, 4, 5, 8
Bisexuality, 72, 79, 142, 149

C

Castration anxiety, 39, 89, 98, 108, 116, 134, 137, 138, 163
 evidence for, 87
 and oral and anal fears, 114
 origins of, 86, 87
 in phallic stage, 86
 as separation fear, 4
 universality of, 114, 115
 (*See also* Anxiety)
Cathexis, 136, 137
 counter-, 103–106, 108, 139, 149, 159, 180
 ego, 102
 object, 102
Censorship, 21
Character, 157, 165, 166, 169, 189
 aggressive, 173, 181, 187
 anal, 159, 161–163, 174, 180, 184, 185, 187
 average, 170, 181, 187
 and basic personality structure, 177, 181, 188
 classification of, 158, 180
 compliant, 172, 173, 181, 187
 creative, 171, 181, 187
 definition of, 156, 174, 180, 182
 detached, 174, 181, 187
 and ego identity, 179, 180, 182, 188
 eliminating, 178, 179, 181, 188
 exploitative, 175, 181, 187
 extraverted, 167, 168, 181, 186, 187
 genital, 159, 164, 180, 187
 hoarding, 176, 181, 187
 impulsive, 140
 intaking, 178, 179, 181, 188
 introverted, 167, 168, 181, 186, 187
 marketing, 176, 181, 187
 national, 188
 neurotic, 170, 171, 181
 oral, 159–161, 180, 183, 184, 187
 and personality, 182
 phallic, 159, 163, 164, 180
 productive, 176, 181, 187
 receptive, 175, 181, 187
 retaining, 178, 179, 181, 188
 social, 174, 181
 types, 159, 181
 urethral, 159, 163, 180
Character armor, 158

Character defenses, 158
Chum, 132, 133, 147
Collective unconscious, 32
  definition of, 23, 29
  function of, 24, 25
  (*See also* Unconscious)
Comanches, feeding practices
  among, 56
Compulsion, 173, 176
  repetition, 18, 108
  and undoing, 107, 108
  and will, 168
Condensation, 21, 163
Conscience, authoritarian, 100–102,
  113
  humanistic, 100–102, 113, 114
  (*See also* Guilt; Superego)
Conscious, 19, 31, 103, 121
  time relations in, 20
  and the unconscious, 168
Consensual validation, 77, 80, 84,
  147
Constancy principle, 18
Constitutional factors, and birth
  trauma, 4, 5
  in character structure, 157
  in fixation, 49
  lip service to, 59
  in predisposition to anxiety, 1
Countercathexis, 103–106, 108, 139,
  149, 159, 180
"Creative man," 171, 187
Creativity, 171, 174, 176, 186
  as adolescent defense, 145, 146,
  150
  and will, 170
Cultural variation, in adolescent expression of sexuality, 151, 152
  in attitudes toward physical sex
  differences, 116
  in feeding practices, 41
  in latency, 134
  in reaction to first menstruation,
  152
  in sequence of psychosexual stages,
  71, 83
  in toilet training, 71, 82

D

Dating, 152
Daydreams, 146, 153
Death, and departure, 65
  fear of, 180

Death instinct, 17–19, 29–31
Defense mechanisms (*see* Mechanisms)
Denial, 103, 113
  in fantasy, 46, 48, 52, 75, 77, 80
  in word and act, 75, 77, 80
Dependency, 95, 112, 137, 160, 170,
  173
Depression, 175
  in adolescent fantasies, 152
  anaclitic, 53
  in oral character, 160, 184
  in phallic character, 163
Deprivation, 34, 44, 49, 51, 53, 60,
  82, 160
Derivatives, 106
Disassociation, 109, 110, 113, 126,
  148
Displacement, 21, 99, 103, 109, 113,
  120, 162
Dreams, 78, 79, 81, 110
  and birth trauma, 6
  and the collective unconscious, 24,
  29
  displacement in, 109
  latent meaning of, 20, 31
  in parataxic mode, 67
  "prenatal," 2, 7
  (*See also* Daydreams)

E

Ego, 22, 26, 44, 46, 47, 50, 51, 53,
  54, 62, 64–66, 75, 77, 78, 82, 94,
  96, 97, 99, 100, 107, 108, 112,
  118, 164, 168–170
  in adolescence, 139–141, 153
  archaic, 33–36, 99
  and character structure, 156–159,
  180, 182
  energy of, 102, 103
  functions of, 98, 103, 106, 157, 180
  and id, 103, 139, 149
  judging, 63
  in latency, 127–130, 132
  in preadolescence, 139, 143
  and superego, 99, 103
Ego defense, 124, 133, 139, 140
Ego ideal, 125, 145, 146
Ego identity, 179, 180, 182, 189
Ego psychology, 156, 185
Ego regression, 60
Ego strength, 133
Ego threat, 123

Electra complex (*see* Oedipus complex)
Empathy, 46, 68
  age levels in, 45, 52, 57
  explanations of, 45, 52
  research on, 56–57
Energy, complications in concept of, 150
  discharge of, 104
  distribution of, 102, 103
  fixed quantity of, 16, 28, 102, 150
  inherited organization of, 24
  in latency period, 129, 132
  mental, 35, 46, 50, 136, 149, 180
  pregenital, 159
  (*See also* Libido)
Eros, 18
Euphoria, 46
  and anxiety, 68, 79
Exhibitionism, 111, 114, 136, 163
Expulsiveness, 69, 70, 79
Externalization, 172
Extravert, 167, 168, 181, 186, 187

F

Feces, 70, 71, 73, 79, 83, 108, 175
  attitudes toward, 72
  and money, 65, 81, 162
Feeling, 166, 167, 181
Fetal activity, 1, 2, 11, 12
  and conditioning, 9
  physiology of, 9
  and postnatal motor development, 10
  and susceptibility to external stimulation, 8, 9
Fixation, 16, 46, 138, 149, 158, 180
  anal, 73
  conditions leading to, 49
  consequences of, 49, 50
  as defense against anxiety, 50
  definition of, 52
  mother, 94, 95
  oral, 49, 50, 160
  and regression, 49
"Flight from womanhood," 90
Forepleasure, 38, 164
Frustration tolerance, 18, 60, 184

G

Genital character, 158, 159, 164, 180, 187

Genital factors, 86, 105, 130, 137, 138
Genital lust mechanism, 147, 150
Genital primacy, 104, 159, 164
Genital stage, 120
Guiding fictions, 165
Guilt, 45, 50, 91, 92, 94, 97, 99–101, 103, 111, 121, 138, 143, 170, 171, 189
  in adolescent fantasies, 152
  and anxiety, 98
  masturbation, 89, 125
  and projection, 58
  sex differences in, 119
  unconscious readiness toward, 22
  (*See also* Conscience; Superego)

H

Homosexuality, 58, 133, 142, 149, 151, 154

I

"I," the, 69
Iatmul, reactions to menstruation among, 152
Id, 14, 19, 98, 106, 108, 112, 136, 140, 144, 145
  and character structure, 156, 180
  characteristics of, 22, 23
  connotations of, 25
  and ego, 103, 139, 149
  and repressed experiences, 25, 30
  as source or reservoir, 32, 102
  and superego, 99
  and the unconscious, 22, 29
Idealized image, 172
Identification, 67, 98, 112, 113, 125, 127, 158, 161, 170, 180
  in adolescence, 142, 149
  with aggressor, 118
  as defense, 118
  definition of, 97
  and imitation, 118
  and object-choice, 118
  primary, 46, 47
  studies on, 117
Imitation, 118
Incorporation, 98, 112, 164
  oral, 38, 39, 41, 47, 51, 52
Indulgence, 34, 44, 51, 140
  over-, 49, 93, 160

Infantile sexuality, 40, 95, 137, 138, 148, 155
  versus adult sexuality, 37
  climax of, 91
  "polymorphous perverse" aspects of, 37, 51
  theory of, 37, 51
Inferiority, feelings of, 165, 166, 170, 181
  organ, 165, 166
Instincts, aim of, 15, 28
  characteristics of, 15, 28
  classification of, 15, 28
  death, 17–19, 29–31
  definition of, 14, 15, 28
  driving power of, 15
  object of, 15, 28
  as poor translation of *Trieb*, 30
  of self-preservation (ego), 17
  sexual, 15–17, 28
  simple physical, types of, 15, 28
  source of, 15, 28, 32
  split into life and death, 18
Intellectualization, 144, 145, 149, 150
Interpersonal relations, 16, 29–31, 42, 46, 54, 70, 84, 96, 112, 147, 148, 155
  (*See also* Relationships with others)
Introjection, 66, 97, 100, 103, 113, 118, 127
  oral, 46–48, 50, 52
Introvert, 167, 168, 181, 186, 187
Intuition, 166, 167, 181
Isolation, 75, 103, 113, 123
  and ambivalence, 108
  types of, 108, 109

J

Japanese, toilet training among, 184, 185
Judgment, 62, 78
Juvenile era, 131–135

K

Kleptomania, 175

L

Latency period, 131, 132, 135, 136, 140, 144
  cultural variation in, 134

Latency period, ego and superego in, 127–129
  evidence concerning, 133
  mechanisms in, 130
  phases in, 128, 129
  psychosexual development in, 129
  relationships in, 129, 130
Libido, 14, 32, 36, 39, 40, 43–45, 50, 56, 73, 100, 129, 132, 136, 137, 139, 141, 142, 148, 159, 171, 174, 181
  definition of, 16, 28
  fixed quantity of, 16, 27, 28, 30
  id as reservoir of, 22
  as primal energy, 16
  regression, 60
  rejection of, 16, 29
  vicissitudes of, 16, 102
  (*See also* Energy)
Loss of love, fear over, 52, 63, 66, 78, 87, 97, 98, 175

M

Magic, 51, 161, 162, 168
Magic beliefs, 64
Magic gestures, 36, 54
Magic hallucinatory omnipotence, 36, 54
Magic helper, 175, 184
Magic power, of parents, 97
  of words, 65
Magic thoughts and words, 36, 54
Magical undoing, 107
Manus, reactions to menstruation among, 152
"Masculine protest," 90, 116, 166
Masochism, 73, 79, 83, 100, 110, 113, 142, 143, 149, 185
Mastery, active, 62, 63, 78, 89
  belated, 67, 78, 80
  passive-receptive, 35, 51, 62
Masturbation, 87, 88, 93, 111, 129, 133
  in adolescence, 138, 149, 151
  family attitudes toward, 92
  studies on, 115, 116
Masturbation fantasies, 89
Masturbation guilt, 89, 125
"Me, the bad," 69, 79
  the good," 69, 79
  not," 69, 79
"Me-you patterns," early, 74
  multiple, 74, 79

Mechanisms, 33, 36, 47–50, 52, 76–78, 80, 84
  in adolescence, 143–146
  defense, 46, 53, 59, 66, 75, 85, 102–109, 119–126, 139, 149, 156, 157, 180
  successful versus unsuccessful, 103, 113
  versus dynamisms, 46
  of escape, 110, 111
  genetic sequence of, 75
  in latency period, 130, 132
  research on, 119
  types of, 46
Menarche (*see* Menstruation)
Menstruation, first, 138, 152
  interests before and after, 153
Mode, eliminative, 41, 42, 71
  incorporative, 41, 42, 52
  intrusive, 41, 42, 90, 111
  parataxic, 36, 67, 69, 74, 77–80
  prototaxic, 36, 37, 51, 54, 67, 79
  retentive, 41, 42, 71
  syntaxic, 36, 78
"Mothering one," 37, 45, 67
Motus, feeding practices among, 56
Moving, away from people, 172, 174, 181, 186
  toward and against people, 172, 173, 181, 186
Mucous membranes, stimulation of, 38, 51, 55, 70, 79
Mundugumor, feeding practices among, 56
  reactions to menstruation among, 152

N

Narcissism, 16, 98, 102, 143, 149, 160, 189
  in adolescence, 142
  criticism of concept of, 27, 28, 30
  definitions of, 25, 27
  observations of parental, 26, 27, 32
  and penis envy, 185
  in phallic character, 164
  in phallic stage, 86, 111
  primary, 14, 25–28, 32, 35
  secondary, 26, 28, 32
  sex differences in, 139
  urethral, 86

"Neurotic man," 170, 171, 187
Neurotic trends, 172

O

Object-choice, in adolescence, 141–143
  definition of, 97
  of girl, change in, 92, 111
  homosexual, 142
  and identification, 118
  narcissistic features in, 26
  in Oedipus complex, 91, 111
  in resolution of Oedipus complex, 96, 97
Obsession, 77, 128, 141, 176
Oceanic feeling, 26, 30
Oedipus complex, 39, 40, 52, 85, 92, 99, 100, 109, 116, 118, 127, 137, 152, 158, 163
  definition of, 91, 111
  fantasies, 111, 138, 141, 148, 149
  of girl, complications in, 116
  influences on form of, 91
  negative and positive, 91
  object-choice in (*see* Object-choice)
  as possession complex, 93, 112
  as rebirth fantasy, 94, 112
  renunciation of, 96, 97
  in terms of familiarity and strangeness, 96, 112
  universality of, 95, 117
Okinawans, feeding practices among, 41, 56
Omnipotence, 47, 51, 52, 64, 65, 127, 129
  longing for, 35
  by magic gestures, 36, 54
  magic hallucinatory, 36, 54
  unconditional, 35, 54
Oral character, 159–161, 180, 183, 184, 187
Oral eroticism, 38, 39, 160
Oral factors, 97, 109, 114, 136, 144, 163, 164, 171, 189
Oral fears, 38, 51, 86
Oral optimism, 183
Oral pessimism, 183
Oral sadism, 39, 42–44, 51, 72, 100, 125, 134, 160, 183
Oral stage of development, 37–42, 51, 70, 71, 82
Organismic consciousness, 3, 7

P

Pampering, 165
  and Oedipus complex, 93, 112
Paranoia, 57, 58, 72
Parataxic mode, 36, 67, 69, 74, 77–80
Penis envy, 86, 89, 92, 111, 134, 137, 138
  determinants of, 90
  modifications of, 88
  and narcissism, 185
  in phallic female, 164
  primary, 88, 90, 116
Perception, as approach to repression, 124, 125
  and defense, 124
  as ego function, 98
  infantile, 33, 34, 43
Persona, 167, 181
Phallic character, 159, 163, 164, 180
Phallic stage, 71, 85–90, 110, 127
  locomotor, 90, 111
Phylogenetic factors, 21, 23, 24, 29, 31, 32, 92
Pleasure, anal, 69–71, 79, 82, 85
  erogenous, 64, 161, 185
  functional, 64
  seeking of, 34, 51, 86
Pleasure principle, 21, 23, 33–35, 51
Pleasure sucking, 38, 40, 48, 51, 54–56, 70
Polarities, 53
Post-hypnotic suggestion, 20, 31
Power motive, 17, 29, 93, 111, 165, 166
Preadolescence (*see* Prepuberty)
Preconscious, 19–21
Pregenital character, 159
Pregenital factors, 38, 129, 130, 137, 148, 159, 179, 189
Pregenital impulses, 104, 105, 130, 159, 164, 189
Pregenital regression, 129
Pregenital symptoms, 148
Pregenital traits, 159
Prenatal influence, 3, 27, 63
  as illustrated in dreams, 2, 7
  opinions on significance of, 11, 12
  physiology of, 9
  possible research approach to, 10
  as predisposition to anxiety, 1, 2
  principles of, 7
  research evidence for, 9, 10

Prepuberty, 40, 127, 141, 147–152
  conflicting views on, 155
  defenses in, 143
  ego and id in, 139
  in girls, 137
  interests and attitudes in, 154
  psychosexual development in, 136, 137
  trauma, 143
Primal fantasies, 21, 31
Primal horde, 24, 92
Primal repression, 105
Primal scene, 91
Primary process, 21
Primitivation, 60
Primordial images (*see* Archetypes)
Projection, 45–48, 52, 99, 101, 103, 113, 119, 120, 172
  studies of, 57–59
Prototaxic mode, 36, 37, 51, 54, 67, 79
Psychosexual development, 33, 36, 44, 49, 51, 111
  in adolescence, 136–139
  in latency period, 129
  stages of, anal, 69–72
    oral, 37–42
    phallic, 85–90, 110
    urethral, 85, 86
Psychotherapy, 20, 31, 74, 79, 121, 122, 186
Puberty, 93, 134, 137–143, 148, 149, 151
  (*See also* Adolescence; Prepuberty)

R

Reaction formation, 75, 103, 113, 119, 120, 129, 132, 137, 164
  in character structure, 159, 160
  definition of, 107
  in latency period, 127, 130
  prediction in, 125, 126
  and repression, 107
  research on, 126
  and sublimation, 107
  and undoing, 107
Reactive traits, 158, 159, 180
Reality, denial of, 48, 52, 75, 76
  development of sense of, 35
  and ego function, 98
  and fantasy transitions, 75–77
  impairment in sense of, 47

Reality, stages in, 35, 36, 54
Reality principle, 35, 51, 66
Reality systems, 178
Reality testing, 63, 77, 78, 98, 157
Reflected appraisals, 73, 74, 79
Regression, 16, 46, 50, 61, 90, 103,
    112, 113, 118–120, 129, 130,
    132, 143, 157
  definition of, 49, 52
  ego, 60
  experiments on, 59
  and fixation, 49
  habit, 126
  hypnotic age, 60
  libido, 60
  in object-choice, 97
Relationships with others, 33, 36, 39,
    46, 92–96, 111
  in adolescence, 141–143, 146
  ambivalence in, 43, 44
  in evolution of the self, 73, 74
  in latency period, 129, 130
  mother as first object in, 43–45, 52,
    91
  (*See also* Interpersonal relations)
Repression, 16, 19, 29, 31, 75, 90,
    103, 104, 109, 113, 119, 126,
    129, 131, 138, 139, 167, 170,
    172, 173, 181
  and asceticism, 144
  chronology of, 84
  criteria for, 121
  effectiveness of, 106, 107
  experiments on, 120–125
  and id forces, 25, 30
  and personal unconscious, 23
  primal, 105
  proper, 105, 121
  and reaction formation, 107
  secondary, 106
  and symbolism, 66
  views on, 105
Retentiveness, anal, 69, 70, 85, 125,
    161

S

Sadism, 73, 79, 85, 100, 110–114,
    133, 142, 179, 185
  (*See also* Anal sadism; Oral sad-
    ism)
Samoans, reaction to menstruation
    among, 152
Secondary process, 21

Selective inattention, 109, 110, 113,
    126
Selective vigilance, 124
Self, 34, 37, 57, 73, 101, 109, 110,
    167, 172
  "I" as, 69
  knowledge of, 170
  personifications of, 79
  sense of, 146, 150
  (*See also* Self-esteem)
Self-actualization, 32
Self-esteem, 34, 35, 51, 63, 158, 173
  in anal character, 162
  decrease in, 98
  and ego identity, 180, 189
  in oral character, 160
  regulation of, 99
Self-love (*see* Narcissism)
Self-system, 74, 148
Sensation, 166, 167, 181
Sexual act, 38, 143, 164, 173
  attitudes toward, 138
  child's observation of, 91
  sado-masochistic interpretation of,
    137
  as symbolic reunion with mother,
    4
Shame, 72, 86, 113, 163
Sibling rivalry, 92, 116, 125, 134
"Significant other," 45
Slips of speech, 20, 31
"Sphincter morals," 66
Stimulus hunger, 34, 53
"Style of life," 164
Sublimation, 16, 44, 76, 113, 148,
    150, 155, 160, 164, 180
  controversies over, 104
  definition of, 104
  forerunners of, 120
  and identification, 105
  partial, 127, 129, 130, 132
  and reaction formation, 107
  research on, 120
  as successful defense, 103
Sublimation category of character
    traits, 158, 159
Sucking, research on, 54–56
  rhythmic movements in, 40, 56
  as sexual instinct, 38
  thumb, 38, 54–56
Sucking drive, 54–56
Suicide, 18, 19, 29
Superego, 22, 33, 36, 48, 50, 51, 62,
    85, 105, 162

Superego, in adolescence, 140, 141, 153, 155
    and character structure, 157, 180
    development of, 96–98
        stages in, 100
    and ego, 99, 103
    energy of, 103
    externalized pre-, 66
    "fatherly," 97, 118, 119
    forerunners of, 66, 78, 97
    functions of, 98
    and id, 99, 103
    in latency period, 127–129, 132
    "motherly," 97, 118, 119
    and Oedipus complex, 96, 97, 112
    toilet-training, 66
    (*See also* Conscience; Guilt)
Symbolism, 24, 29, 65–68, 81, 93
Symptoms, hysterical, 144
    mental, 20
    neurotic, 139
    obsessional, 128
    physical, 20
    pregenital, 148
    unconscious meaning of, 20, 31
Syntaxic mode, 36, 78

T

Talion principle, 63, 73, 78, 86
Tanala, toilet training in, 184
Tchambuli, feeding practices among, 56
    reaction to menstruation among, 152
Thanatos, 18
Thinking, 62, 64, 157, 162, 166, 181
    advanced, 65
    concerete versus abstract, 134
    and isolation, 108
    in marketing orientation, 176
    original, 174
    prelogical, 65, 78, 80, 81
    stages of logical, 81
    symbolism in, 65
Toilet training, 66, 68, 72, 79, 92, 100, 161, 175, 177
    and adult personality, 184, 185
    factors in, 82
    research on effects of, 82, 83
Toilet-training practices, 82
Transference, 67, 79

U

Unconscious, attributes of, 20, 21
    collective (*see* Collective unconscious)
    connotations of, 25, 29
    and the conscious, 168
    content in, nature of, 21, 22
        origin of, 21, 31
    definition of, 19
    and the id, 22
    importance of, 19, 20
    personal versus collective, 23, 29
    reasons for belief in, 20
    timelessness in, 20, 31
Unconscious emotions, 22
Unconscious fantasies, 36, 51, 54
Undoing, 75, 103, 113
    and anal eroticism, 108
    and reaction formation, 107
Urethral ambition, 185
Urethral versus anal training, 113
Urethral character, 163, 180
Urethral eroticism, 85

V

Vector analysis, 179
"Visceral ethics," 66
Voyeurism, 114

W

Will, 171, 181
    counter-, 169, 170
    definition of, 168
    steps in development of, 169
Wish fulfillment, hallucinatory, 65, 75

Y

Yurok, personality traits in, 185

Z

Zones, erogenous, 37, 38, 88
    anal, 41, 69
    anal-urethral, 71, 72
    genital, 41
    oral-sensory, 41, 52